P O R T A B L E

Puerto Vallarta, Manzanillo & Guadalajara

2nd Edition

by David Baird and Lynne Bairstow

Macmillan • USA

ABOUT THE AUTHORS

David Baird (chapters 6 and 7) is a writer, editor, and translator based in Austin, Texas. He spent part of his childhood in Morelia, Mexico, and later lived for 2 years among the Mazatec Indians in Oaxaca while he was doing graduate fieldwork.

Lynne Bairstow (chapters 1, 2, 3, 4, 5, and Appendix) is a writer specializing in travel and the Internet, who has lived in Puerto Vallarta, Mexico, at least part-time for the past 9 years. She now lives there year-round, and was assisted in her research for this book by Claudia Velo. In a previous professional life, Lynne was a vice president for Merrill Lynch in Chicago and New York.

They are also the authors of *Frommer's Mexico* and *Frommer's Cancún, Cozumel & the Yucatán*.

MACMILLAN TRAVEL

Macmillan General Reference USA, Inc.
1633 Broadway
New York, NY 10019

Find us online at **www.frommers.com**

Copyright © 2000 by Macmillan General Reference USA, Inc.
Maps copyright © by Macmillan General Reference USA, Inc.

ISBN 0-02-863129-3
ISSN 1093-6998

Editors: Kelly Regan, Justin Lapatine
Production Editors: Mike Thomas, Christina Van Camp
Photo Editor: Richard Fox
Design by Michele Laseau
Staff Cartographers: John Decamillis, Roberta Stockwell
Page creation: Pete Lippincott, Angel Perez

SPECIAL SALES

Bulk purchases (10+ copies) of Frommer's and selected Macmillan travel guides are available to corporations, organizations, mail-order catalogs, institutions, and charities at special discounts, and can be customized to suit individual needs. For more information write to Special Sales, Macmillan General Reference, 1633 Broadway, New York, NY 10019.

Manufactured in the United States of America

5 4 3 2 1

Contents

List of Maps

AN INVITATION TO THE READER

In researching this book, we discovered many wonderful places—resorts, inns, restaurants, shops, and more. We're sure you'll find others. Please tell us about them, so we can share the information with your fellow travelers in upcoming editions. If you were disappointed with a recommendation, we'd love to know that, too. Please write to:

Frommer's Portable Puerto Vallarta, Manzanillo & Guadalajara
Macmillan Travel
1633 Broadway
New York, NY 10019

AN ADDITIONAL NOTE

Please be advised that travel information is subject to change at any time—and this is especially true of prices. We therefore suggest that you write or call ahead for confirmation when making your travel plans. The authors, editors, and publisher cannot be held responsible for the experiences of readers while traveling. Your safety is important to us, however, so we encourage you to stay alert and be aware of your surroundings. Keep a close eye on cameras, purses, and wallets, all favorite targets of thieves and pickpockets.

A FEW WORDS ABOUT PRICES

The peso's value continues to fluctuate—at press time it was slightly less than 10 pesos to the dollar. Prices in this book (which are always given in U.S. dollars) have been converted to U.S. dollars at 10 pesos to the dollar. Most hotels in Mexico— with the exception of places that receive little foreign tourism—quote prices in U.S. dollars. Thus, currency fluctuations are unlikely to affect the prices charged by most hotels.

Mexico has a **Value-Added Tax** of 15% (*Impuesto de Valor Agregado,* or IVA, pronounced "ee-bah") on most everything, including restaurant meals, bus tickets, and souvenirs. Hotels charge the usual 15% IVA, plus a locally administered bed tax of 2% (in many but not all areas), for a total of 17%. IVA will not necessarily be included in the prices quoted by hotels and restaurants. You may find that upper-end properties (three stars and above) quote prices without IVA included, while lesser-priced hotels include IVA in their quotes. Always ask to see a printed price sheet, and always ask if the tax is included.

WHAT THE SYMBOLS MEAN

✪ Frommer's Favorites

Our favorite places and experiences—outstanding for quality, value, or both.
The following abbreviations are used for credit cards:

AE	American Express	EURO	Eurocard
CB	Carte Blanche	JCB	Japan Credit Bank
DC	Diners Club	MC	MasterCard
DISC	Discover	V	Visa
ER	enRoute		

FIND FROMMER'S ONLINE

Arthur Frommer's Budget Travel Online (www.frommers.com) offers more than 6,000 pages of up-to-the-minute travel information—including the latest bargains and candid, personal articles updated daily by Arthur Frommer himself. No other Web site offers such comprehensive and timely coverage of the world of travel.

Planning a Trip to Mid-Pacific Mexico

*A*long the Pacific coast of Mexico, palm-studded jungles sweep down to meet the deep blue of the Pacific Ocean, providing spectacular backdrops for three modern resort cities and smaller coastal villages. This lovely stretch of coastline extending from Puerto Vallarta down to Manzanillo is known as the Mexican Riviera. Modern hotels, easy air access, and a growing array of activities and adventure tourism attractions have transformed this region of Mexico into one of the country's premier resort areas.

A little advance planning can make the difference between a good trip and a great trip. When should you go? What's the best way to get there? How much should you plan on spending? What festivals or special events will be taking place during your visit? What safety or health precautions are advised? We'll answer these and other questions for you in this chapter.

In addition to these basics, I highly recommend taking a little time to learn a little about the culture and traditions of Mexico. It can make the difference between simply "getting away" and truly adding understanding to the experience.

1 The Region in Brief

Few regions in Mexico vary in terrain as dramatically as the country's Pacific Coast. At **Puerto Vallarta,** tropical-forested mountains meet the sea on the stunningly beautiful and wide Banderas Bay. With its colonial Mexican architecture and gold-sand beaches, Vallarta is currently the second most visited resort in Mexico (trailing only Cancún). To the south of Puerto Vallarta and continuing to **Manzanillo,** the coastline alternates between fields of banana, mango, and coconut palm plantations and tropical forests. Tiny towns and luxury, superexclusive resorts also dot the coastline. This area encompasses laid-back **Barra de Navidad** and its sister town **Melaque,** both on good-sized bays, rimmed by cream-colored beaches.

Both Puerto Vallarta and Manzanillo have come of age. They are linked to major cities by air and offer a charming mix of traditional Mexico and sophisticated tourist services. Although the resorts

Mexico

UNITED STATES

Tijuana Mexicali
Ensenada
**BAJA
CALIFORNIA
NORTE**
San
Quintin

Puerto
Penasco

Nogales

Ciudad
Juárez

SONORA

Hermosillo

CHIHUAHUA

Ojinaga

Cuauhtémoc

Chihuahua

COAHUILA

*Isla
Cedros*

Guerrero
Negro

Santa
Rosalia

Cuidad
Obregon

Delicias

Monclova

Mulegé

Hidalgo
del Parral

**BAJA
CALIFORNIA
SUR**

Loreto

SINALOA

Torreon

Saltillo

Los
Mochis

DURANGO

Culiacán

Sea of Cortez

Durango

Fresnillo

La Paz

Todos Santos San José
del Cabo

Mazatlán

ZACATECAS

Zacatecas

San
Luis
Potosi

Cabo San Lucas

*Islas
Marias*

San Blas Tuxpan
Tepic

AGUASCALIENTES

Aguascalientes

Leon

NAYARIT

Puerto Vallarta

Guadalajara

Guanajuato

**GUANA
JUATO**

Morelia

JALISCO

*Lake
Chapala*

Barra de Navidad

Colima

Uruapan

Pátzcuare

MICHOACAN

Manzanillo **COLIMA**

Lazaro
Cardenas
Zihuatanejo
& Ixtapa

Pacific Ocean

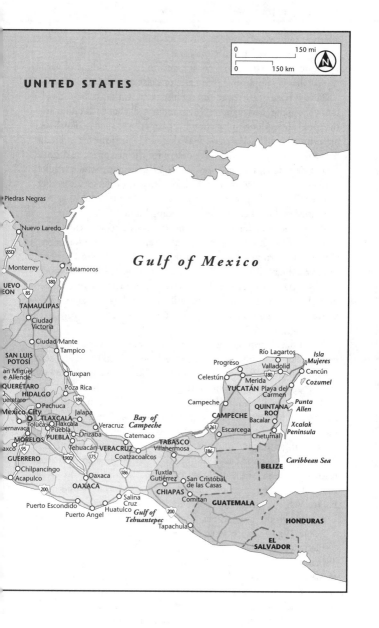

UNITED STATES

Gulf of Mexico

Piedras Negras

Nuevo Laredo

850

Monterrey Matamoros

UEVO
EON 85 180

TAMAULIPAS

Ciudad
Victoria

Ciudad Mante

SAN LUIS Tampico
POTOSÍ

an Miguel Tuxpan
e Allende

QUERÉTARO Poza Rica
HIDALGO 180

ueretaro Pachuca

Mexico City Jalapa

TLAXCALA Tlaxcala

Toluca Veracruz

uernavaca Puebla Orizaba

MORELOS PUEBLA Catemaco

axco 95 Tehuacán VERACRUZ

GUERRERO 1900 175 Coatzacoalcos

Chilpancingo 186

Acapulco Oaxaca

200 OAXACA

Puerto Escondido Salina
Cruz

Puerto Angel Huatulco *Gulf of
Tehuantepec*

*Bay of
Campeche*

Río Lagartos *Isla
Mujeres*

Progreso Valladolid

Celestún Merida Cancún

180 *Cozumel*

YUCATÁN Playa del
Carmen

Campeche QUINTANA *Punta
Allen*

CAMPECHE ROO

261 Bacalar Xcalak

Escarcega *Peninsula*

Chetumal

TABASCO
Villahermosa

Tuxtla *Caribbean Sea*
Gutiérrez San Cristóbal
de las Casas BELIZE

CHIAPAS

Comitán GUATEMALA

200

Tapachula HONDURAS

EL
SALVADOR

0   150 mi
0   150 km

N

advertise somewhat homogeneous beach holidays, each city possesses its own distinctive Mexican *ambiente.*

Mexico's central Pacific Coast caters to so many kinds of vacationers that it's impossible to suggest one city over the other. Puerto Vallarta is both picturesque and sophisticated, with excellent restaurants, shopping, and nightlife. Manzanillo is all about relaxation and the simple life. Along this section of coast, villages such as **San Blas, Sayulita, Bucerías, Barra de Navidad,** and **Melaque** are still laid back, almost undiscovered, and, except for the new, superluxurious Grand Bay Hotel, relatively inexpensive. Excursions to these smaller villages, whether easy day-trips or extended stays, offer an altogether different kind of experience. Several are so close together that you can easily explore them all before heading home.

If you're looking for a more "authentic" Mexican experience, head inland over the mountains to **Guadalajara,** Mexico's second-largest city and the birthplace of many of the country's traditions.

International airports at all three cities make getting to each easier; Guadalajara and Puerto Vallarta have the most frequent connections. Distances in the region are easily managed by car; most drives between major points take from 45 minutes to 6 hours on roads that are generally good.

If you decide to visit this region, you have several choices about how to allot your time. Most people pick one coastal resort and stay there for the duration of their vacations, but you can easily enjoy more than one resort during your time in Mexico.

Barra de Navidad, for example, is so close to Manzanillo that it's easy to combine several days there with a stay in Manzanillo. From Puerto Vallarta, Bucerías, Yelapa, San Sebastian, and San Blas all offer a change of pace and scenery. With the exception of Las Alamandas (which is closer to Puerto Vallarta), the luxury coastal resorts between Manzanillo and Puerto Vallarta are nearer to Manzanillo. There are more frequent flights, however, to and from Puerto Vallarta, and many people find Puerto Vallarta provides the best access to the coastal area. Beginning in December 1999, new scheduled flight service aboard a Cessna Caravan Turbo-prop will connect Puerto Vallarta with the resorts in Careyes, Isla Navidad, and Tamarindo (contact **Air Adventures,** ☎ **322/1-0657** or 322/1-0658 for details). The resorts located between the cities are self-contained and far from anything else, so they are intended as vacation destinations in their own right (see the "Side Trips. . ." sections in the various chapters). Although these resorts can arrange transportation from either Manzanillo or Puerto Vallarta, renting a car may be more economical if you plan to be exploring on your own.

2 Visitor Information, Entry Requirements & Money

SOURCES OF INFORMATION

The **Mexico Hot Line** (☎ **800/44-MEXICO**) is an excellent source for general information, requesting brochures on the country, and for answers to the most commonly asked questions. If you have a fax, Mexico's Ministry of Tourism also offers **Fax-Me-Mexico** (☎ **541/385-9282**). Call, key in your fax number, and then select from a variety of topics from general destination information to accommodations (the service lists 400 hotels), shopping, dining, sports, sightseeing, festivals, and nightlife. They'll then fax you the materials you're interested in.

More information (15,000 pages worth, they say) about Mexico is available on the Mexico Ministry of Tourism's Web site: **http://mexico-travel.com**.

The **U.S. State Department** (☎ **202/647-5225** for travel information and Overseas Citizens Services) offers a **Consular Information Sheet** on Mexico, with a compilation of safety, medical, driving, and general travel information gleaned from reports by official U.S. State Department offices in Mexico. You can also request the Consular Information Sheet by fax (☎ **202/647-3000**). The State Department is also on the Internet; check out **http://travel. state.gov/mexico.html** for the Consular Information Sheet on Mexico; **http://travel.state.gov/travel_warnings.html** for other Consular Information sheets and travel warnings; and **http://travel. state.gov/tips_mexico.html** for the State Department's *Tips for Travelers to Mexico.*

The **Centers for Disease Control Hot Line** (☎ **404/332-4559**) is another source for medical information affecting travelers to Mexico and elsewhere. The center's Web site, **www.cdc.gov/**, provides lengthy information on health issues for specific countries.

MEXICAN GOVERNMENT TOURIST OFFICES

Mexico's foreign tourist offices (MGTO) throughout the world—with the exception of the United States and Canada—were closed effective January 1997. Those operating in North America include the following:

United States: Chicago, IL (☎ **312/606-9252**); Houston, TX (☎ **713/780-3740**); Los Angeles, CA (☎ **213/351-2069;** fax 213/

351-2074); Miami, FL (☎ **305/443-9160**); New York, NY (☎ **800/446-3942**); and the Mexican Embassy Tourism Delegate, 1911 Pennsylvania Ave., Washington, DC 20005 (☎ **202/728-1750**). The MGTO offices have been combined with Mexican Consulate offices in the same cities, providing one central source for official information on Mexico.

Canada: 1 Place Ville-Marie, Suite 1931, Montréal, PQ, H3B 2C3 (☎ **514/871-1052**); 2 Bloor St. W., Suite 1502, Toronto, ON, M4W 3E2 (☎ **416/925-2753**); 999 W. Hastings, Suite 1110, Vancouver, BC, V6C 2W2 (☎ **604/669-2845**).

OTHER SOURCES

The following newsletters may be of interest to readers: *Mexican Meanderings,* P.O. Box 33057, Austin, TX 78764, aimed at readers who travel to off-the-beaten-track destinations by car, bus, or train (six to eight pages, published six times annually; subscription $18); *Travel Mexico,* Apdo. Postal 6-1007, 06600 Mexico, D.F., from the publishers of the *Traveler's Guide to Mexico,* the book frequently found in hotel rooms in Mexico, covers a variety of topics from archaeology news to hotel packages, new resorts and hotels, and the economy (six times annually; subscription $18).

For other newsletters, see "For Seniors" and "For Gay & Lesbian Travelers" under "Tips for Travelers with Special Needs," below.

ENTRY REQUIREMENTS
DOCUMENTS

Canadian and U.S. travelers to Mexico are required to present **proof of citizenship,** such as an original birth certificate with a raised seal, a valid passport, or naturalization papers. Those using a birth certificate should also have a current photo identification such as a driver's license or official ID. Those whose last name on the birth certificate is different from their current name (women using a married name, for example) should also bring a photo identification card *and* legal proof of the name change, such as the *original* marriage license or certificate. This proof of citizenship may also be requested when you want to reenter either the United States or Mexico. Photocopies are *not* acceptable.

Citizens of Western European countries, Australia, and New Zealand need a passport to enter Mexico. No visa is required.

You must also carry a **Mexican Tourist Permit (FMT),** which is issued free of charge by Mexican border officials after proof of citizenship is accepted. The tourist permit is more important than a passport

Don't Pass on the Passport

We've heard that a number of readers have had trouble entering Mexico using a birth certificate or voter registration card in place of a passport; in some cases people have been turned away at the border or point of entry. While the U.S. State Department endorses the entry requirements we have outlined above, it is strongly recommended that to minimize hassle you bring your passport as proof of identification and citizenship.

in Mexico, so guard it carefully. If you lose it, you may not be permitted to leave the country until you can replace it—a bureaucratic hassle that can take anywhere from a few hours to a week. (If you do lose your tourist permit, get a police report from local authorities indicating that your documents were stolen; having one *might* lessen the hassle of exiting the country without all your identification.)

A tourist permit can be issued for up to 180 days, although your stay south of the border may be shorter than that. Sometimes officials don't ask—they just stamp a time limit, so be sure to say "6 months" (or at least twice as long as you intend to stay). If you decide to extend your stay, request that additional time be added to your permit at an official immigration office in Mexico.

Note that children under age 18 traveling without parents or with only one parent must have a notarized letter from the absent parent or parents authorizing the travel.

LOST DOCUMENTS   To replace a **lost passport,** contact your embassy or nearest consular agent (see "Fast Facts: Mexico," below). You must establish a record of your citizenship and also fill out a form requesting another Mexican Tourist Permit (assuming it, too, was lost). Without the **tourist permit** you can't leave the country, and without an affidavit affirming your passport request and citizenship, you may have problems at Customs when you get home. So it's important to clear everything up *before* trying to leave. Mexican Customs may, however, accept the police report of the loss of the tourist permit and allow you to leave.

CUSTOMS

ALLOWANCES   When you enter Mexico, Customs officials will be tolerant as long as you have no illegal drugs or firearms. You're allowed to bring in two cartons of cigarettes, or 50 cigars, plus a kilogram (2.2 lb.) of smoking tobacco; the liquor allowance is two

1-liter bottles of anything, wine or hard liquor; you are also allowed 12 rolls of film. A laptop computer, camera equipment, and sporting equipment (golf clubs, scuba gear, a bicycle) that could feasibly be used during your stay are also allowed. The underlying guideline is that they will disallow anything that they feel you will be attempting to resell in Mexico.

When you reenter the **United States,** federal law allows you to bring in up to $400 in purchases duty-free every 30 days. The first $1,000 over the $400 allowance is taxed at 10%. You may bring in a carton (200) of cigarettes or 100 cigars or 2 kilograms (4.4 lb.) of smoking tobacco, plus 1 liter of wine, beer, or spirits.

Canadian citizens are allowed $20 in purchases after a 24-hour absence from the country or $100 after a stay of 48 hours or more.

British travelers returning from outside the European Union are allowed to bring in £145 worth of goods, in addition to the following: up to 200 cigarettes, 50 cigars or 250 grams of tobacco; 2 liters of wine; 1 liter of liqueur greater than 22% alcohol by volume; and 60cc/milliliters of perfume. If any item worth more than the limit of £145 is brought in, payment must be made on the full value, not just on the amount above £145.

Citizens of **New Zealand** are allowed to return with a combined value of up to NZ$1,000 in goods, duty-free.

GOING THROUGH CUSTOMS   Mexican Customs inspection has been streamlined. At most points of entry, tourists are requested to press a button in front of what looks like a traffic signal, which alternates on touch between red and green signals. Green light and you go through without inspection; red light and your luggage or car may be inspected briefly or thoroughly. If you have an unusual amount of luggage or an oversized piece, you may be subject to inspection despite the traffic signal routine.

MONEY
CASH/CURRENCY

The currency in Mexico is the Mexican **peso.** Paper currency comes in denominations of 20, 50, 100, 200, and 500 pesos. Coins come in denominations of 1, 2, 5, 10, and 20 pesos and 20 and 50 **centavos** (100 centavos equal 1 peso). The current exchange rate for the U.S. dollar is around 10 pesos; at that rate, an item that costs 10 pesos would be equivalent to US$1.

Getting **change** continues to be a problem in Mexico. Small-denomination bills and coins are hard to come by, so start collecting

Mexico's Mid-Pacific Coast

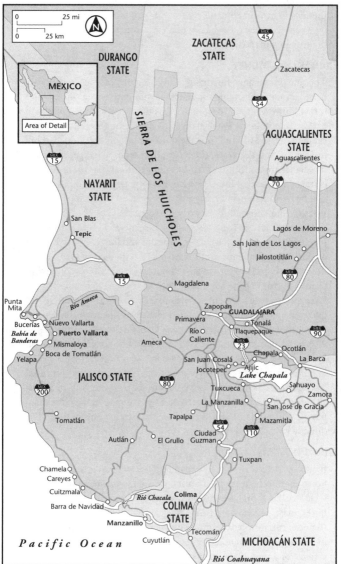

them early in your trip and continue as you travel. Shopkeepers everywhere seem always to be out of change and small bills; that's doubly true in a market.

EXCHANGING MONEY

The rate of exchange fluctuates a tiny bit daily, so you probably are better off not exchanging too much of your currency at once. Don't forget, however, to have enough pesos to carry you over a weekend or Mexican holiday, when banks are closed. In general, avoid carrying the U.S. $100 bill. It is the most commonly counterfeited bill in Mexico, and therefore, the most difficult to exchange, especially in smaller towns. Since small bills and coins in pesos are hard to come by in Mexico, the U.S. $1 bill is very useful for tipping.

The bottom line on exchanging money of all kinds: It pays to ask first and shop around. Banks pay the top rates.

Exchange houses (*casas de cambio*) are generally more convenient than banks since they have more locations and longer hours; the rate of exchange may be the same as a bank or only slightly lower. *Note:* Before leaving a bank or exchange-house window, always count your change in front of the teller before the next client steps up.

Large airports have currency-exchange counters that often stay open whenever flights are arriving or departing. Though convenient, these generally do not offer the most favorable rates.

A hotel's exchange desk commonly pays less favorable rates than banks; however, when the currency is in a state of flux, higher-priced hotels are known to pay *higher* than bank rates, in their effort to attract dollars. The bottom line: It pays to shop around, but in almost all cases you receive a better exchange by changing money first, then paying for goods or services, rather than by paying with dollars directly to an establishment.

BANKS & ATMS

Banks in Mexico are rapidly expanding and improving services. New hours tend to be from 9am until 5 or 6pm, with many open for at least a half day on Saturday, and some even offering limited hours on Sunday. The exchange of dollars, which used to be limited until noon, can now be accommodated anytime during business hours in the larger resorts and cities. Some, but not all, banks charge a service fee of about 1% to exchange traveler's checks. However, most purchases can be paid for directly with traveler's checks at the stated exchange rate of the establishment. Don't even bother with personal checks drawn on a U.S. bank—although theoretically they may be

Money Matters

Note: The **universal currency sign ($)** is used to indicate pesos in Mexico. The use of this symbol in this book, however, denotes U.S. currency. Many establishments dealing with tourists, especially in coastal resort areas, quote prices in dollars. To avoid confusion, they use the abbreviations "Dlls." for dollars and "M.N." (moneda nacional, or national currency) for pesos. All dollar equivalencies in this book were based on an exchange rate of 10 pesos per dollar.

cashed, it's not without weeks of delay, and the bank will wait for your check to clear before giving you your money.

Travelers to Mexico can also access money from **automated teller machines (ATMs),** now available in most major cities and resort areas in Mexico. Universal bank cards (such as the Cirrus and PLUS systems) can be used, and this is a convenient way to withdraw money from your bank and avoid carrying too much with you at any time. There is often a service fee charged by your bank for each transaction, but the exchange rate is generally more favorable than one found at a currency house. Most machines offer Spanish/English menus and dispense pesos, but some offer the option of withdrawing dollars. Be sure to check the daily withdrawal limit before you depart, and ask your bank whether you need a new personal ID number. For Cirrus locations abroad, call ☎ **800/424-7787** or check out MasterCard's Web site (**www.mastercard.com/atm/**). For PLUS usage abroad, call ☎ **800/843-7587** or visit Visa's Web site (**www.visa.com/atms**).

TRAVELER'S CHECKS

Traveler's checks are readily accepted nearly everywhere, but they can be difficult to cash on a weekend or holiday or in an out-of-the-way place. Their best value is their easy replacement in case of theft. Frequently in Mexico, a bank or establishment will provide a better rate for traveler's checks than for cash dollars.

CREDIT CARDS

You'll be able to charge most hotel, restaurant, and store purchases, as well as almost all airline tickets, on your credit card. You can get cash advances of several hundred dollars on your card, but there may be a wait of 20 minutes to 2 hours. You generally can't charge gasoline purchases in Mexico; however, with the new franchise system of Pemex stations taking hold, this may change as well. Visa

("Bancomer" in Mexico), MasterCard ("Carnet" in Mexico), and American Express are the most accepted cards.

Credit-card charges will be billed in pesos, then later converted into dollars by the bank issuing the credit card. Generally you receive the favorable bank rate when paying by credit card.

CRIME, BRIBES & SCAMS
CRIME

Crime in Mexico has received much attention in the North American press over the past 2 years (1997 to 1999). Many in Mexico feel this unfairly reflects the real dangers of traveling there, but it should be noted that crime is in fact on the rise, including taxi robberies, kidnappings, and highway car-jackings. The most severe crime problems are concentrated in Mexico City, located far away from this region; however, the city of Guadalajara has experienced an increase in street crime.

Precautions are necessary, but travelers should be realistic. When traveling anyplace in the world, common sense is essential. I have lived in and traveled throughout Mexico for 8 years now, without incident. The crime rate is on the whole much lower in Mexico than in most parts of the United States, and the nature of crimes in general is less violent—most crime is motivated by robbery, or by jealousy. Random, violent crime or serial crime is essentially unheard of in Mexico. You are much more likely to meet kind and helpful Mexicans than you are to encounter those set on thievery and deceit. A good rule of thumb is that you can generally trust people whom you approach for help, assistance, or directions—but be wary of anyone who approaches you offering the same. The more insistent they are, the more cautious you should be.

BRIBES & SCAMS

As is the case around the world, there are the occasional bribes and scams, targeted at people believed to be naive in the ways of the place—i.e., obvious tourists. For years Mexico was known as a place where bribes—called *propinas* (tips) or *mordidas* ("bites")—were expected; however, the country is rapidly changing. Offering a bribe today, especially to a police officer, is frequently considered an insult, and it can land you in deeper trouble.

If you believe a bribe is being requested, here are a few tips on dealing with the situation. Even if you speak Spanish, don't utter a word of it to Mexican officials. That way you'll appear innocent, all the while understanding every word.

When you are crossing the border, should the man who inspects your car ask for a tip, you can ignore this request—but understand that the official may suddenly decide that a complete search of your belongings is in order. If faced with a situation where you feel you're being asked for a *propina,* how much should you offer? Usually $3 to $5 or the equivalent in pesos will do the trick. To **report irregularities with Customs officials,** call ☎ **01/800-0-014800** in Mexico. Your call will go to the office of the Comptroller and Administrative Development Secretariat (SECODAM); however, be forewarned that most personnel do not speak English. Be sure you have some basic information—such as the name of the person who requested a bribe or acted in a rude manner, as well as the place, time, and day of the event.

Whatever you do, **avoid impoliteness;** under no circumstances should you insult a Latin American official. Mexico is ruled by extreme politeness, even in the face of adversity. In Mexico, *gringos* have a reputation for being loud and demanding. By adopting the local custom of excessive courtesy, you'll have greater success in negotiations of any kind. Stand your ground, but do it politely.

As you travel in Mexico, you may encounter several types of **scams,** which are typical throughout the world. One involves some sort of a **distraction** or feigned commotion. While your attention is diverted, a pickpocket makes a grab for your wallet. In another common scam, an **unaccompanied child** pretends to be lost and frightened and takes your hand for safety. Meanwhile the child, or an accomplice, manages to plunder your pockets. A third involves **confusing currency.** A shoe-shine boy, street musician, guide, or other individual might offer you a service for a price that seems reasonable—in pesos. When it comes time to pay, they tell you the price is in dollars, not pesos, and become very hostile if payment is not made. Be very clear on the price and currency when services are involved.

3 When to Go

SEASONS

Mexico has two principal travel seasons: high and low. **High season** begins around December 20 and continues to Easter, although in some places high season can begin as early as mid-November. **Low season** begins the day after Easter and continues to mid-December; during low season, prices may drop 20% to 50%. In beach destinations, the prices may also increase during the months of July and

August, the traditional national summer vacation period. Prices in inland cities, such as Guadalajara, seldom fluctuate from high to low season, but may rise dramatically during **Easter** and **Christmas** weeks.

THE CLIMATE

From Puerto Vallarta south to Huatulco, Mexico offers one of the world's most perfect winter climates—dry, balmy, and with temperatures ranging from the 80s during the day to the 60s at night. From Puerto Vallarta south, you can swim year-round.

High mountains shield Pacific beaches from *nortes* (northers—freezing blasts out of Canada via the Texas Panhandle). The states of Jalisco and Colima, like most of Mexico, have the most rain from May through September; the rainiest month is September. Tropical showers generally begin around 4 or 5pm and last a few hours. Though these rains can come on suddenly and be quite strong, they usually end just as fast and cool off the air for the evening.

For more on climate, see the "Fast Facts" sections in the destination chapters.

HOLIDAYS & SPECIAL EVENTS

On national holidays, banks, stores, and businesses are closed; hotels fill up quickly; and transportation is crowded.

January
- **New Year's Day (Año Nuevo).** National holiday. Parades, religious observances, parties, and fireworks welcome in the New Year everywhere. In traditional indigenous communities, new tribal leaders are inaugurated with colorful ceremonies rooted in the pre-Hispanic past. January 1.
- **Three Kings Day.** Commemorates the Three Kings' bringing of gifts to the Christ Child. On this day, children receive gifts, much like the traditional gift giving that accompanies Christmas in the United States. Friends and families gather to share the *Rosca de Reyes,* a special cake. Inside the cake there is a small doll representing the Christ Child; whoever receives the doll in his or her piece must host a tamales-and-*atole* party the next month. January 6.

February
- **Candlemas.** Music, dances, processions, food, and other festivities lead up to a blessing of seed and candles, a ritual that mixes

pre-Hispanic and European traditions marking the end of winter. All those who attended the Three Kings Celebration reunite to share *atole* and tamales at a party hosted by the recipient of the doll found in the Rosca. February 2.

- **Ash Wednesday.** The start of Lent and time of abstinence. It's a day of reverence nationwide, but some towns honor it with folk dancing and fairs. February 2.

March

- **Benito Juárez's Birthday.** National holiday. March 21.
- ✪ **Holy Week.** Celebrates the last week in the life of Christ, from Palm Sunday through Easter Sunday, with somber religious processions almost nightly, spoofings of Judas, and reenactments of specific biblical events, plus food and craft fairs. Businesses close during this week of Mexican national vacations.

  If you plan on traveling to or around Mexico during Holy Week, make your reservations early. Airline seats on flights into and out of the country will be reserved months in advance. Buses to almost anywhere in Mexico will be full, so try arriving on the Wednesday or Thursday before Good Friday. Easter Sunday is quiet. In 2000, March 15 through 18 is Holy Week, Easter Sunday is March 19, and the week following is a traditional vacation period.

May

- **Labor Day.** Workers' parades countrywide and everything closes. May 1.
- **Holy Cross Day** (Día de la Santa Cruz). Workers place a cross on top of unfinished buildings and celebrate with food, bands, folk dancing, and fireworks around the work site. May 3.
- **Cinco de Mayo.** A national holiday that celebrates the defeat of the French at the Battle of Puebla. May 5.

June

- **National Ceramics Fair and Fiesta,** Tlaquepaque, Jalisco. This pottery center on the outskirts of Guadalajara offers craft demonstrations and competitions as well as mariachis, dancers, and colorful parades. June 14.
- **Día de San Pedro** (St. Peter and St. Paul's Day). Celebrated wherever St. Peter is the patron saint, and honors anyone named Pedro or Peter. It's especially festive at San Pedro Tlaquepaque, near Guadalajara, with numerous mariachi bands, folk dancers, and parades with floats. In Mexcatitlan, Nayarit, shrimpers hold a regatta to celebrate the season opening. June 29.

September
- **Mariachi Festival,** Guadalajara, Jalisco. Public mariachi concerts, including visiting mariachi groups from around the world (even Japan!). Workshops and lectures are given on the history, culture, and music of the mariachi in Mexico. Plans for an extension of this festival in Puerto Vallarta were being worked out—call ☎ **800-44MEXICO** to confirm dates and schedule of performances. September 1 to 15.
- **Independence Day.** Celebrates Mexico's independence from Spain. A day of parades, picnics, and family reunions throughout the country. At 11pm on September 15, the president of Mexico gives the famous independence *grito* (shout) from the National Palace in Mexico City, which is duplicated by every *presidente municipal* (mayor) in every town plaza in Mexico. Both Guadalajara and Puerto Vallarta have great parties in the town plaza on the nights of September 15 and 16.

October
- **Fiestas de Octubre** (October Festivals), Guadalajara. This "most Mexican of cities" celebrates for a whole month with its mariachi music trademark. A bountiful display of popular culture and fine arts, and a spectacular spread of traditional foods, Mexican beers, and wines adds to the celebration. All month.

November
- ✪ **Day of the Dead.** What's commonly called the Day of the Dead is actually 2 days, All Saints' Day—honoring saints and deceased children—and All Souls' Day, honoring deceased adults. Relatives gather at cemeteries countrywide, carrying candles and food, and often spend the night beside the graves of loved ones. Weeks before, bakers begin producing bread shaped like mummies or round loaves decorated with bread "bones." Decorated sugar skulls emblazoned with glittery names are sold everywhere. Many days ahead, homes and churches erect special altars laden with Day of the Dead bread, fruit, flowers, candles, and favorite foods and photographs of saints and of the deceased. On the 2 nights, children, dressed in costumes and masks, carry mock coffins and pumpkin lanterns through the streets, expecting people to drop money in them. November 1 to 2.
- **Fiesta del Mar,** Puerto Vallarta. A monthlong calendar of activities including art festivals, sports competitions, the Mexico Boat Show, the Governor's Cup golf tournament, and a gourmet dining festival. Among the sporting events are sailing regattas,

windsurfing exhibitions, and beach volleyball competitions. November 10 to 30.

- **Revolution Day.** Commemorates the start of the Mexican Revolution in 1910 with parades, speeches, rodeos, and patriotic events. November 20.

December

✪ **Feast of the Virgin of Guadalupe.** Throughout the country the patroness of Mexico is honored with religious processions, street fairs, dancing, fireworks, and masses. It is one of Mexico's most moving and beautiful displays of traditional culture. The Virgin of Guadalupe appeared to a young man, Juan Diego, in December 1531, on a hill near Mexico City. He convinced the bishop that he had seen the apparition by revealing his cloak, upon which the Virgin was emblazoned. It's customary for children to dress up as Juan Diego, wearing mustaches and red bandannas. December 12.

In Puerto Vallarta, the celebration begins on December 1 and extends through December 12, with traditional processions to the church for a brief *misa* (mass) and blessing. In the final days, the processions and festivities take place around the clock, with many of the processions featuring floats, mariachis, Aztec dancers, and fireworks. The central plaza is filled with street vendors and a festive atmosphere, and a major fireworks exhibition takes place on December 12 at 11pm.

- **Christmas Posadas.** On each of the 9 nights before Christmas, it's customary to reenact the Holy Family's search for an inn, with door-to-door candlelit processions in cities and villages nationwide. Most business and community organizations host them in place of the northern tradition of a Christmas party. December 15 to 24.
- **Christmas.** Mexicans extend this celebration, often beginning 2 weeks before Christmas, all the way through New Year's. Many businesses close, and resorts and hotels fill up. December 24 and 25.
- **New Year's Eve.** As in the rest of the world, New Year's Eve in Mexico is celebrated with parties, fireworks, and plenty of noise. December 31.

4 Active Vacations

The diverse geography of the area has made it a natural favorite of travelers looking for more active vacations, offering a wealth of eco- and adventure-tour options.

Excellent **golf** courses are located in Guadalajara, Puerto Vallarta, and along the coastline down to Manzanillo, with its excellent Las

Hadas course. **Tennis, water-skiing, surfing, biking,** and **horseback riding** are all sports visitors can enjoy in this region. **Scuba diving** is excellent along the Pacific Coast at Puerto Vallarta and Manzanillo, where a wide array of sea life can be observed, including dolphins, sea turtles, and giant mantas.

OUTDOORS ORGANIZATIONS & TOUR OPERATORS

There's a new association in Mexico of eco- and adventure-tour operators called **AMTAVE** (Asociación Mexicana de Turismo de Aventura y Ecoturismo, A.C.). They publish an annual catalog of participating firms and their offerings, all of which must meet certain criteria for security, quality and training of the guides, as well as for sustainability of natural and cultural environments. For more information, contact them (in Mexico City) at ☎ 5/661-9121 (fax 5/662-7354; www.amtave.com.mx; e-mail: ecomexico@compuserve. com.mx); ask for Marlene Ehrenberg or Daniel Martínez.

Bike Mex Adventures, calle Guerrero s/n, 48300 Puerto Vallarta, Jalisco (☎ **322/3-1680;** www.bikemex.com; e-mail: bikemex@ zonavirtual.com.mx), offers day or overnight mountain-biking excursions in the Sierra Madre foothills near Puerto Vallarta. One overnight trip travels to the old mountain mining towns of Mascota, Talpa de Allende, and San Sebastian. This excellent trip is a combination of van transport and biking between towns, with stays in old haciendas.

Culinary Adventures, 6023 Reid Dr. NW, Gig Harbor, WA 98335 (☎ **253/851-7676;** fax 253/851-9532), offers a short but special list of cooking tours of particular regions of Mexico known for excellent cuisine, and featuring well-known cooks. The owner, Marilyn Tausend, is the coauthor of *Mexico the Beautiful Cookbook,* and *Cocinas de la Familia* (Family Kitchens), published by Simon & Schuster in 1997.

Mexico Sportsman, 14427 Brook Hollow, 124, San Antonio, TX 78232 (☎ and fax **210/494-9916**), is sportfishing central for anyone interested in advance arrangements for fishing in Puerto Vallarta, Manzanillo, or Mazatlán. The company also books excellent bass and flats fishing trips. Mexico Sportsman will arrange the trips through local outfitters, and provide you with everything you will need to know, including cost and length of a fishing trip; kind of boat, line, and tackle used; and whether or not bait, drinks, and lunch are included. Prices are as good as you will get on site in Mexico.

One World Workforce, P.O. Box 3188, La Mesa, CA 91944 (☎ **800/451-9564**), has weeklong "hands-on conservation trips" that offer working volunteers a chance to help with sea-turtle conservation along the Majahuas beach 60 miles south of Puerto Vallarta during the summer and fall.

Open Air Expeditions, calle Guerrero 339, Col. Centro, Apdo. Postal 105-B, Puerto Vallarta, Jal. C.P. 48300 (☎ **322/2-3310;** fax 322/3-2407; www.vivamexico.com; e-mail: openair@vivamexico.com), offers true eco-adventures guided by experts trained as marine biologists, oceanographers, or geologists. Their specialty is whale-watching tours (December through May); they have documented the returning whale population in an annual photo-ID study for the past 5 years. Other offerings include tours to sea turtle preservation camps, hiking, sea kayaking, and bird watching. All are in small groups, with minimal environmental impact and great sensitivity to the natural surroundings.

Trek America, P.O. Box 189, Rockaway, NJ 07866 (☎ **800/ 221-0596** or 973/983-1144; fax 973/983-8551) organizes lengthy, active trips that combine trekking, hiking, van transportation, and camping in the Yucatán, Chiapas, Oaxaca, the Copper Canyon, and Mexico's Pacific coast, and touching on Mexico City and Guadalajara.

Vallarta Adventure, Edif. Marina Golf Local 13c, Marina Vallarta, Puerto Vallarta, Jal., C.P. 48354 (☎ **322/1-0657** or 322/ 1-0658; fax 322/1-1117; www.vallarta-adventures.com; e-mail: adventure@tag01.acnet.net), Puerto Vallarta's premier adventure tour company, offers expeditions by boat to the Marietas Islands nature preserve, by land to the foothills of the Sierra Madre, and by air to the remote mining village of San Sebastian. They also have a dolphin-swim facility, with an emphasis on education and interactive communication, and a day spa at the private cove of Caletas, the former home of film great John Huston. All adventures are top quality, led by enthusiastic guides who mix adventure with spirited fun.

5 Health, Safety & Insurance

STAYING HEALTHY

BUG OFF   Mosquitoes and **gnats** are prevalent along the coast. Insect repellent (*repelente contra insectos*) is a must, and it's not always available in Mexico. If you'll be in these areas and are prone to bites, bring a repellent along that contains the active ingredient DEET. Avon's "Skin So Soft" also works extremely well. If you're sensitive to bites, pick up some antihistamine cream from a drugstore at home.

Most readers won't ever see a scorpion (*alacrán*). But if you're stung, go immediately to a doctor.

ALTITUDE BLUES   Travelers to certain regions of Mexico occasionally experience **elevation sickness,** which results from the relative lack of oxygen and the decrease in barometric pressure that characterizes high elevations (over 5,000 ft./1,500m). Symptoms include shortness of breath, fatigue, headache, insomnia, and even nausea. At high elevations it takes about 10 days to acquire the extra red blood corpuscles you need to adjust to the scarcity of oxygen. To help your body acclimate to the higher elevation, drink plenty of fluids, avoid the consumption of alcoholic beverages, which tend to exaggerate conditions, and don't overexert yourself with physical activity during the first few days. If you have heart or lung problems, talk to your doctor before going above 8,000 feet.

MORE SERIOUS DISEASES   You shouldn't be overly concerned about tropical diseases if you stay on the normal tourist routes and don't eat street food. However, both dengue fever and cholera have appeared in Mexico in recent years. Talk to your doctor, or a medical specialist in tropical diseases, about any precautions you should take. You can also get medical bulletins from the U.S. State Department and the Centers for Disease Control (see "Sources of Information," above). You can protect yourself by taking some simple precautions. Watch what you eat and drink; don't swim in stagnant water (ponds, slow-moving rivers, or wells); and avoid mosquito bites by covering up, using repellent, and sleeping under mosquito netting. The most dangerous areas seem to be on Mexico's west coast, away from the big resorts (which are relatively safe).

EMERGENCY CARE   Puerto Vallarta also has a modern, U.S.-standards health care facility that offers insured care while in Mexico. **Ameri-Med,** Plaza Neptuno, in Marina Vallarta (☎ **800/815-1921** or 322/1-0023; fax 322/1-0026; www.amerimed-hospitals.com), provides complete, 24-hour, emergency health care adhering to U.S.

Over-the-Counter Drugs

Antibiotics and other drugs that you'd need a prescription to buy in the States are sold over-the-counter in Mexican pharmacies. Mexican pharmacies also have common over-the-counter cold, sinus, and allergy remedies, although not the broad selection we're accustomed to finding easily in the States.

medical standards. Facilities include CAT scan, radiology, ultra-sound, and emergency air-evacuation services. Prices are in line with the standard of care, meaning that it's more costly than other medical facilities in Mexico.

For extreme medical emergencies, there's a service from the United States that will fly people to American hospitals: **Air-Evac,** a 24-hour air ambulance (☎ **888/554-9729,** or call collect 510/293-5968). You can also contact the service in Guadalajara (☎ **01-800/305-9400,** 3/616-9616, or 3/615-2471).

SAFETY

I have lived and traveled in Mexico for over 8 years, have never had any serious trouble, and rarely feel suspicious of anyone or any situation. You will probably feel physically safer in most Mexican cities and villages than in any comparable place at home. See "Crime, Bribes & Scams," and "Sources of Information," above, for more information and how to access the latest **U.S. State Department advisories.**

INSURANCE

Even the most careful of us can still experience a traveler's nightmare: You discover you've lost your wallet, your passport, your airline ticket, or your tourist permit. Always keep a photocopy of these documents in your luggage—it makes replacing them easier. To be reimbursed for insured items once you return, you'll need to report the loss to the Mexican police and get a written report. If you don't speak Spanish, take along someone who does. If you lose official documents, you'll need to contact both Mexican and U.S. officials in Mexico before you leave the country.

Health Care Abroad, Wallach and Co. Inc., 107 W. Federal St. (P.O. Box 480), Middleburg, VA 20118 (☎ **800/237-6615** or 540/687-3166), and **World Access,** 6600 W. Broad St., Richmond, VA 23230 (☎ **800/628-4908** or 804/285-3300), offer medical and accident insurance as well as coverage for trip cancellation. Always read the fine print on the policy to be sure that you're getting the coverage you want.

6 Tips for Travelers with Special Needs

FOR FAMILIES

Children are considered the national treasure of Mexico, and Mexicans will warmly welcome and cater to your children. Where many parents were reluctant to bring young children into Mexico in the past, primarily due to health concerns, I can't think of a better place

---

Turista on the Toilet: What to Do If You Get Sick

It's called "travelers' diarrhea" or *turista,* the Spanish word for "tourist": the persistent diarrhea, often accompanied by fever, nausea, and vomiting, that used to attack many travelers to Mexico. Some in the United States call this "Montezuma's revenge," but you won't hear it referred to this way in Mexico. Widespread improvements in infrastructure, sanitation, and education have practically eliminated this ailment, especially in well-developed resort areas. Most travelers make a habit of drinking only bottled water, which also helps to protect against unfamiliar bacteria. In resort areas, and generally throughout Mexico, only purified ice is used. Doctors say it's not caused by just one "bug," but by a combination of consuming different foods and water, upsetting your schedule, lack of sleep, and the stresses of travel. A good high-potency (or "therapeutic") vitamin supplement, and even extra vitamin C is a help; yogurt is good for healthy digestion. If you do happen to come down with this ailment, nothing beats Pepto Bismol, readily available in Mexico.

How to Prevent It: The U.S. Public Health Service recommends the following measures for preventing travelers' diarrhea:

---

today to introduce children to the exciting adventure of exploring a different culture. Hotels can often arrange for a baby-sitter. Some hotels in the moderate-to-luxury range have small playgrounds and pools for children and hire caretakers with special activity programs during the day. Few budget hotels offer these amenities.

Before leaving, you should check with your doctor to get advice on medications to take along. Disposable diapers cost about the same in Mexico but are of poorer quality. You can get Huggies Supreme and Pampers identical to the ones sold in the United States, but at a higher price. Gerber's baby foods are sold in many stores. Dry cereals, powdered formulas, baby bottles, and purified water are all easily available in midsize and large cities and resorts.

Cribs, however, may present a problem. Only the largest and most luxurious hotels provide cribs. However, rollaway beds to accommodate children staying in the room with parents are often available. Child seats or high chairs at restaurants are common, and most restaurants will go out of their way to accommodate your child.

- **Drink only purified water.** This means tea, coffee, and other beverages made with boiled water; canned or bottled carbonated beverages and water; or beer and wine. Most restaurants with a large tourist clientele use only purified water and ice.
- **Choose food carefully.** In general, avoid salads, uncooked vegetables, and unpasteurized milk or milk products (including cheese). However, salads in a first-class or tourist restaurant are generally safe to eat. Choose food that is freshly cooked and still hot. Peelable fruit is ideal. Don't eat undercooked meat, fish, or shellfish.
- In addition, something so simple as **clean hands** can go a long way toward preventing turista.
- Since **dehydration** can quickly become life threatening, the Public Health Service emphasizes the importance of replacing fluids and electrolytes (potassium, sodium, and the like) during a bout of diarrhea. Do this by drinking Pedialyte, a rehydration solution available at most Mexican pharmacies, glasses of natural fruit juice (high in potassium) with a pinch of salt added, or a glass of boiled pure water with a quarter teaspoon of sodium bicarbonate (baking soda) added.

FOR GAY & LESBIAN TRAVELERS

Mexico is a conservative country, with deeply rooted Catholic religious traditions. As such, public displays of same-sex affection are rare and still considered shocking for men, especially outside of urban or resort areas. Women in Mexico frequently walk hand in hand, but anything more would cross the boundary of acceptability. However, gay and lesbian travelers are generally treated with respect and should not experience any harassment, assuming the appropriate regard is given to local culture and customs.

Puerto Vallarta is perhaps the most welcoming and accepting destination in Mexico, with a selection of accommodations and nightlife oriented especially toward gay and lesbian travelers. **Vicki Skinner's Doin' It Right in Puerto Vallarta** is a special travel service that rents gay-friendly condos and villas for individuals and groups up to 75. She also has a newsletter, "The PV Purple Pages," that offers travel specials and features tips, special events, and activities. It's free to Doin' It Right clients, or $10 plus a SASE with

$1.01 postage to nonclients. To subscribe, write to 1010 University Ave. #C113-741, San Diego, CA 92103 (☎ **800/936-3646** or 619/297-3642). The newsletter is also available online at GayPVR@aol.com.

Arco Iris is a gay-owned, full-service travel agency and tour operator specializing in Mexico packages and special group travel, including to Puerto Vallarta. Contact them by phone, ☎ **800/795-5549,** or through their Web site: www.freeyellow.com/members/arco/index.html. **The International Gay & Lesbian Travel Association** (IGLTA) (☎ **800/448-8550** or 954/776-2626; fax 954/776-3303; www.iglta.org), can provide helpful information and additional tips. The **Travel Alternative Group (TAG)** maintains a database and Gay-Friendly Accommodations Guide. For details, call ☎ **415/437-3800** or e-mail info@mark8ing.com.

FOR PEOPLE WITH DISABILITIES

Mexico may seem like one giant obstacle course to travelers in wheelchairs or on crutches. At airports, you may encounter steep stairs before finding a well-hidden elevator or escalator—if one exists. Airlines will often arrange wheelchair assistance for passengers to the baggage area. Porters are generally available to help with luggage at airports and large bus stations, once you've cleared baggage claim. Few airports offer the luxury of boarding an airplane from the waiting room. You either descend stairs to a bus that ferries you to the waiting plane that's boarded by climbing stairs, or you walk across the airport tarmac to your plane and ascend the stairs. Deplaning presents the same problem in reverse.

Few rest rooms are equipped for travelers with disabilities, or when one is available, access to it may be via a narrow passage that won't accommodate a wheelchair or someone on crutches. Many deluxe hotels (the most expensive) now have rooms with baths for people with disabilities. Those traveling on a budget should stick with one-story hotels or those with elevators. Even so, there will probably still be obstacles somewhere. Stairs without handrails abound in Mexico, and escalators (there aren't many in the country) are often out of operation. Generally speaking, no matter where you are, someone will lend a hand, although you may have to ask for it.

FOR SENIORS

Mexico is a popular country for retirees. For decades, North Americans have been living indefinitely in Mexico by returning to the border and recrossing with a new tourist permit every 6 months. Mexican immigration officials have caught on, and now limit the maximum time in the country to 6 months within any year. This is to encourage even partial residents to comply with the proper documentation.

Some of the most popular places for long-term stays are Guadalajara, Lake Chapala, Ajijic, and Puerto Vallarta—all in the state of Jalisco; and to a lesser extent Manzanillo, in Colima.

AIM, Apdo. Postal 31–70, 45050 Guadalajara, Jalisco, Mexico, is a well-written, candid, and very informative newsletter on retirement in Mexico. Subscriptions cost $18 to the United States and $21 to Canada. Back issues are three for $5.

Sanborn Tours, 2015 S. 10th St., Post Office Drawer 519, McAllen, TX 78505-0519 (☎ **800/395-8482**), offers a "Retire in Mexico" Guadalajara orientation tour. American Express, Discover, MasterCard, and Visa are accepted.

One of the most enjoyable ways to take a sneak peak at retired life in Mexico is to read *Tales of Retirement in Paradise,* by Polly Vicars, an entertaining account of the pleasures of "retired" (but amazingly active) life in Puerto Vallarta. Proceeds of the book benefit the America-Mexico Foundation (www.puerto-vallarta.com/amf/), which provides scholarships to needy and deserving Mexican students. Buy the $20 book online through Amazon (www.amazon.com), or e-mail the author directly at phvicars@pvnet.com.mx.

FOR SINGLES

Mexico may be an old favorite for romantic honeymoons, but it's also a great place to travel on your own without really being or feeling alone. Although offering an identical room rate regardless of single or double occupancy is slowly becoming a trend in Mexico, many of the hotels mentioned in this book still offer singles at lower rates.

Mexicans are very friendly, and it's easy to meet other foreigners. But if you don't like the idea of traveling alone, try **Travel Companion Exchange,** P.O. Box 833, Amityville, NY 11701 (☎ **800/392-1256** or 516/454-0880; fax 516/454-0170), which brings prospective travelers together. Members complete a profile, then place an anonymous listing of their travel interests in the newsletter. Prospective traveling companions then make contact through the exchange. Membership costs $99 for 6 months or $159 for a year. They also offer an excellent booklet on avoiding theft and scams while traveling abroad, for $3.95. Order through the same number listed above.

FOR WOMEN   As a female traveling alone, I can tell you firsthand that I feel safer traveling in Mexico than in the United States. But I use the same commonsense precautions I use traveling anywhere else in the world, and I am alert to what's going on around me.

Mexicans in general, and men in particular, are nosy about single travelers, especially women. If a taxi driver or anyone else with whom you don't want to become friendly asks about your marital status, family, etc., my advice is to make up a set of answers (regardless of the truth): "I'm married, traveling with friends, and I have three children."

Saying you are single and traveling alone may send out the wrong message about availability. Movies and television shows exported from the United States have created an image of sexually aggressive North American women. If bothered by someone, don't try to be polite—just leave or head into a public place.

FOR STUDENTS

Because higher education is still considered more of a luxury than a birthright in Mexico, a formal network of student discounts and programs does not exist in this country. Also, most students within the country travel with their families, rather than with other students—thus student discount cards are not commonly recognized here.

For those wishing to study in Mexico, however, there are a number of university-affiliated and independent programs for intensive Spanish-language study. Frequently, these will also assist with accommodations, usually putting you up with a local family in their home. One such program is **KABAH Travel and Education Tourism,** based in Guadalajara, which offers study and travel programs throughout the country. You can receive faxed information by calling ☎ **800/596-4768.** More information is available at their Web site: **http://mexplaza.com.mx/kabah/**.

The University of Guadalajara has offered a respected language program for over 50 years, with credits accepted at major universities worldwide and with campuses in both Guadalajara and Puerto Vallarta. Details are available by calling ☎ **523/616-4399;** faxing 3/616-4013, or through their Web site: www.cepe.udg.mx.

7 Getting There

BY PLANE

The airline situation in Mexico is changing rapidly, with many new regional carriers offering scheduled service to areas previously not served. In addition to regularly scheduled service, charter service direct from U.S. cities to resorts is making Mexico more accessible. It has become much easier to fly to destinations without having to go through Mexico City than in the past.

THE MAJOR INTERNATIONAL AIRLINES   The main airlines operating direct or nonstop flights from the United States to points in Mexico include **Aerocalifornia** (☎ 800/237-6225), **Aeromexico** (☎ 800/237-6639), **Alaska Airlines** (☎ 800/426-0333), **America West** (☎ 800/235-9292), **American** (☎ 800/433-7300), **Continental** (☎ 800/231-0856), **Lacsa** (☎ 800/225-2272), **Mexicana** (☎ 800/531-7921), **Northwest** (☎ 800/225-2525), **United** (☎ 800/241-6522), and **US Airways** (☎ 800/428-4322).

CYBERDEALS FOR NET SURFERS

A great way to find the cheapest fare is by searching through the Internet. There are too many companies to mention them all, but a few of the better-respected ones are **Travelocity** (**www.travelocity. com**), **Microsoft Expedia** (**www.expedia.com**), and **Yahoo's Flifo Global** (**travel.yahoo.com/travel**). Each has its own little quirks—several require you to register with them, for example—but they all provide variations of the same service. Just enter the dates you want to fly and the cities you want to visit, and the computer looks for the lowest fares. The Yahoo site has a feature called "Fare Beater," which will check flights on other airlines or at different times or dates in hopes of finding an even cheaper fare. Expedia's site will e-mail you the best airfare deal once a week if you so choose. Travelocity uses the SABRE computer reservations system that most travel agents use, and has a "Last-Minute Deals" database that advertises really cheap fares for those who can get away at a moment's notice.

Great last-minute deals are also available directly from the airlines themselves through a free e-mail service called **E-savers.** Each week, the airline sends you a list of discounted flights, usually leaving the upcoming Friday or Saturday, and returning the following Monday or Tuesday. You can sign up for most of the major airlines at once by logging on to **Smarter Living** (www.smarterliving.com), or go to each individual airline's Web site:

- **Aeromexico:** www.aeromexico.com
- **Alaska Airlines:** www.alaskaair.com
- **American Airlines:** www.americanair.com
- **America West:** www.americawest.com
- **Continental Airlines:** www.flycontinental.com

- **Mexicana:** www.mexicana.com
- **Northwest Airlines:** www.nwa.com

One caveat: Charter airfares and those offered through wholesalers (like Apple Vacations, Funjet, etc.) are generally not included in these online services, meaning you still may want to check with a travel agent to ensure you have the best all-around package price.

BY CAR

Driving is not the cheapest way to get to Mexico, but it is the best way to see the country. Even so, you may think twice about taking your own car south of the border once you've pondered the bureaucratic requirements that affect foreign drivers here. One option would be to rent a car, for touring around a specific region, once you arrive in Mexico. Rental cars in Mexico are now generally new, clean, and very well maintained. Although pricier than in the United States, discounts are often available for rentals of a week or longer, especially when arrangements are made in advance from the United States. (See "Car Rentals" under "Getting Around," below, for more details.)

CAR DOCUMENTS

You must carry your temporary car-importation permit, tourist permit (see "Entry Requirements," above), and, if you purchased it, your proof of Mexican car insurance (see "Mexican Auto Insurance," below) in the car at all times. The temporary car-importation permit papers will be issued for 6 months to a year, while the tourist permit is usually issued for 30 days. It's a good idea to overestimate the time you'll spend in Mexico, so that if something unforeseen happens and you have to (or want to) stay longer, you'll have avoided the hassle of getting your papers extended. Whatever you do, don't overstay either permit. Doing so invites heavy fines and/or confiscation of your vehicle, which will not be returned. Remember also that 6 months does not necessarily work out to be 180 days—be sure to return before the expiration date

To drive your car into Mexico, you'll need a **temporary car-importation permit,** which is granted after you complete a strictly required list of documents (see below). The permit can be obtained either through Banco del Ejército (*Banjercito*) officials, who have a desk, booth, or office at the Mexican Customs (*Aduana*) building after you cross the border into Mexico. Or, you can obtain the permit before you travel, through Sanborn's Insurance (☎ **800/ 395-8482**) or the American Automobile Association (AAA) (☎ **800/222-4357**), each of which maintains border offices in

Texas, New Mexico, Arizona, and California. These companies may charge a fee for this service, but it will be worth it to avoid the uncertain prospect of traveling all the way to the border without proper documents for crossing. However, even if you go through Sanborn's or AAA, your credentials *may* be reviewed again by Mexican officials at the border—you must take them all with you since they are still subject to questions of validity.

The following requirements for border crossing were accurate at press time:

- **A valid driver's license,** issued outside of Mexico.
- **Current, original car registration and a copy of the original car title.** If the registration or title is in more than one name and not all the named people are traveling with you, then a notarized letter from the absent person(s) authorizing use of the vehicle for the trip is required; have it ready just in case. The car registration and your credit card (see below) must be in the same name.
- **A valid international major credit card.** With a credit card, you are required to pay only a $11.50 car-importation fee. The credit card must be in the same name as the car registration. If you do not have a major credit card (Visa, MasterCard, American Express, or Diners Club), you will have to post a bond or make a deposit equal to the value of the vehicle. Check cards are not accepted.
- **Original immigration documentation.** This will either be your tourist permit (FMT) or the original immigration booklet, FM2 or FM3, if you hold this more permanent status.
- **A signed declaration promising to return to your country of origin with the vehicle.** This form (Carta Promesa de Retorno) is provided by AAA or Sanborn's before you go or by Banjercito officials at the border. There's no charge. The form does not stipulate that you must return through the same border entry you came through on your way south.
- **Temporary Importation Application.** Upon signing this form, you are stating that you are only temporarily importing the car for your personal use, and will not be selling the vehicle. I find it's easier to deal with bureaucracy when the reasons behind the rules are clear—here, the strict entry requirements are in place to help regulate the entry and restrict the resale of unauthorized cars and trucks. Vehicles in the U.S. are much less expensive, and for years, were bought, brought into Mexico, and then sold.

If you receive your documentation at the border (rather than through Sanborn's or AAA), Mexican border officials will make two copies of everything and charge you for the copies. For up-to-the minute information, a great source is the Customs office in Nuevo Leon (Modulo de Importacion Temporal de Automoviles, Aduana Nuevo Leon), at ☎ **52-8/712-2071.**

Important reminder: Someone else may drive the car, but the person (or relative of the person) whose name appears on the car-importation permit must *always* be in the car at the same time. (If stopped by police, a nonregistered family member driving without the registered driver must be prepared to prove familial relationship to the registered driver—no joke.) Violation of this rule makes the car subject to impoundment and the driver to imprisonment and/ or a fine. You can drive a car with foreign license plates only if you have an international (non-Mexican) driver's license.

If you have any additional questions or you want to confirm the current rules, call your nearest Mexican consulate, Mexican Government Tourist Office, AAA, or **Sanborn's** (☎ **800/395-8482**). To check on road conditions or to get help with any travel emergency while in Mexico, call ☎ **01-800/903-9200,** or 5/250-0151 in Mexico City. Both numbers are staffed by English-speaking operators.

In addition, check with the **U.S. State Department** (see "Sources of Information," at the beginning of this chapter) for their warnings about dangerous driving areas.

MEXICAN AUTO INSURANCE

Auto insurance is not legally required in Mexico. U.S. insurance is invalid in Mexico; to be insured in Mexico, you must purchase Mexican insurance. Any party involved in an accident who has no insurance may be sent to jail, and his or her car will be impounded until all claims are settled. This is true even if you just drive across the border to spend the day. U.S. companies that broker Mexican insurance are commonly found at the border crossing, and several will quote daily rates.

Car insurance can also be purchased through **Sanborn's Mexico Insurance,** P.O. Box 52840, 2009 S. 10th, McAllen, TX 78505-2840 (☎ **800/638-9423** or 956/686-0711 in Texas; fax 956/ 686-1417). The company has offices at all of the border crossings in the United States. Its policies cost the same as the competition's do, but you get legal coverage (attorney and bail bonds if needed) and a detailed mile-by-mile guide for your proposed route. Most of Sanborn's border offices are open Monday through Friday, and a few are staffed on Saturday and Sunday. **AAA** auto club also sells insurance.

RETURNING TO THE UNITED STATES WITH YOUR CAR

The car papers you obtained when you entered Mexico *must* be returned when you cross back with your car or at some point within the time limit of 180 days. (You can cross as many times as you wish within the 180 days.) If the documents aren't returned, heavy fines are imposed ($250 for each 15 days late), and your car may be impounded and confiscated or you may be jailed if you return to Mexico. You can only return the car documents to a Banjercito official on duty at the Mexican Customs (*Aduana*) building *before* you cross back into the United States. Some border cities have Banjercito officials on duty 24 hours a day, but others do not; some also do not have Sunday hours. On the U.S. side, customs agents may or may not inspect your car from stem to stern.

BY SHIP

Numerous cruise lines serve Mexico's Central Pacific coast, known as the Mexican Riviera. Ships from California cruise down to the Baja Peninsula (including specialized whale-watching trips) and ports of call along the Pacific Coast.

If you don't mind taking off at the last minute, several cruise-tour specialists arrange substantial discounts on unsold cabins. One such company is **The Cruise Line,** 150 NW 168 St., North Miami Beach, Miami, FL 33169 (☎ **800/777-0707** or 305/521-2200).

BY BUS

Greyhound-Trailways (or its affiliates) offers service from around the United States to the Mexican border, where passengers disembark, cross the border, and buy a ticket for travel into the interior of Mexico. At many border crossings there are scheduled buses from the U.S. bus station to the Mexican bus station.

8   The Pros & Cons of Package Tours

Say the word "package tour" and many people automatically feel as though they're being forced to choose: your money or your lifestyle. This isn't necessarily the case. Most Mexican packages let you have both your independence *and* your in-the-black bank-account balance. Package tours are not the same thing as escorted tours. They are simply a way of buying your airfare, accommodations, and other pieces of your trip (usually airport transfers, and sometimes meals and activities) at the same time.

For popular destinations like Mexico's beach resorts they're often the smart way to go, because they can save you a ton of money. In many cases, a package that includes airfare, hotel, and transportation to and from the airport will cost you less than just the hotel alone if you booked it yourself. That's because packages are sold in bulk to tour operators, who resell them to the public.

You can buy a package at any time of the year, but the best deals usually coincide with low season—May to early December—when room rates and airfares plunge. But packages vary widely. Some offer a better class of hotels than others. Some offer the same hotels for lower prices. Some offer flights on scheduled airlines while others book charters. In some packages, your choices of accommodations and travel days may be limited. Each destination usually has some packagers that are better than the rest because they buy in even bigger bulk. Not only can that mean better prices, but it can also mean more choices—a packager that just dabbles in Mexico may have only a half-dozen or so hotels for you to choose from.

WARNINGS

- **Read the fine print.** Make sure you know *exactly* what's included in the price you're being quoted, and what's not.
- **Don't compare Mayas and Aztecs.** When you're looking over different packagers, compare the deals that they're offering on similar properties. Most packagers can offer bigger savings on some hotels than others.
- **Know what you're getting yourself into—and if you can get yourself out of it.** Before you commit to a package, make sure you know how much flexibility you have.
- **Use your best judgment.** Stay away from fly-by-nights and shady packagers. Go with a reputable firm with a proven track record. This is where your travel agent can come in handy.

WHERE TO BROWSE

- For one-stop shopping on the Web, go to **www.vacation packager.com**, an extensive search engine that'll link you up with more than 30 packagers offering Mexican beach vacations—and even let you custom design your own package.
- At **www.2travel.com** you'll find a page with links to a number of the big-name Mexico packagers, including several of the ones listed here.

PACKAGERS PACKIN' A PUNCH

- **Aeromexico Vacations** (☎ 800/245-8585; www.aeromexico. com): Year-round packages for Puerto Vallarta, including connections to Guadalajara, with a large selection of hotels in these destinations in a variety of price ranges.

- **Alaska Airlines Vacations** (☎ **800/426-0333;** www.alaskair. com) sells packages to Puerto Vallarta from Los Angeles, San Diego, San Jose, San Francisco, Seattle, Vancouver, Anchorage, and Fairbanks.

- **American Airlines Vacations** (☎ **800/321-2121;** www. americanair.com): American has year-round deals for Puerto Vallarta. You don't have to fly with American if you can get a better deal on another airline; land-only packages include hotel, airport transfers, and hotel room tax. American's hubs to Mexico are Dallas/Fort Worth, Chicago, and Miami, so you're likely to get the best prices—and the most direct flights—if you live near those cities.

- **America West Vacations** (☎ **800/356-6611;** www. americawest.com) has deals to Manzanillo and Puerto Vallarta, mostly from its Phoenix gateway.

- **Apple Vacations** (☎ **800/365-2775**): Apple offers inclusive packages with the largest choice of hotels: 6 in Manzanillo and 31 in Puerto Vallarta. Apple perks include baggage handling and the services of an Apple representative at the major hotels.

- **Continental Vacations** (☎ **800/634-5555;** www.fly continental.com): With Continental, you've got to buy air from the carrier if you want to book a room. The airline has year-round packages available to Puerto Vallarta, and the best deals are from Houston; Newark, New Jersey; and Cleveland.

- **Friendly Holidays** (☎ **800/344-5687;** www.2travel.com/ friendly/mexico.html): This major player in the Mexico field is based in upstate New York, but also has offices in California and Houston. They offer trips to all the resorts, including Puerto Vallarta and Manzanillo. Their Web site is very user-friendly, listing both a starting price for 3 nights in a hotel and a figure for air add-ons, so at least you have a rough idea of what your trip is likely to cost you.

- **Funjet Vacations** (bookable through travel agents or online at **www.funjet.com**): One of the largest vacation packagers in the United States, Funjet has packages to Mexico's resorts, including Puerto Vallarta. You can choose a charter or fly on American, Continental, Aeromexico, Alaska Airlines, or TWA.

- **Mexicana Vacations (or MexSeaSun Vacations)** (☎ **800/ 531-9321;** www.mexicana.com) offers getaways to Puerto Vallarta from Los Angeles, Chicago, and Denver.

• **TWA Vacations** (☎ 800/438-2929; www.twa.com) runs seasonal deals to Puerto Vallarta from their St. Louis hub.

REGIONAL PACKAGERS

From the East Coast: Liberty Travel (☎ 888/271-1584; www.libertytravel.com) frequently runs Mexico specials. Here, the best bet is to check the ads in your Sunday travel section or go to a Liberty rep near you.

From the West Coast: Sunquest Holidays (☎ 800/357-2400 or 888/888-5028 for departures within 14 days) is one of the largest packagers for Mexico on the West Coast, arranging regular charters to Puerto Vallarta from Los Angeles paired with a large selection of hotels.

From the Southwest: Town and Country (bookable through travel agents) packages regular deals to Puerto Vallarta and Manzanillo with America West, from the airline's Phoenix and Las Vegas gateways.

RESORTS   The biggest hotel chains and resorts also sell packages. The Mexican-owned Fiesta Americana/Fiesta Inns, for example, run **Fiesta Break** deals that include airfare from New York, Los Angeles, Dallas, or Houston, airport transfers, optional meal plans, and more. In 1999, a high-season Fiesta Break package from Dallas to Puerto Vallarta cost $495 per person, based on double occupancy, and includes airfare, tax, transfers, and 3 nights in the Fiesta Americana Puerto Vallarta. Call ☎ **800/9-BREAK-9** for details, or ☎ 800/FIESTA-1 for land-only packages.

9 Getting Around

An important note: If your travel schedule depends on an important connection, say a plane trip between points or a ferry or bus connection, use the telephone numbers in this book or other information resources mentioned here to find out if the connection you are depending on is still available. Although we've done our best to provide accurate information, transportation schedules can and do change.

BY PLANE

To fly from point to point within Mexico, you'll rely on Mexican airlines. Mexico has two privately owned large national carriers: **Mexicana** (☎ 800/366-5400) and **Aeromexico** (☎ 800/021-4000), in addition to several up-and-coming regional carriers.

Mexicana and Aeromexico both offer extensive connections to the United States as well as within Mexico.

Several of the new regional carriers are operated by or can be booked through Mexicana or Aeromexico. Regional carriers are **Aerocaribe** (see Mexicana); **Aerolitoral** (see Aeromexico); and **Aero Mar** (see Mexicana). The regional carriers are expensive, but they go to difficult-to-reach places. In each applicable section of this book, we've mentioned regional carriers with all pertinent telephone numbers.

Because major airlines can book some regional carriers, read your ticket carefully to see if your connecting flight is on one of these smaller carriers—they may leave from a different airport or check in at a different counter, especially true in the Guadalajara airport.

AIRPORT TAXES   Mexico charges an airport tax on all departures. Passengers leaving the country on an international departure pay $17.25—in dollars or the peso equivalent. It has become a common practice to include this departure tax in your ticket price, but double-check to make sure. Taxes on each domestic departure you make within Mexico cost around $12.50, unless you're on a connecting flight and have already paid at the start of the flight; you shouldn't be charged again if you have to change planes for a connecting flight. These taxes are usually included in the price of your ticket.

RECONFIRMING FLIGHTS   Although airlines in Mexico say it's not necessary to reconfirm a flight, it's still a good practice. To avoid getting bumped on popular, possibly overbooked flights, check in for an international flight an hour and a half in advance of travel.

BY CAR

Most Mexican roads are not up to U.S. standards of smoothness, hardness, width of curve, grade of hill, or safety marking. Driving at night is dangerous—the roads aren't good enough and are rarely lit; the trucks, carts, pedestrians, and bicycles usually have no lights; and you can hit potholes, animals, rocks, dead ends, or bridges out with no warning.

The "spirited" style of Mexican driving sometimes requires super vision and reflexes. Be prepared for different behavior, as when a truck driver flips on his left-turn signal when there's not a crossroad for miles. He's probably telling you the road's clear ahead for you to pass—after all, he's in a better position to see than you are. Another custom that's very important to respect is how to make a left turn. Never turn left by stopping in the middle of a highway with your left signal on. Instead, pull off the highway onto the right shoulder, wait for traffic to clear, then proceed across the road.

GASOLINE   There's one government-owned brand of gas and one gasoline station name throughout the country—**Pemex** (Petroleras Mexicanas). There are two types of gas in Mexico: *magna,* an 87-octane unleaded gas; and the newer premium 93-octane. In Mexico, fuel and oil are sold by the liter, which is slightly more than a quart (40 liters equals about 10^{1}/$_{2}$ gal.). *Important note:* No credit cards are accepted for gas purchases. There is a new trend toward franchise Pemex stations, many of which have bathroom facilities and convenience stores—a great improvement over the old Pemex stations.

TOLL ROADS   Mexico charges among the highest tolls in the world for its network of new toll roads. As a result, they are little used. Generally speaking, using the toll roads will cut your travel time between destinations. Older toll-free roads are generally in good condition but travel times are usually longer, since they tend to be mountainous and clotted with slow-moving trucks.

BREAKDOWNS   Your best guide to repair shops is the Yellow Pages. For specific makes and shops that repair cars, look under "Automoviles y Camiones: Talleres de Reparación y Servicio"; auto-parts stores are listed under "Refacciones y Accesorios para Automoviles." To find a mechanic on the road, look for a sign that says TALLER MECÁNICO.

If your car breaks down on the road, help might already be on the way. Radio-equipped, green repair trucks operated by uniformed English-speaking officers patrol the major highways during daylight hours to aid motorists in trouble. These **"Green Angels"** will perform minor repairs and adjustments for free, but you pay for parts and materials.

MINOR ACCIDENTS   When possible, many Mexicans drive away from minor accidents to avoid hassles with police, or try to make an immediate settlement to avoid involving the police. If the police arrive while the involved persons are still at the scene, everyone may be locked in jail until blame is assessed. In any case, you have to settle up immediately, which may take days of red tape. Foreigners who don't speak fluent Spanish are at a distinct disadvantage when trying to explain their side of the event. Three steps may help the foreigner who doesn't wish to do as the Mexicans do: If you're in your own car, notify your Mexican insurance company, whose job it is to intervene on your behalf. If you're in a rental car, notify the rental company immediately and ask how to contact the nearest adjuster. (You did buy insurance with the rental, right?) Finally, if all else fails, ask to contact the nearest Green Angel, who may be able to explain to officials that you are covered by insurance.

See also "Mexican Auto Insurance" in "Getting There," above.

CAR RENTALS

You'll get the best price if you reserve a car a week in advance in the United States. U.S. car-rental firms include **Avis** (☎ **800/331-1212** in the U.S.; 800/TRY-AVIS in Canada), **Budget** (☎ **800/ 527-0700** in the U.S. and Canada), **Hertz** (☎ **800/654-3131** in the U.S. and Canada), and **National** (☎ **800/CAR-RENT** in the U.S. and Canada). For European travelers, **Kemwel Holiday Auto** (☎ **800/678-0678**) and **Auto Europe** (☎ **800/223-5555**) can arrange Mexican rentals, sometimes through other agencies. These and some local firms have offices in Mexico City and most other large Mexican cities. You'll find rental desks at airports, all major hotels, and many travel agencies.

Cars are easy to rent if you have a major credit card, are 25 or over, and have a valid driver's license and passport with you. Without a credit card you must leave a cash deposit, usually a big one. Rent-here/leave-there arrangements are usually simple to make but more costly.

Car-rental costs are high in Mexico, because cars are more expensive here. The condition of rental cars has improved greatly over the years, however, and clean, comfortable, new cars are the norm. The basic cost of a 1-day rental of a Volkswagen Beetle, with unlimited mileage (but before 17% tax and $15 daily insurance) was $40 in Puerto Vallarta. Renting by the week gives you a lower daily rate. Avis was offering a basic 7-day weekly rate for a VW Beetle (before tax or insurance) of $190 in Puerto Vallarta. Prices may be considerably higher if you rent around a major holiday.

Car-rental companies usually write up a credit-card charge in U.S. dollars.

DEDUCTIBLES   Be careful—these vary greatly in Mexico; some are as high as $2,500, which comes out of your pocket immediately in case of car damage. Hertz's deductible is $1,000 on a VW Beetle; Avis's is $500 for the same car.

INSURANCE   Insurance is offered in two parts: **Collision and damage** insurance covers your car and others if the accident is your fault, and **personal accident** insurance covers you and anyone in your car. Read the fine print on the back of your rental agreement and note that insurance may be invalid if you have an accident while driving on an unpaved road.

DAMAGE   Always inspect your car carefully and note every damaged or missing item, no matter how minute, on your rental agreement, or you may be charged.

TROUBLE NUMBER   It's advisable to carefully note the rental company's trouble number, as well as the direct number of the agency where you rented the car.

BY TAXI

Taxis are the preferred way to get around almost all of the resort areas of Mexico, and also within Guadalajara. Short trips within towns are generally charged by preset zones, and are quite reasonable compared with U.S. rates. For longer trips or excursions to nearby cities, taxis can generally be hired for around $10 to $15 per hour, or for a negotiated daily rate. Even drops to different destinations, say between Puerto Vallarta and Barra de Navidad, can be arranged. A negotiated one-way price is usually much less than the cost of a rental car for a day, and service is much faster than traveling by bus. For anyone who is uncomfortable driving in Mexico, this is a convenient, comfortable route. An added bonus is that you have a Spanish-speaking person with you in case you run into any car or road trouble. Many taxi drivers speak at least some English. Your hotel can assist you with the arrangements.

BY BUS

Mexican buses are frequent, readily accessible, and can get you to almost anywhere you want to go. They're often the only way to get from large cities to other nearby cities and small villages. Don't hesitate to ask questions if you're confused about anything.

Dozens of Mexican companies operate large, air-conditioned, Greyhound-type buses between most cities. Travel class is generally labeled first (*primera*), second (*segunda*), and deluxe, which is referred to by a variety of names. The deluxe buses often have fewer seats than regular buses, show video movies en route, are air-conditioned, and have few stops; some have complimentary refreshments. Many run express from the origin to the final destination, and they are well worth the few dollars more that you'll pay. In rural areas, buses are often of the school-bus variety, with lots of local color.

Travel Tip

There's little English spoken at bus stations, so come prepared with your destination written down, then double-check the departure.

Whenever possible, it's best to buy your reserved-seat ticket, often via a computerized system, a day in advance on many long-distance routes and especially before holidays. Schedules are fairly dependable, so be at the terminal on time for departure. Current information must be obtained from local bus stations.

See the Appendix for a list of helpful bus terms in Spanish.

FAST FACTS: Mexico

Abbreviations   Dept. (apartments); Apdo. (post office box); av. (avenida; avenue); c/ (calle; street); calz. (calzada; boulevard). "C" on faucets stands for *caliente* (hot), and "F" stands for *fría* (cold). PB (*planta baja*) means ground floor, and most buildings count the next floor up as the first floor (1).

Business Hours   In general, businesses in larger cities are open between 9am and 7pm; in smaller towns many close between 2 and 4pm. Most are closed on Sunday. Bank hours are Monday through Friday from 9 or 9:30am to 5 or 6pm. Increasingly, banks are offering Saturday hours for at least a half-day.

Cameras/Film   Film costs about the same as in the United States. Tourists wishing to use a video or still camera at any archaeological site in Mexico and at many museums operated by the Instituto de Antropología e Historia (INAH) will be required to pay $4 per video camera and/or still camera in their possession at each site or museum visited. Such fees are noted in the listings for specific sites and museums. It's courteous to ask permission before photographing anyone.

Customs   See "Visitor Information, Entry Requirements & Money," earlier in this chapter.

Doctors/Dentists   Every embassy and consulate can recommend local doctors and dentists with good training and modern equipment; some of the doctors and dentists even speak English. See the list of embassies and consulates under "Embassies/consulates," below. Hotels with a large foreign clientele can often recommend English-speaking doctors. Almost all first-class hotels in Mexico have a doctor on call.

Drug Laws   To be blunt, don't use or possess illegal drugs in Mexico. Mexican officials have no tolerance for drug users, and jail is their solution, with very little hope of getting out until the sentence (usually a long one) is completed or heavy fines or bribes are paid. Remember—in Mexico the legal system assumes you are guilty until proven innocent. (*Important note:* It isn't uncommon to be befriended by a fellow user, only to be turned in by that "friend"—he's collected a bounty for turning you in.) Bring prescription drugs in their original containers. If possible, pack a copy of the original prescription with the generic name of the drug.

U.S. Customs officials are also on the lookout for diet drugs that are sold in Mexico but are illegal in the U.S. If you buy antibiotics over the counter (which you can do in Mexico)—say, for a sinus infection—and still have some left, you probably won't be hassled by U.S. Customs.

Drugstores   Drugstores (*farmacias*) will sell you just about anything you want, with a prescription or without one. Most drugstores are open Monday through Saturday from 8am to 8pm. There are generally one or two 24-hour pharmacies in each major resort area. If you are in a smaller town and need to buy medicines after normal hours, ask for the *farmacia de turno;* pharmacies take turns staying open during off-hours.

Electricity   The electrical system in Mexico is 110 volts A/C (60 cycles), as in the United States and Canada. However, in reality it may cycle more slowly and overheat your appliances. To compensate, select a medium or low speed for hair dryers. Many older hotels still have electrical outlets for flat two-prong plugs; you'll need an adapter for any modern electrical apparatus that has an enlarged end on one prong or that has three prongs. Many first-class and deluxe hotels have the three-holed outlets (*trifásicos* in Spanish). Those that don't may have loan adapters, but to be sure, it's always better to carry your own.

Embassies/Consulates   They provide valuable lists of doctors and lawyers, as well as regulations concerning marriages in Mexico. Contrary to popular belief, your embassy cannot get you out of a Mexican jail, provide postal or banking services, or fly you home when you run out of money. Consular officers can provide you with advice on most matters and problems, however. Most countries have a representative embassy in Mexico City, and many have consular offices or representatives in the provinces.

The Embassy of the **United States** in Mexico City is next to the Hotel María Isabel Sheraton at Paseo de la Reforma 305, at the corner of Río Danubio (☎ **5/209-9100**). There is a U.S. Consulate General in Guadalajara, Progreso 175 (☎ **3/825-2998**); and a consular agency in Puerto Vallarta (☎ **322/2-0069**).

The Embassy of **Canada** in Mexico City is at Schiller 529, in Polanco (☎ **5/724-7900**); it's open Monday through Friday from 9am to 1pm and 2 to 5pm (at other times the name of a duty officer is posted on the embassy door). Additionally, Canada has consular services in Guadalajara (☎ **3/615-6270** or 3/615-6215) and in Puerto Vallarta at Zaragoza 160, 1st floor (☎ **322/2-5398**).

The Embassy of the **United Kingdom** in Mexico City is in Río Lerma 71, Col. Cuahutemoc (☎ **5/207-2089** or 5/207-2189); it's open Monday through Friday from 8:30am to 3:30pm. There's also a UK consular office in Guadalajara (☎ **3/761-6405**).

Irish and **South African** citizens must go to the British Consulate.

The Embassy of **Australia** in Mexico City is at Ruben Darío 55, Col. Polanco (☎ **5/531-5225;** fax 5/531-9552); it's open Monday through Friday from 9am to 1pm.

The Embassy of **New Zealand** in Mexico City is at José Luis Lagrange 103, 10th floor, Col. Los Morales Polanco (☎ **5/281-5304** or 5/281-5486); it's open Monday through Thursday from 9am to 2pm and 3 to 5pm, and Friday from 9am to 2pm.

Emergencies   In most areas **060** is the number for police. The 24-hour **Tourist Help Line** in Mexico City is ☎ **800/903-9200** or 5/250-0151. A tourist legal assistance office (Procuraduria del Turista) is located in Mexico City (☎ **5/625-8153** or 5/625-8154). They offer 24-hour service, and there is always an English-speaking person available.

Legal Aid   International Legal Defense Counsel, 111 S. 15th St., 24th Floor, Packard Building, Philadelphia, PA 19102 (☎ **215/977-9982**), is a law firm specializing in legal difficulties of Americans abroad. See also "Embassies/Consulates" and "Emergencies," above.

Newspapers/Magazines   Two English-language newspapers, the *News* and the *Mexico City Times,* are published in Mexico City, distributed nationally, and carry world news and commentaries, plus a calendar of the day's events, including concerts, art shows, and plays. In Puerto Vallarta, the English-language *Vallarta Today* is published daily, and the *Tribune* is published weekly. The

Guadalajara Reporter is an excellent English-language weekly that also has a Puerto Vallarta supplement. Newspaper kiosks will also carry a selection of English-language magazines.

Pets   Taking a pet into Mexico is easy, but requires a little preplanning. For travelers coming from the United States and Canada, your pet needs to be checked for health within 30 days of arrival in Mexico. Most veterinarians in major cities have the appropriate paperwork—an official health certificate, to be presented to Mexican Customs officials, which ensures that the pet is up-to-date on its vaccinations. When you and your pet return from Mexico, the same type of paperwork will be required by U.S. Customs officials. If your stay extends beyond the 30-day time frame of your U.S.-issued certificate, you'll need to get an updated Certificate of Health issued by a veterinarian in Mexico that also states the condition of your pet, and the status of its vaccinations. To be certain of any last-minute changes in requirements, consult the Mexican Government Tourist Office nearest you (see "Visitor Information, Entry Requirements & Money," earlier in this chapter).

Police   In Mexico City, police are to be suspected as frequently as they are to be trusted; however, you'll find many who are quite honest and helpful. In the rest of the country, especially in the tourist areas, the majority are very protective of international visitors. Several cities, including Puerto Vallarta, have gone as far as to set up a special corps of English-speaking Tourist Police to assist with directions, guidance, and more.

Taxes   There's a 15% IVA tax on goods and services in most of Mexico, and it's supposed to be included in the posted price. There is an exit tax of around $17.25 imposed on every foreigner leaving the country, usually included in the price of airline tickets.

Telephone/Fax   Telephone area codes are gradually being changed all over the country. The change may affect the area code and first digit or only the area code. Some cities are even adding exchanges and changing whole numbers. Courtesy messages telling you that the number you dialed has been changed do not exist. You can call operator assistance (**040**) for difficult-to-reach numbers. Many fax numbers are also regular telephone numbers; you have to ask whoever answers your call for the fax tone (*"tono de fax, por favor"*).

The **country code** for Mexico is **52.** For instructions on how to call Mexico from the United States, call the United States from

Phone Update

In mid-1999, the Mexico telephone system was changed to require seven-digit local telephone numbers. It will probably take several years before listing numbers as such becomes commonplace. Until then, here's an easy way to understand the change: Wherever you are in Mexico, add the appropriate number of digits from the area code to make up a seven-digit number. For example: if a phone number in Puerto Vallarta appears as: 322/1-2345, you would dial 221-2345 to reach this number locally.

Mexico, place calls within Mexico, or use a pay phone, consult "Telephones & Mail" in the Appendix.

Time Zone   Central standard time prevails throughout most of Mid-Pacific Mexico, but the state of Nayarit, including Nuevo Vallarta, is on Mountain Standard Time. Mexico observes **daylight saving time.**

Water   Most hotels have decanters or bottles of purified water in the rooms, and the better hotels have either purified water from regular taps or special taps marked *agua purificada.* Some hotels will charge for in-room bottled water. Virtually any hotel, restaurant, or bar will bring you purified water if you specifically request it, but you'll usually be charged for it. Bottled purified water is sold widely at drugstores and grocery stores (popular brands include Santa Maria, Ciel, Agua Pura, Pureza, and Bonafit).

2

Settling into Puerto Vallarta

*P*uerto Vallarta was never the "sleepy little fishing village" that many proclaim. It began life as a port for processing the silver brought down from mines in the Sierra Madre—then was forever transformed by a movie director and two star-crossed lovers. In 1963, John Huston brought stars Ava Gardner and Richard Burton here to film the Tennessee Williams play *Night of the Iguana*. Burton's new love, Elizabeth Taylor, came along to ensure the romance remained in full bloom—despite the fact both were married to others at the time. Titillated, the international paparazzi arrived, and when they weren't shooting photos of the famous couple—or of Ava Gardner water-skiing back from the set, surrounded by a bevy of beach boys—they photographed the beauty of Puerto Vallarta.

This seaside town was never the same, and the later addition of a highway and airport helped it mature into the resort it is today. At press time, Vallarta was braced for another *Iguana* invasion; a remake of the film is set to be filmed here in late 1999.

Luxury hotels and shopping centers have sprung up to the north and south of the original town, allowing Vallarta to grow to a sizable city of 250,000 without sacrificing its considerable charms. Today, it boasts the services and infrastructure of a modern city—over 250 restaurants, a sizzling nightlife, and enough shops and galleries to tempt even jaded consumers—as well as the authenticity of a colonial Mexican village.

Cool breezes flow down from the mountains along the Río Cuale, which runs through the center of town. The main waterfront street, or *malecón,* is graced with fanciful public sculptures and bordered by lively restaurants, shops, and bars. The malecón is a magnet for both residents and visitors, who stroll the broad walkway to take in an ocean breeze, a multihued sunset, or a moonlit, perfect wave.

If I sound partial, it's not just because Puerto Vallarta is my favorite of Mexico's sunny resorts; this has been my home for the past 8 years. I live here in good company—there's a considerable colony of American and Canadian residents. Perhaps they feel as I do, that the surrounding mountains offer the equivalent of a continual, comforting embrace, adding to that sense of welcome that so many visitors feel as well.

1 Puerto Vallarta Essentials

620 miles NW of Mexico City; 260 miles W of Guadalajara; 175 miles NW of Manzanillo; 300 miles SE of Mazatlán; 112 miles SW of Tepic

GETTING THERE & DEPARTING

BY PLANE   For a list of international carriers serving Mexico, see chapter 1, "Planning a Trip to Mid-Pacific Mexico." Some local numbers of international carriers serving Puerto Vallarta: **Alaska Airlines** (☎ **322/1-1350** or 322/1-1353), **American Airlines** (☎ **322/1-1972** or 322/1-1799; fax 322/1-1032), **America West** (☎ **322/1-1333**), **Continental** (☎ **322/1-1025;** fax 322/1-1096).

From other points in Mexico, **Aeromexico** (☎ **322/4-2777** or 322/1-1055) flies from Aguascalientes, Guadalajara, La Paz, León, Mexico City, Morelia, and Tijuana. **Mexicana** (☎ **322/4-8900,** 322/1-1266, or 322/1-0243) has direct or nonstop flights from Guadalajara, Mazatlán, Los Cabos, and Mexico City.

BY CAR   The coastal **Highway 200** is the only choice between Mazatlán to the north (6 hr. away) or Manzanillo to the south ($3^{1}/2$ to 4 hr.). The 6-hour journey from Guadalajara through Tepic can be shortened to 4 to 5 hours by taking Highway 15A from Chapalilla to Compostela (this bypasses Tepic and saves 2 hr.), then continuing south on Highway 200 to Puerto Vallarta.

BY BUS   A new bus station, **Central Camionera de Puerto Vallarta,** opened in early 1998 and has centralized bus travel in and out of Puerto Vallarta. Located just north of the airport, approximately 7 miles from downtown, it offers ticketing, long-distance telephone and fax service, restaurants, overnight guarded parking, baggage storage, and local transportation into town. A large, marble-floored waiting area offers ample seating in air-conditioned comfort. Most major first-class bus lines operate from here, with transportation to points throughout Mexico including Mazatlán, Tepic, Manzanillo, Guadalajara, and Mexico City. Taxis into town cost approximately $3.50 and are readily available; public buses have a regular stop in front of the arrivals hall, operating from 7am to 11pm.

ORIENTATION

ARRIVING BY PLANE   The airport is close to the north end of town near Marina Vallarta, about 6 miles from downtown.

Transportes Terrestres minivan (colectivo) and **Aeromovil** taxis make the trip. Costs for both are determined by zones—clearly posted at the respective ticket booths. **Colectivo** fares are $3, $4.50, $5.50, and $7 (for the farthest zone, the southern Hotel Zone). Colectivos to town run only when they fill up, so you may have to wait a bit to obtain transportation. **Airport taxis** are federally licensed taxis that operate exclusively to provide transportation from the airport. Their fares are almost three times as high as city (yellow) taxis. A trip to downtown Puerto Vallarta costs $8, whereas a return trip using a city taxi will cost only $3. Yellow cabs are restricted to picking up passengers leaving the airport.

VISITOR INFORMATION   The **Municipal Tourism Office,** at Juárez and Independencia (☎ **322/3-2500;** ask for the Tourism office), is in a corner of the white Presidencia Municipal building (city hall) on the north end of the main square. In addition to offering a listing of current events and a collection of promotional brochures for local activities and services, they can also assist with specific questions—there's always an English-speaking person on staff. This is also the office of the tourist police. It's open Monday through Friday from 8am to 8pm.

The **State Tourism Office,** at Plaza Marina L 144, 2nd floor (☎ **322/1-2676,** 322/1-2677, or 322/1-2678), also offers promotional brochures, and can assist with specific questions about Puerto Vallarta and other points within the state of Jalisco, including Guadalajara, the Costa Alegre, and the town of Tequila. It's open Monday through Friday from 9am to 7pm and Saturday from 9am to 1pm.

GETTING AROUND   By Taxi   Taxis are plentiful and relatively inexpensive. Most trips from downtown to the northern Hotel Zone and Marina Vallarta cost between $3.50 and $5; to or from Marina Vallarta to Mismaloya Beach to the south costs $7. Rates are charged by zone, and are generally posted in the lobbies of hotels. Taxis can also be hired by the hour or day for longer trips, when you'd prefer to leave the driving to someone else. Rates run between $10 and $12 per hour, with discounts available for full-day rates. At publication time there was talk of switching to the use of meters.

By Car   Rental cars are available at the airport and through travel agencies, but unless you're planning a distant side trip, don't bother. Car rentals are expensive, averaging $60 per day, and parking around town is difficult.

Puerto Vallarta: Hotel Zone & Beaches

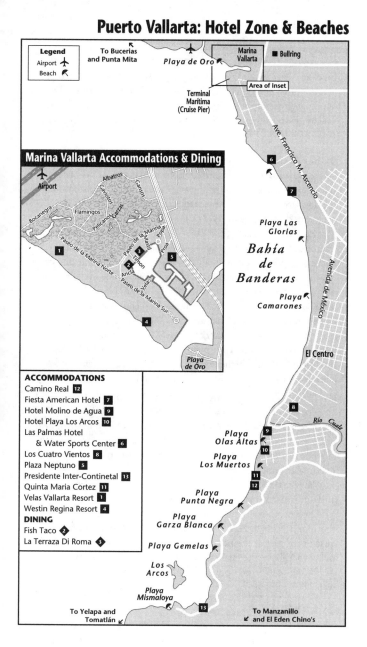

Legend
Airport ✈
Beach ↖

To Bucerías and Punta Mita

Playa de Oro

Marina Vallarta

■ Bullring

Terminal Marítima (Cruise Pier)

Area of Inset

Marina Vallarta Accommodations & Dining

✈ Airport

Albatros

Bocanegra

Flamingos

Gaviotas

Pelícanos

Garzas

Canos

Paseo de la Marina

Proa

Popa

Paseo de la Marina Norte

Ancla

Timón

Vela

Paseo de la Marina Sur

Playa de Oro

Ave. Francisco M. Ascencio

Playa Las Glorias

Bahía de Banderas

Playa Camarones

Avenida de México

El Centro

Río Cuale

Playa Olas Altas

Playa Los Muertos

Playa Punta Negra

Playa Garza Blanca

Playa Gemelas

Los Arcos

Playa Mismaloya

To Yelapa and Tomatlán

To Manzanillo and El Eden Chino's

ACCOMMODATIONS
Camino Real 12
Fiesta American Hotel 7
Hotel Molino de Agua 9
Hotel Playa Los Arcos 10
Las Palmas Hotel
& Water Sports Center 6
Los Cuatro Vientos 8
Plaza Neptuno 5
Presidente Inter-Continetal 13
Quinta Maria Cortez 11
Velas Vallarta Resort 1
Westin Regina Resort 4
DINING
Fish Taco 2
La Terraza Di Roma 3

Steer Clear of the Rambo Bus!

Buses in Vallarta tend to be rather aggressive, and some even sport names—including "Terminator," "Rambo," and "Tornado." Don't tempt fate by assuming these buses will stop for pedestrians. Although Vallarta is an extremely low-crime city, bus accidents are frequent.

By Bus & Colectivo   City buses run from the airport through the Hotel Zone along Morelos street (1 block inland from the malecón), across the Río Cuale, and inland on Vallarta, looping back through the downtown hotel and restaurant districts on Insurgentes and several other downtown streets. To get to the northern hotel strip from old Puerto Vallarta, take the "Zona Hoteles," "Ixtapa," or "Aeropuerto" bus. These same buses may also post the names of hotels they pass such as Krystal, Fiesta Americana, Sheraton, and others. Buses marked MARINA VALLARTA will travel inside this area, stopping at the major hotels there. These buses, costing about 30¢, will serve just about all your transportation needs frequently and inexpensively. Buses run generally from 6am to 11pm, and it's rare to wait more than a few minutes for one. Another bus route travels south every 10 to 15 minutes to either Mismaloya Beach or Boca de Tomatlán (the destination will be indicated in the front window) from Plaza Lázaro Cárdenas, a few blocks south of the river at Cárdenas and Suárez.

By Boat   The cruise ship pier (*muelle*), also called Terminal Marítima, is where **excursion boats** to Yelapa, Las Ánimas, Quimixto, and the Marietas Islands depart. It's north of town near the airport and an inexpensive taxi or bus ride from town. Just take any bus marked IXTAPA and tell the driver to let you off at the Terminal Marítima.

   Water taxis offering direct transportation to Yelapa, Las Ánimas, and Quimixto leave at 10:30 and 11am from the pier at Los Muertos Beach (south of downtown) on Rodolfo Rodríguez next to the Hotel Marsol. Another water taxi departs at 11am from the beachfront pier at the northern edge of the malecón. A round-trip ticket to Yelapa (the farthest point) costs $12. Return trips usually depart between 3 and 4pm, but confirm the pick-up time with your water-taxi captain.

CITY LAYOUT

The seaside promenade (the malecón) borders the street **paseo Díaz Ordaz,** which runs north to south through the central downtown area. From the waterfront, the town stretches back into the hills a half a dozen blocks. The areas bordering the **Río Cuale** are the oldest parts of town—the original Puerto Vallarta. The area immediately south of the river, called **Olas Altas** after its main street (and sometimes, Los Muertos, after the beach of the same name), is now home to a growing selection of sidewalk cafes, fine restaurants, espresso bars, and hip nightclubs, many with live music. Once you're in the center of town, you'll find nearly everything within walking distance both north and south of the river. The two sections of downtown are linked by **bridges** on Insurgentes (northbound traffic) and Ignacio Vallarta (southbound traffic).

Beyond downtown, Puerto Vallarta has grown along the beach to the north and south. **Nuevo Vallarta,** a planned resort, is north of the airport, across the Ameca River in the state of Nayarit (about 8 miles north of downtown). It also has hotels, condominiums, and a yacht marina, but very little in the way of restaurants, shopping, or other attractions. Most hotels there are all-inclusive, and guests usually plan to travel the distance into Puerto Vallarta (about an $8 cab ride) for anything other than poolside or beach action—however, these hotels do enjoy some of the finest beaches in the bay. There is regularly scheduled public bus service for about 25¢, which runs until 10pm.

Marina Vallarta, a resort city within a city, is at the northern edge of the Hotel Zone not far from the airport—you pass it on the right as you come into town from the airport. It boasts the most modern luxury hotels plus condominiums and residential homes, a huge marina with 450 yacht slips, a golf course, restaurants and bars, a water park, and several shopping plazas. Because the area began life as a swamp, filled in for development, the beaches are the least desirable in the area, with darker sand and seasonal inflows of cobblestones. They are, however, more than made up for by exquisite pools at the oceanfront hotels. Here, you're on a peninsula facing the open ocean and in a completely separate world from the rest of Puerto Vallarta.

Don't Let Taxi Drivers Steer You the Wrong Way

Beware of restaurant recommendations offered by taxi drivers—many receive a commission from restaurants where they discharge passengers. Be especially wary if a driver tries to talk you out of a restaurant you've already selected.

Linking downtown to the airport is **avenida Francisco Medina Ascencio** (formerly called **avenida de las Palmas**). Along this main thoroughfare are many luxury hotels (in an area called the **Zona Hotelera,** or Hotel Zone), plus several shopping centers with casual restaurants.

Bucerías, a small beachfront village of cobblestone streets, villas, and small hotels, is farther north along Banderas Bay, 19 miles beyond the airport. Past Bucerías, following the curved coastline of Banderas Bay, is **Punta de Mita.** Once a truly rustic village of fishermen and bamboo houses, it is on the verge of imminent development as a series of luxury resorts, private villas, and golf courses.

Going in the other direction from downtown is the southern coastal highway, home to more luxury hotels. Immediately south of town lies the exclusive residential and rental district of **Conchas Chinas.** Six miles south, on **Playa Mismaloya** (where *Night of the Iguana* was filmed), lies the Jolla de Mismaloya Resort. There's no road servicing the southern shoreline of Banderas Bay, but three small coastal villages are popular attractions for visitors to Puerto Vallarta: **Las Ánimas, Quimixto,** and **Yelapa,** all accessible only by boat. Yelapa, located on a beautiful sheltered cove, has been a popular haven for long-term ex-pat visitors and artists, due to its seclusion, natural beauty, and simplicity of life. Offering a selection of primitive accommodations, Yelapa—which has only solar-powered electricity—also offers beachside restaurants and hikes to one of two jungle waterfalls. Quimixto and Las Ánimas are popular day excursions aboard tour boats or water taxis. The tiny, pristine cove of **Caletas,** site of John Huston's former home, is a popular day or nighttime excursion (see "Boat Tours" in chapter 3).

FAST FACTS: Puerto Vallarta

American Express   The local office is located in town at Morelos 660, at the corner of Abasolo (☎ **01-800/333-3211** in Mexico, or 322/3-2955). It's open Monday through Friday from 9am to 6pm and Saturday from 9am to 1pm, and offers excellent, efficient travel agency services in addition to money exchange and traveler's checks.

Area Code   The telephone area code is **322.**

Climate   It's warm all year, with tropical temperatures; however, evenings in the winter months can turn quite cool. Summers are sunny, but with an increase in humidity during the rainy season, between May and October. Rains come almost every afternoon in June and July but are usually brief and strong—just enough to cool off the air for evening activities. September is the month in which heat and humidity are least comfortable, and rains are the heaviest.

Consumer Assistance   Tourists with complaints about taxis, stores, or other matters should contact **PROFECO,** the consumer protection office (☎ **322/5-0000** or 322/5-0018). They are open from 9am to 5pm, Monday through Friday.

Currency Exchange   Banks are found throughout downtown, and also in the other prime shopping areas of Vallarta. Most banks are open from 9am to 5pm Monday through Friday, with partial-day hours on Saturday. ATMs are commonly found throughout Vallarta, including on the central plaza downtown. Money-exchange houses (*casas de cambio*) are also located throughout town, and offer longer hours than the banks with only slightly lower exchange rates.

Embassies/Consulates   Both the U.S. and Canadian consulates maintain offices here, in the building on the southern border of the central plaza (you'll see the U.S. and Canadian flags). The **U.S. Consular Agency** office (☎ **322/2-0069,** fax 322/3-0074; 24 hours for emergencies) is open Monday through Friday from 10am to 2pm. The **Canadian Consulate** (☎ **322/2-5398** or 322/3-0858; emergencies 01-800-706-2900, 24 hours) is open Monday through Friday from 9am to 5pm.

Emergencies   **Police Emergency** ☎ 060; **local police** ☎ 322/1-2588 or 322/1-0759; **Tourist Protection** ☎ 01-800-90-39200; **Intensive Care Ambulance** ☎ 322/5-0386; **Ameri-Med Urgent Care** (U.S.-standards health care service, available 24 hours) ☎ 322/1-0023 or 322/1-0026; www.amerimed.com.mx; **Red Cross** ☎ 322/2-1533.

Internet Access   Puerto Vallarta is one of the better-connected destinations in Mexico when it comes to Internet access. Of the several cybercafes around town, one of the most popular is **Puerto Net,** Juarez 388, 1 block north of the main square (☎ **322/2-0204**), open Monday through Saturday from 9am to 11pm and Sunday from 3pm to 9pm.

Newspapers & Magazines   *Vallarta Today,* a daily English-language newspaper (☎ **322/5-3303**), is an excellent source for local information and upcoming events. The quarterly city magazine *Vallarta Lifestyles* (☎ **322/1-0106**) is also very popular, but provides listings only of services from those who advertise, so is not comprehensive. Both are available for sale at area newsstands and hotel gift shops. The weekly *P. V. Tribune* (☎ 322/3-0585) is distributed free, throughout town, and offers more of an objective, local viewpoint.

Pharmacies (late night)   **CMQ Farmacia,** Basilio Badillo 365, is open 24 hours (☎ 322/2-1330).

Post Office   The post office (*correo*) is at Mina 188 (☎ 322/2-1888). It's open Monday through Friday from 9am to 7:30pm, Saturday from 9am to 1pm.

Safety   Puerto Vallarta enjoys a very low crime rate throughout the city. Public Transportation is perfectly safe to use, and Tourist Police (dressed in white safari uniforms with white hats) are available to answer questions, give directions, and offer assistance. Most crimes or encounters with the police are linked to using or purchasing drugs—so simply don't do it here (see chapter 1, "Planning a Trip to Mid-Pacific Mexico").

2 Where to Stay

Beyond a varied selection of hotels, Puerto Vallarta has many other types of accommodations. Oceanfront or marina-view condominiums or elegant private villas are also available; both can offer a better value and more ample space for families or small groups. For more information on short-term rentals, contact **Bill Taylor Real Estate,** International Yachting Center, Royal Pacific Yacht Club, Local 1, calle Timóm s/n, Marina Vallarta (☎ 322/1-0923 or 322/1-1085; www.tristarrentals.com). Prices start at $99 a night for nonbeachfront condos and go to $1,000 for penthouse condos or private villas. **Vicki Skinner's Doin' It Right in Puerto Vallarta** (☎ 800/936-3646 or 619/297-3642; e-mail: GayPVR@aol.com) is a special service that rents gay-friendly condos and villas for individuals and groups (up to 75 people), and can package private chef and tour services with accommodations.

The following listings of the hotels are provided in directional order, moving south along Banderas Bay from the airport.

MARINA VALLARTA

Marina Vallarta is the most modern and deluxe area of hotel development in Puerto Vallarta. Located immediately south of the airport and just north of the Maritime (cruise-ship) Terminal, it's a planned development whose centerpiece is a 450-slip modern marina. The boardwalk surrounding the marina is filled with excellent restaurants, bars, galleries, and shops. A stay here is a world apart from the quaintness of downtown Puerto Vallarta.

The hotels reviewed below are located on the beachfront of the peninsula. The beaches here are much less attractive than beaches in other parts of the bay; the sand is darker and firmly packed, and, during certain times of the year, also quite rocky. The hotels in this zone make up for this shortfall with oversized pool areas and exotic landscaping. Still, if you're longing for a beautiful beach, try one of the southern hotel options. This area is better for families, or for those looking for lots of centralized activity. Marina Vallarta is also home to an 18-hole **golf course** designed by Joe Finger, and the **Vidafel Waterpark,** with water slides and tubes, pools, inner-tube canal, and snack-bar facilities. Open to the public daily from 11am to 6pm, it costs $8 for adults and $6 for kids, and is located across from the Mayan Palace Resort.

Because of traffic more than distance, a taxi from the Marina to downtown takes 20 to 30 minutes.

✪ **Velas Vallarta Grand Suite Resort.** paseo de la Marina 485, Marina Vallarta, 48354 Puerto Vallarta, Jal. ☎ **800/659-8477** in the U.S. and Canada, or 322/1-0091. Fax 322/1-0755. www.velasvallarta.com. E-mail: velasv@pvnet.com.mx. 361 units. A/C TV TEL. High season $220 double, $300–$540 suite. Low season $150 double, $220–$380 suite. AE, DC, MC, V. Free indoor parking.

Velas Vallarta is an excellent choice for families, as each suite offers a full-size, fully equipped kitchen, ample living and dining areas, separate bedroom(s), and a large balcony with seating. The apartments are tastefully decorated with light-wood furnishings, cool terrazzo floors, bright fabrics, and marble tub/shower-combination bathrooms. This property is actually part hotel, part full-ownership condominiums, which means each suite is the size of a true residential unit, offering the feeling of a home away from home. The suites all have partial ocean views, as they face onto a central area where three free-form swimming pools, complete with bridges and waterfalls, meander through tropical gardens. A full range of services—including restaurants, minimarket, deli, tennis courts, spa, and boutiques—means you'd never need to leave the place if you didn't want to. The Marina Golf Club is across the street, and special packages are available to Velas guests.

Dining: An excellent and elegant Italian restaurant, **Andrea,** offers indoor or patio dining and has an exhibition kitchen. The beachfront restaurant, **La Ribera,** offers casual, international fare, with grilled steaks and lobsters as specialties. Both are open for breakfast, lunch, and dinner. Poolside, the **Aquabar** swim-up bar serves beverages, light fare, and free drinks from 6 to 7pm.

Amenities: Beachfront with water-sports rental equipment, fitness center with sauna and massage service, minimarket, deli, boutique, beauty salon, activities program for children and adults, three lighted tennis courts, bicycle rentals, golf privileges at Marina Vallarta Golf Club, laundry, room service, car rental, concierge, travel agency. A new, expansive meeting facility, with its own catering kitchen, opened in mid-1999.

✪ **Westin Regina Resort.** paseo de la Marina Sur 205, Marina Vallarta, 48321 Puerto Vallarta, Jal. ☎ **800/228-3000** in the U.S., or 322/1-1100. Fax 322/1-1121. 280 units. A/C MINIBAR TV TEL. High season $195–$295 double, $415–$520 suite. Low season $160–170 double, $335–$420 suite. AE, DC, MC, V. Free parking.

Stunning architecture and vibrant colors are the hallmark of this award-winning property, considered Puerto Vallarta's finest. Though the grounds are large—over 21 acres with 850 feet of beachfront—the warm service and gracious hospitality are more befitting an intimate resort. The central free-form pool is spectacular, with hundreds of tall palms surrounding it. Hammocks are strung between the palms closest to the beach, where there's also an elaborate wooden playground for kids. Rooms are contemporary in style, brightly colored in textured fabrics with oversized wood furnishings, tile floors, original art, tub/shower-combination bathrooms, and in-room safes. Balconies have panoramic views. Eight junior suites have Jacuzzis, and the five grand suites and presidential suite are two-level, with ample living areas. Two floors of rooms are designated as their Royal Beach Club, with VIP services including private concierge, plush bathrobes, continental breakfast, newspaper, cocktails, and canapés. The fitness center here is one of the most modern, well-equipped facilities of its kind in Vallarta.

Dining/Diversions: Two restaurants serve all three meals; **Garibaldi** specializes in seafood and nouveau Mexican cuisine, and offers outdoor, beachfront dining, or indoor dining under a giant palapa. **El Palmar** offers international cuisine and an exceptional Sunday brunch buffet. Two poolside bars also offer snacks and sandwiches; and the **La Cascada Lobby Bar,** overlooking the pool and beach, features live music during its nightly happy hour.

Amenities: Ocean-side pool; full-service, state-of-the-art health club with treadmills, Stairmasters, resistance equipment, sauna, steam room, solarium, whirlpool, three grass tennis courts (lighted for night play), massage services, and salon; golf privileges at Marina Vallarta Golf Club; Kid's Club; laundry; 24-hour room service; travel agency; car rental; shopping arcade.

THE HOTEL ZONE

The main street running between the airport and town is named avenida Francisco Medina Ascencio, but is commonly referred to as avenida de las Palmas, for the stately palm trees that line the dividing strip. The hotels built along this road were the result of the tourism boom that Vallarta enjoyed in the early 1980s, and most have been exceptionally well maintained. All offer excellent, wide beachfronts with generally tranquil waters for swimming. From here it's a quick taxi or bus ride into downtown Vallarta.

Fiesta Americana Puerto Vallarta. blvd. Fco. Medina Ascencio, km 2.5, 48300 Puerto Vallarta, Jal. ☎ **800/FIESTA-1** in the U.S., or 322/4-2010. Fax 322/4-2108. 291 units. A/C MINIBAR TV TEL. High season $180 double, $250–$700 suite. Low season $120–$160 double, $180–$430 suite. AE, DC, MC, V. Limited free parking.

The Fiesta Americana's towering, three-story, thatched palapa lobby is a landmark in the Hotel Zone, and the hotel is known for its excellent beach and friendly service. An abundance of plants, splashing fountains, constant breezes, and comfortable sitting areas in the lobby evoke a casual South Seas ambiance. The nine-story, terra cotta–colored building embraces a large plaza with a pool facing the beach. Marble-trimmed rooms, in neutral tones with pastel accents, come with carved headboards and comfortable rattan and wicker furniture. All have private balconies with ocean views.

Dining/Diversions: The hotel's three restaurants include two for casual dining and one, **La Hacienda,** for fine dining featuring excellent Mexican cuisine. There's live music nightly in the lobby bar. **Friday López** is a popular karaoke and sports bar, located on the highway at the entrance to this hotel. It's open from 10:30pm to 3am.

Amenities: Large pool with cushioned lounges and towel service, pool activities, and children's activities in high season; laundry, room service, travel agency, boutiques, beauty shop. A modern meeting center opened in late 1998.

DOWNTOWN TO LOS MUERTOS BEACH

This part of town has recently undergone a renaissance; accommodations here are dominated by economically priced hotels and good-value guesthouses. Several blocks off the beach you can find numerous budget inns offering clean, simply furnished rooms; most will discount long-term stays. The neighborhood is older, but very friendly and generally safe. Most of Vallarta's nightlife activity is now centered in the areas south of the Río Cuale, and along Olas Altas Avenue.

✪ **Hotel Molino de Agua.** Vallarta 130 (Apdo. Postal 54), 48380 Puerto Vallarta, Jal. ☎ **322/2-1957.** Fax 322/2-6056. www.molinodeagua.com. E-mail: molinodeagua@acnet.net. 50 units, including bungalows and suites. A/C. High season garden bungalows $80, oceanfront rooms and suites $95–$130. Low season bungalows $75, suites $80–$109 (all double). AE, MC, V. Free secured parking.

With an unrivaled location adjacent to both the Río Cuale and the ocean, this hotel is actually a mix of stone and stucco-walled bungalows and small beachfront buildings, spread out among winding walkways and lush tropical gardens. It's located immediately past the Río Cuale—after crossing the southbound bridge, it's on your right. Although centrally located on a main street, open spaces, big trees, birds, and lyrical fountains lend it tranquillity. The individual bungalows are located in the gardens, between the entrance and the ocean. They are well-maintained and simply furnished, with a bed, wooden desk and chair, Mexican tile floors, beamed ceilings, and beautiful tile bathrooms. Wicker rocking chairs grace their private patios. Rooms and suites in the two small two- and three-story buildings on the beach have double beds and private terraces.

Facilities include the poolside garden restaurant/bar, **The Lion's Court.** There's a whirlpool beside the beachside pool and another pool with Jacuzzi beside the Lion's Court restaurant.

✪ **Hotel Playa Los Arcos.** Olas Altas 380, 48380 Puerto Vallarta, Jal. ☎ **800/648-2403** in the U.S., or 322/2-1583. Fax 322/2-2418. www.playalosarcos. com. E-mail: losarcos@pvnet.com.mx. 185 units. A/C TV TEL. High season $63–$85 double, $105 suite. Low season $51–$65 double, $75 suite. AE, MC, V.

This is one of Vallarta's perennially popular hotels, and a favorite of mine, with a stellar location in the heart of Los Muertos beach, central to the Olas Altas sidewalk-cafe action and close to downtown. The four-story structure is in a U shape, facing the ocean, with a small swimming pool in the courtyard. Rooms with private balconies overlook the pool, while the 10 suites have ocean views and five of these have kitchenettes. The standard rooms are small but pleasantly decorated and immaculate, with carved wooden furniture painted pale pink. On the premises are a palapa beachside bar with occasional live entertainment, a coffee shop, and the popular Maximilian's gourmet restaurant. Other services include a boutique, tour desk, car-rental services, laundry, baby-sitting services, and safe-deposit boxes and money exchange at the front desk. It's 7 blocks south of the river.

Los Cuatro Vientos. Matamoros 520, 48300 Puerto Vallarta, Jal. ☎ **322/2-0161.** Fax 322/2-2831. www.cuatrovientos.com. E-mail: fourwinds@pvnet.com.mx. 13 units. $55 double, $69 suites. Rates include continental breakfast. Ask about low-season discounts. MC, V.

This quiet, secluded inn is located in the center of downtown on a hillside overlooking Banderas Bay and features rooms built around a small central patio and pool. A short flight of stairs takes you to the second-floor patio, pool, flowering trees, and the cozy Chez Elena restaurant, open in the evenings. The cheerful, spotless, colorful rooms have fans, small tiled bathrooms, brick ceilings, red-tile floors, and glass-louvered windows. Each is decorated with simple Mexican furnishings, folk art, and antiques. The rooftop, with a panoramic view of the city, is great for sunning, and it's the best place in the city for sunset drinks. Continental breakfast is served in the restaurant for guests only from 7 to 11am.

The hotel is favored by solo women travelers, and even offers weeklong "Women's Getaway" packages several times a year, with cultural discussions and recreational activities.

SOUTH TO MISMALOYA

✪ **Camino Real.** Carr. Barra de Navidad, km 3.5, Playa Las Estacas, 48300 Puerto Vallarta, Jal. ☎ **800/722-6466** in the U.S. and Canada, or 322/1-5000. Fax 322/1-6000. www.caminoreal.com. E-mail: pvr@caminoreal.com. 337 units. A/C MINIBAR TV TEL. High season $180–$240 double, $670–$1100 suite. Low season $140–$200 double, $550–$950 suite. AE, DC, MC, V.

The original luxury hotel in Puerto Vallarta, the Camino Real has retained its place as a premier property here despite newer arrivals. Scores of loyal guests think only of staying here, and its free monthly classical concerts (held the first Thursday of each month) have earned an integrated place in the local community. It unquestionably has the nicest beach of any Vallarta hotel, with soft, white sand in a private cove. Set apart from other properties, with a lush mountain backdrop, it retains the exclusivity that made it popular from the beginning—yet it's only a 5- to 10-minute ride to town. The hotel consists of two buildings: the 250-room main hotel, which curves gently with the shape of the Playa Las Estacas, and a newer 11-story Camino Real Club tower, also facing the beach and ocean. An ample pool fronts the main building. Standard rooms in the main building are large, some with sliding doors opening onto the

beach and others with balconies. The two-story Presidential suite in
the main building has a large private pool. Royal Beach Club rooms
from the sixth floor up feature balconies with whirlpool tubs. The
top floor is divided among six two-bedroom Fiesta Suites, each with
a private swimming pool. All rooms are accented with the vibrant
colors of Mexico and come with in-room safe-deposit boxes.

Dining/Diversions: There are two restaurants: Open for dinner
only are **La Finestra,** offering Italian cuisine and seafood, and the
elegant, award-winning **La Perla,** a classic gourmet favorite. Camino
Real Club guests enjoy a complimentary full buffet breakfast on a
beautiful open-air patio beside the ocean. Live bands frequently
entertain in the lobby bar in the evening. Adjacent is a specialty
cantina and shop, **Mi Amiga El Tequila,** serving a broad selection
of premium tequilas.

Amenities: Swimming pool; beach palapas with chair, towel, and
dining service; two lighted grass tennis courts; health club with
weights; boutiques; convenience store. Camino Real Club guests
enjoy separate check-in and concierge, daily complimentary breakfast, and evening cocktails and hors d'oeuvres. Laundry; 24-hour
room service; travel agency; car rental; children's program December, July, and August.

Presidente Inter-Continental. carr. Barra de Navidad, km 8.5, 48300 Puerto
Vallarta ☎ **800/327-0200** or 322/8-0507. Fax 322/8-0609. www.interconti.
com. 120 units. A/C TV TEL. High season $330–$360 double, $470–$700 suite.
Low season $260–$300 double, $380–$650 suite. Rates are all-inclusive. AE, DC,
MC, V. Limited free parking.

Presidente Inter-Continental is taking the all-inclusive concept
upscale. Meals, drinks, and sports are included here—a convenient
necessity, as this welcoming hotel is 20 minutes south of Puerto
Vallarta, secluded from the activity of town. Backed by a jungle
mountain landscape and fronted by a beautiful white-sand beach,
the 11-story building is draped in flowering bougainvillea. Deluxe
rooms all have large, furnished balconies with ocean views, tile
floors, white wood furnishings, and muted colored textiles. Marble
tub/shower-combination bathrooms are extra-large, with separate
vanity areas. The 19 suites have in-room Jacuzzis; the three Master
suites have two separate bedrooms and Jacuzzis; the Presidential suite
has its own swimming pool. A large mosaic pool with swim-up bar
is on a terrace overlooking the beach, adjacent to the grass tennis
court and small fitness room. Guests aren't limited to buffet dining,
but can order a la carte from a selection of two restaurants, plus

enjoy premium drinks at their choice of bars. It's a top choice for honeymooners looking for romantic seclusion.

Dining/Diversions: El Coral restaurant serves a la carte, international gourmet cuisine; the more casual terrace restaurant **El Caribeño** offers three meals daily with choice of menu or buffet dining. A poolside restaurant/bar offers light fare and drinks. The lobby **Sunset Bar** has a terrific ocean view with live music in the evenings. There are also two theme nights every week; one, a Mexican Fiesta, the second, a poolside barbecue, both with live music.

Amenities: Beachfront pool with water-sports equipment for rent; lighted grass tennis court; fitness room with sauna and steam; full adults' activities program; year-round Kid's Club; game room; laundry and valet; travel agency; tobacco shop; car rental.

✪ **Quinta María Cortez.** Sagitario 132, Playa Conchas Chinas, 48300 Puerto Vallarta, Jal. ☎ **888/640-8100** or 801/536-5848 in the U.S., or 322/1-5317. Fax 322/1-5327. www.quintamaria.com. E-mail: qmc@pvnet.com.mx. 7 units. MINIBAR TEL. High season $120–$220 double. Low season $80–$185 double. Rates include breakfast. AE, MC, V.

An eclectic, sophisticated, and imaginative B&B on the beach, this is Puerto Vallarta's most original place to stay—and one of Mexico's most unique inns. Seven large suites, uniquely decorated in antiques, whimsical curios, and original art, all feature private bathrooms, and most include a kitchenette and a balcony. Sunny terraces, a small pool, and a central gathering area with fireplace and palapa-topped dining area (where breakfast is served) occupy different levels of this seven-story house. Located on a beautiful cove on Conchas Chinas beach, the rocks just offshore form tranquil tide pools, perfect for wading and snuggling. A terrace fronting the beach supports Roman columns draped in ivy and accommodates chairs for taking in the sunset.

For years, this intimate inn was owned and run by a legendary Vallarta resident and Texan named Silver, who welcomed celebrity guests and allowed the house to be used as a location for fashion shoots and several films, including *Revenge,* starring Kevin Costner. The new owners have lovingly maintained its singular sense of style while significantly upgrading amenities and remodeling common areas in 1997. The Quinta María wins my highest recommendation (in fact, I enjoyed living here for a few years, when it accepted long-term stays), but admittedly it's not for everyone. There's no air-conditioning, and all the rooms are very open—part of the expansive penthouse suite is completely open to a view of the sun and stars above. Breakfast is served under the midlevel thatched-roof area, overlooking the pool and ocean below. Those who love it return year after year, charmed by this remarkable place. Not appropriate for children.

3 Where to Dine

Puerto Vallarta has the most exceptional dining scene of any resort town in Mexico. Over 200 restaurants serve cuisine from around the world, in addition to fresh seafood and regional dishes. Chefs from France, Switzerland, Germany, Italy, and Argentina have come for visits and then stayed on to open restaurants of their own. In celebration of the diversity of dining experiences available, Vallarta's culinary community hosts a 2-week-long Gourmet Dining Festival as part of its annual SeaFest each November.

Nonetheless, dining is not limited to high-end options—there are plenty of small, family-owned restaurants, local Mexican kitchens, and vegetarian cafes. Vallarta also has its branches of the imported world food-and-fun chains: Hard Rock Cafe, Planet Hollywood, and even Hooters. I won't bother to review these restaurants, as the consistency and decor are so familiar.

Of the inexpensive local spots, one of the long-standing favorites for light meals and fresh fruit drinks is **Tutifruti,** Morelos 552 (☎ **322/2-1068**). It's open Monday through Saturday from 8am to 8pm. No credit cards. A new favorite for cheap eats is **Archi's,** serving only (great) char-grilled burgers and homemade fries in a surfer-inspired atmosphere. It's located at Morelos 799 at Pípila, behind Carlos O'Brian's (☎ **322/2-4383**). Open Tuesday to Sunday, 11am to 1am. Inexpensive and absolutely fresh seafood cocktails and cerviche tostados are served up in the locally popular **Ocho Tosdados** (☎ **322/2-1510**), located almost across from the American Express office, at Morelos 685A; it's open Monday to Saturday from noon to 5pm.

MARINA VALLARTA

Contrary to conventional travel wisdom, most of the best restaurants in the Marina are located in hotels. Especially notable are **Andrea,** at Velas Vallarta, for fine Italian cuisine, and **Garibaldi,** on the beachfront of the Westin Regina Resort, for exceptional seafood. Other choices are found along the boardwalk bordering the marina yacht harbor. My pick for the best "cheap eats" in the area are the fish tacos served at **Marina Fish Taco,** located in the Las Palmas II commercial center, at the eastern entrance to the marina malecón. A variety of fish and seafood tacos are just $1.50 per order. Open Monday through Saturday from noon to 8pm.

La Terraza di Roma. Puesta del Sol, Local no. 2 (Marina Vallarta malecón). ☎ **322/1-0560.** Main courses $4–$15. AE, MC, V. Daily 8am–11pm. ITALIAN.

One of the first restaurants in the marina, this remains a favorite here, serving authentically flavorful Italian dishes and excellent breakfasts in a casual atmosphere with exceptional service. For starters, their fried calamari is delicately seasoned, and the grilled vegetable antipasta could easily serve as a full meal. Signature pasta dishes include fusilli prepared with fresh mushrooms, olive oil, and garlic; and fettuccini carbonara. They also have a selection of shrimp dishes as well as brick-oven pizzas. Most people prefer the seating on the gazebolike terrace bordering the marina malecón, or on their wooden dock situated over the marina itself. Indoor dining is air-conditioned, and they have live piano music in the evenings.

HOTEL ZONE TO DOWNTOWN
EXPENSIVE

✪ **Chef Roger.** A. Rodríguez 267. ☎ **322/2-5900.** Reservations recommended. Main courses $10–$20. AE, MC, V. Mon–Sat 6:30–11pm. INTERNATIONAL/SWISS.

This sophisticated little dinner-only restaurant has developed a strong following since it opened in 1989, due to Swiss-born chef and owner Roger Dreier. A European-trained chef, he's combined elements of the cuisine of Europe and Mexico to create a highly personal style of cooking. Guests enjoy their meals on the patio or in one of the adjoining dining rooms. There are five or six daily specials using market-fresh ingredients; these might include such interesting combinations as crepes huitlacoche, red snapper fillet with bananas and almonds, or breaded crepes stuffed with spinach and goat cheese in a red-pepper sauce. His freshly made pâtés and terrines are especially notable, as is the fresh fruit and chocolate fondue for desert. The restaurant is cater-cornered from the municipal market between Matamoros and Hidalgo.

MODERATE

✪ **La Dolce Vita.** paseo Díaz Ordaz no. 674, Centro. ☎ **322/2-3852.** Main courses $4–$8.80, wine and mixed drinks $2–$3.60. AE, MC, V. Daily noon–2am. ITALIAN.

This locally popular eatery eminently combines good food, a casually upbeat atmosphere, attentive service, and great entertainment.

Overlooking the malecón, La Dolce Vita offers excellent views and prime people-watching through its oversized windows and second-floor balcony. Despite its choice location and superb food, its prices remain more than reasonable. Owned by an engaging group of Italian friends, the food is authentic in preparation and flavor, from the thin crust, brick-oven pizzas to savory homemade pastas—my favorite is the Braccio de Fiero, topped with spinach, black olives, and fresh tomatoes. Sultry jazz by "The Sweet Life" (the house band) plays Thursday through Friday evenings.

Owned by a related group, **Pan & Vino** (calle Independencia 225, 2nd floor, ☎ 322/2-3272) offers the same great food, but in a quieter, more romantic atmosphere. Tables are set up on the ample balcony overlooking the central plaza, or with views of the Guadalupe Cathedral. The inside dining room is cozy; aromas waft from the brick oven, and the air fills with Italian chatter. It's the ultimate venue for watching the annual Guadalupe processions each December (see "Holidays & Special Events," in chapter 1).

Las Palomas. paseo Díaz Ordaz 594. ☎ **322/2-3675.** Breakfast $2.60–$6.20, lunch $4.40–$8.30, main courses $5.30–$16. AE, MC, V. Daily 8am–11pm. MEXICAN.

One of Puerto Vallarta's first restaurants, this is the power-breakfast place of choice for local movers and shakers—and a generally popular hangout for everyone else throughout the day. Authentic in atmosphere and menu, it's one of Puerto Vallarta's few genuine Mexican restaurants, with the atmosphere of a gracious home. Breakfast is the best value here, with mugs of steaming coffee spiced with cinnamon poured as soon as you're seated. Try the classic huevos rancheros or *chilaquiles* (tortilla strips, fried and topped with a red or green spicy sauce, cream cheese, and fried eggs). Lunch and dinner offer other traditional Mexican specialties, plus a selection of stuffed crepes. The best place for checking out the malecón and watching the sun set while sipping an icy margarita is in the spacious bar or the new upstairs terrace.

✪ **Rito's Baci.** Domínguez 181. ☎ **322/2-6448.** Pasta $6.50–$8.90, salads and sandwiches $1–$5.60, pizza $13–$14.50. MC, V. Daily 1–11:30pm. ITALIAN.

If the food weren't reason enough to come here (and it definitely is!), then Rito himself would be, with his gentle, devoted way of caring for every detail of this cozy *trattoria*. His grandfather emigrated from Italy, so the recipes and tradition of Italian food come naturally to him. So does his passion for food—obvious as he describes the specialties, which include lasagna (vegetarian, *verde*, or meat-filled);

ravioli stuffed with spinach and ricotta cheese; spaghetti with garlic, anchovy and lemon zest; or a side of homemade Italian sausage.
Everything, in fact, is made by hand from fresh ingredients. Pizza
lovers favor the Piedmonte, with that famous sausage and mushrooms, and the Horacio, a cheeseless pizza with tomatoes, oregano,
and basil. Sandwiches come hot or cold; but arrive hungry, as they're
a two-handed operation. Because Rito offers home and hotel delivery, I enjoy his food more than any other restaurant in town! It's
1½ blocks off the malecón, on Josefa de Domínguez between
Morelos and Juárez.

✪ **Trio.** Guerrero 264. ☎ **322/2-2196.** Reservations recommended. Main
courses $5–$14. AE, MC, V. Lunch Mon–Sat noon–4pm, dinner daily 6pm–
midnight. INTERNATIONAL.

Trio is the current darling of Vallarta restaurants, and I believe diners beat a path to this modest but stylish cafe because chef/owner
Bernhard Güth's undeniable passion for food is imbued into each
dish. Partners Bernhard and Chef Peter Lodes have combined local
ingredients with impressive culinary experience; the result is such
memorable entrees as San Blas shrimp with eggplant in a roasted
red-pepper sauce, risotto with wild mushrooms and braised sweet-
breads, and grilled sea bass with chile vegetables, served in a black-
olive salsa. The restaurant is noted for its perfected melding of Mexican and Mediterranean flavors. What's great about Trio is that
despite a sophisticated menu, the atmosphere is always comfortable
and welcoming, and Bernhard is regularly seen chatting with guests
at the end of an evening. A real treat!

SOUTH OF THE RÍO CUALE TO OLAS ALTAS

South of the river is the most condensed restaurant area, with the
street Basilio Badillo nicknamed "Restaurant Row." A second main
dining drag has emerged along calle Olas Altas, where you can find
all varieties of food types and price categories. Its wide sidewalks
lined with cafes are concentrated with espresso bars, generally open
from 7am to midnight.

While you're in the area, stop by **Nina's Bodega,** calle Pulpito
220 (☎ **90-329-27324**), for scrumptious muffins, coffee, whole
cakes, and tarts to go, even home-baked dog treats. The Bodega is
also a gourmet cookware shop that sells such pantry treats as dress-
ings and pestos, plus an impressive assortment of imported wines.
It's a great place to find a uniquely Vallartan gift. Open Tuesday
through Saturday from 9am to 4pm.

EXPENSIVE

Kit Kat Club. Pulpito 120, Playa Los Muertos. ☎ **322/3-0093.** Reservations recommended in high season. Main courses $6.50–$15. MC, V. Daily 11am–2am. INTERNATIONAL.

It's swank and sleek and reminiscent of a New York high-styled club, but don't be fooled—it also has a terrific sense of humor. In the golden glow of candlelight, lounge around in cushy, leopard-patterned chairs or cream-colored, overstuffed banquettes, listening to swinging tunes while you sip a martini—shaken, not stirred, of course. Not only is the place very hip, the food is great too. The manageable menu has an ample selection of starters, which can double as light meals. Don't pass up the coconut crab cakes, served with dill tartar and mango catsup. The top entree is the Big Daddy shrimp—Cajun spiced, skewered, and served in a grilled pineapple. Also popular is the Gibson pork tenderloin with garlic mashed potatoes. Michael, the owner, describes his lounge and cafe as cool, crazy, wild, jazzy, and sexy. I agree. Martini T dances daily, from 5 to 7pm.

MODERATE

✪ **Adobe Café.** Badillo 252. ☎ **322/2-6720** or 322/3-1925. Reservations recommended in high season. Main courses $9–$15. AE, MC, V. Wed–Mon 6–11pm. Closed Aug–Sept. INTERNATIONAL.

Adobe Café offers a classically chic atmosphere in which to enjoy innovative cuisine based on traditional Mexican specialties. The Santa Fe–style decor with rustic wood accents provides a serene backdrop, and tables are comfortably large for enjoying a leisurely meal. Waiters possess that ideal skill of being attentive without being intrusive. The menu features imaginative dishes, including grilled jumbo shrimp battered in coconut and served with home-made apple sauce, penne pasta with Italian sausage in a creamy tequila sauce, and tenderloin of beef stuffed with huitlacoche (Mexican truffles) in a cheese sauce—to name just a few specialties. Owner Rodolfo Choperena is almost always on hand, which accounts for the consistently fine food and service. Adobe Café is located at the corner of calles Basilio Badillo and Ignacio Vallarta, opposite Los Pibes restaurant, on the "calle de los cafés," or restaurant row.

✪ **Archie's Wok.** Francisco Rodríguez 130, ¹/₂ block from the Los Muertos pier. ☎ **322/2-0411.** Main courses $6–$12. AE, MC, V. Mon–Sat 2–11pm. ASIAN/SEAFOOD.

Since 1986, Archie's has been legendary in Puerto Vallarta for serving original cuisine influenced by the intriguing flavors of Thailand, China, and the Philippines. "Archie" was Hollywood director John

Huston's private chef during the years he spent in the area. Today, his wife Cindy continues his legacy as she welcomes guests to this tranquil retreat. Their Thai Mai Tai and other tropical drinks are made from only fresh fruit and juices, and they are a good way to kick off a meal here, as are the Filipino spring rolls, consistently crispy and delicious. The popular Singapore Fish Fillet features lightly battered fillet strips in a sweet-and-sour sauce, while the Thai Garlic Shrimp are prepared with fresh garlic, ginger, cilantro, and black pepper. Vegetarians have plenty of options, including the Broccoli, Tofu, Mushroom, & Cashew Stir-Fry in a black-bean–and-sherry sauce. Finish things off with the signature Spice Islands coffee or a slice of lime cheese pie. Thursday through Saturday from 8 to 11pm, live classical guitar and flute set the atmosphere in Archie's Oriental garden.

El Palomar de los González. Aguacate 425. ☎ **322/2-0795** or 322/2-2795. Reservations recommended in high season. Main courses $8–$16. MC, V. Daily 6–11pm. INTERNATIONAL/SEAFOOD.

The atmosphere and view are the principal attractions to one of the most romantic restaurants in town. Located in a hillside villa, it has sweeping views of the town and bay. The former González family home has remained much as it was when they lived here; only now, tables deck the balconies and border the pool for guests to enjoy dining under the stars. The menu offers traditional international fare, including fish, steaks, and jumbo shrimp, prepared grilled, with several choices of sauces. Specialty coffees, served flaming at your table, or their excellent bananas flambé, make for an entertaining end to the meal. Generally, there's a trio on the premises serenading couples.

La Palapa. Pulpito 103. ☎ **322/2-5225.** Reservations recommended in high season. Breakfast $1.50–$3, main courses $4–$20, salad or sandwiches $3–$8. AE, MC, V. Daily 8am–11pm. SEAFOOD/MEXICAN.

This colorfully decorated, open-air and palapa-roofed restaurant on the beach is a decades-old local favorite. Enjoy a tropical breakfast by the sea, lunch on the beach, cocktails at sunset, or a romantic dinner—at night they set cloth-covered tables in the sand. Once a rather rustic restaurant with mediocre food, owner Alberto Pérez has updated the menu and upgraded the atmosphere. For lunch and dinner, seafood is the specialty, with featured dishes including grilled shrimp in a *guajillo* (chile)–and-mango sauce, and poached red snapper with fresh cilantro sauce. Its location in the heart of Los Muertos beach makes it an exceptional place to either start or end the day; I favor it for either breakfast or, better, a late-night sweet temptation and specialty coffee, enjoyed while watching the moon over the bay, with the sand at your feet. There's acoustic guitar and vocals nightly from 8 to 11pm, generally performed by Alberto himself.

INEXPENSIVE

Café San Angel. Olas Altas 449, corner of Francisco Rodríguez. ☎ **322/ 3-2160.** Breakfast $2.50–$3.50, main courses $2.50–$4. Daily 8am–midnight. CAFE.

This comfortable, classic sidewalk cafe has become a local gathering place from sunrise to sunset. For breakfast, choose between a burrito stuffed with eggs and chorizo sausage, a three-egg western omelet, crepes filled with mushrooms, or a tropical fruit plate. Deli sandwiches, crepes, and pastries round out the small but ample menu. They also have exceptional fruit smoothies, like the Yelapa—a blend of mango, banana, and orange juice—and perfectly made espresso drinks. Bar service and Internet access are also available.

✪ **Fajita Republic.** Pino Suárez 321, corner of Basilio Badillo. ☎ **322/ 2-3131.** Main courses $3.75–$12. MC, V. Daily 4–11pm. MEXICAN/SEAFOOD/ STEAKS.

Lines for a table were so common at this wildly popular spot, the owners had to expand after their first year. . . and they're still bringing in the crowds. Fajita Republic has hit on a winning recipe: delicious food, ample portions, welcoming atmosphere, and low prices. The specialty is, of course, fajitas, grilled to perfection in every variety: steak, chicken, shrimp, combo, and vegetarian. All come with a generous tray of salsas and toppings. This "tropical grill" also serves sumptuous barbecue ribs, Mexican *molcajetes* with incredibly tender strips of marinated beef fillet, and grilled shrimp. Starters include fresh guacamole served in a giant spoon and the ever-popular Mayan cheese sticks (cheese, breaded and deep-fried). Try a Fajita Rita Mango Margarita—or one of their other spirited temptations—served in oversized mugs or by the pitcher. Partners Fernando and Carlos have created a casual, fun, and festive atmosphere in a garden of mango and palm trees. Now located on Basilio Badillo, Restaurant Row, 1 block north of Olas Altas.

✪ **Red Cabbage Café (El Rebpollo Rojo).** calle Rivera del Río 204A, across from the Cuale River. ☎ **322/3-0411.** Main courses $3–$10. No credit cards. Daily 5–11pm. MEXICAN.

The tiny, hard-to-find cafe is worth the effort—a visit here will reward you with not only exceptional, traditional Mexican cuisine, but also with a whimsical crash course in the contemporary culture of this country. The small room is covered wall to wall and table to table with photographs, paintings, movie posters, and news clippings about the cultural icons of Mexico. Frida Kahlo figures prominently in the decor, and there's a special menu that duplicates dishes she and husband Diego Rivera prepared for guests.

Specialties from all over Mexico are featured, including the divine *chiles en nogada* (poblano chiles stuffed with ground beef, pine nuts, and raisins, topped with a sweet cream sauce and served cold), an intricate chicken mole from Puebla, and the hearty *carne en su jugo* (steak in its juice). In addition, chef/owner Lola serves probably the most diverse, tasty vegetarian menu in town (she offers cooking classes for interested groups of four or more). There's a piano with occasional live music; talented (and not so talented!) diners are also welcome to play. This is not the place for an intimate conversation, however—the poor acoustics cause everyone's conversations to blend together. Though generally what you're hearing from adjacent tables are raves about the food.

JUNGLE RESTAURANTS

One of the unique attractions of Puerto Vallarta is its "jungle restaurants," located to the south of town, toward Mismaloya. Each offers open-air dining in a tropical setting by the sea or beside a mountain river. A stop for swimming and lunch is included in the many varieties of "Jungle" or "Tropical" tours (see "Organized Tours" in chapter 3). If you travel on your own, a taxi is the best transportation, as the restaurants are all located quite a distance from the main highway. Taxis are usually waiting for return patrons. The restaurants up the hill from the entrance to Mismaloya are **Chino's Paraíso** and **El Edén** (no phones). Both are located up the mountain road at km 6.5, Highway 200, and feature mediocre restaurants in once-beautiful natural settings of tropical jungle next to a stream. El Edén, further up the road from Chino's, was the site of several key scenes in the Arnold Schwarzenegger film *Predator*. Both are somewhat unkempt, and during summer months swimming in the river here can be extremely dangerous—flash floods come without warning and take several lives each year.

Just past Boca de Tomatlán, at km 20, Highway 200, is **Chico's Paradise** (☎ **322/2-0747** or 322/3-0413; e-mail: chicos@acnet. net), a better option, offering spectacular views of massive rocks—some marked with petroglyphs—and the surrounding jungle and mountains. There are natural pools and waterfalls for swimming, plus a small mercado selling pricey trinkets. The menu features excellent seafood (the seafood platter for two is excellent, with lobster, clams, giant shrimp, crab, and fish fillet), as well as Mexican dishes. The quality is quite good, and the portions are generous, although prices are higher than in town—remember, you're paying for the setting. It's open daily 10am to 8pm.

The newest and most recommendable of the jungle restaurants is ✪ **El Nogalito** (☎ **322/1-5225**). Located beside a clear jungle stream, this exceptionally clean, beautifully landscaped ranch serves lunch, beverages, and snacks on a shady terrace in a very relaxing atmosphere. There are also several hiking routes that depart from the grounds. If you're accompanied by one of El Nogalito's guides, they'll point out the native plants, birds, and wildlife of the area. To find it, a taxi can easily take you, or travel to Punta Negra, just about 5 miles south of downtown Puerto Vallarta. There's a well-marked sign that leads up Calzada del Cedro, a dirt road, to the ranch. It's much closer to town than the other jungle restaurants mentioned above, and it's open daily noon to 5:30pm.

3

Exploring Puerto Vallarta & Beyond

*B*eyond the cobblestone streets, graceful cathedral, and welcoming atmosphere of this colonial town, Puerto Vallarta offers a wealth of natural beauty and manmade pleasures.

Ecotourism activities are gaining ground—from mountain biking the Sierra foothills to whale watching, ocean kayaking, or diving with giant mantas in Banderas Bay (see "Staying Active," below). Twenty-six miles of beaches extend from the center of town around the bay, many tucked in pristine coves and accessible only by boat. High in the Sierra Madre Mountains, the mystical Huichol Indians still live in relative isolation in an effort to protect their centuries-old culture from outside influences. Their art is both intricate and highly prized; in the "Shopping" section, below, I've given some tips for how to spot the best works.

In the past few years, live music has become a staple of the Vallarta nightlife scene, augmented by the usual crowd of hip dance clubs, bars, cafes, and art galleries. In "Puerto Vallarta After Dark," below, I've pointed you to a few of my favorite spots.

Outside of town, villages such as **San Blas, Bucerías,** and **San Sebastian** are still laid-back, almost undiscovered, and offer travelers a glimpse into the local culture. Excursions to these smaller villages make easy day-trips or extended stays and are starkly different from Vallarta's spirited resort towns.

1 Beaches, Activities & Excursions

Travel agencies can provide information on what to see and do in Puerto Vallarta and can arrange tours, fishing, and other activities.

Special Events in Puerto Vallarta

Each November, **Fiestas del Mar** (SeaFest) is celebrated with a Gourmet Dining Festival, International Boat Show, art exhibitions, tennis tournaments, regattas, and more. Dates vary; call the Tourism Board (☎ **888/384-6822** from the U.S.) for dates and schedule. From December 1 through December 12, the ✪ **Festival of the Virgin of Guadalupe**—Mexico's patron saint—is celebrated in one of the most authentic displays of culture and community in Mexico. Each business, neighborhood, association, or group makes a pilgrimage (called peregrinaciones) to the cathedral, where offerings are exchanged for a brief blessing by the priest. These processions, especially those offered by hotels, often include floats, Aztec dancers, and mariachis, and are followed by fireworks. Hotels frequently invite guests to participate in the walk to the church. It's an event not to be missed.

Most hotels have a tour desk on-site. Of the many travel agencies in town, I highly recommend **Tukari Servicios Turísticos,** av. España 316 (☎ **322/4-7177;** fax 322/4-2350), which specializes in ecological and cultural tours. Another good source for information is **Xplora Adventours** (☎ **322/3-0661**), located in the Sierra Madre shop on the malecón. They have books of all locally available tours with photos, explanations, and costs. **American Express Travel Services,** Morelos 660 (☎ **322/3-2955**), also has a varied selection of high-quality, popular tours.

THE BEACHES

For years, beaches were Puerto Vallarta's main attraction. Although visitors today are exploring more of the surrounding geography, the sands are still a powerful draw. Over 26 miles of beaches extend around the broad Bay of Banderas, ranging from action-packed party spots to secluded coves accessible only by boat.

IN TOWN   The easiest to reach is **Playa Los Muertos** (also known as Playa Olas Altas or Playa del Sol), just off calle Olas Altas, south of the Río Cuale. The water is rough here, but the wide beach is home to a wide array of palapa restaurants with food, beverage, and beach-chair service. On the southern end of this beach is a section known as "Blue Chairs"—the most popular gay beach. Vendors stroll the length of Los Muertos, and beach volleyball, parasailing, and jet skiing are all popular pastimes. The **Hotel Zone** is also known for its broad, smooth beaches, accessible primarily through the associated hotel lobbies.

SOUTH OF TOWN   **Playa Mismaloya** is in a beautiful sheltered cove about 6 miles south of town along Highway 200. The water here is clear and beautiful, ideal for snorkeling off the beach. Entrance to the public beach is just to the left of the Jolla de Mismaloya Hotel. Colorful palapa restaurants dot the small beach and rent beach chairs for sunning. You can also stake out a table under a palapa for the day. Using a restaurant's table and palapa is a reciprocal arrangement—they let you be comfortable, and you buy your drinks, snacks, and lunch there. *Night of the Iguana* was filmed at Mismaloya. La Jolla de Mismaloya Resort and Spa recently opened a restaurant on the restored film set—**La Noche de la Iguana Set Restaurant,** open daily from noon to 11pm. The movie runs continuously in a room below the restaurant, and photo stills from the filming hang in the restaurant. The restaurant is accessible by land on the point framing the south side of the cove. Just below the restaurant is **John Huston's Bar & Grill,** serving drinks and light snacks from 11am to 6pm. La Jolla de Mismaloya Resort and Spa is to the right of the public beach, and restaurants there are available to outsiders as well. The beach at **Boca de Tomatlán,** just down the road, is similar in setup to Mismaloya, but without a large resort looming in the backdrop. The two are accessible by public buses that depart from the corner of Basilio Badillo and Insurgentes every 15 minutes from 5:30am to 10pm, costing just 50¢.

Las Ánimas, Quimixto, and **Yelapa** beaches offer a true sense of seclusion; they are accessible only by boat (see "Getting Around," in chapter 2, for information about water-taxi service). These are each larger than Mismaloya, offer intriguing hikes to jungle waterfalls, and are similarly set up with restaurants fronting a wide beach. Overnight stays are available only at Yelapa (see "Side Trips from Puerto Vallarta," below).

NORTH OF TOWN   The beaches at **Marina Vallarta** are the least desirable in the area, with darker sand and seasonal inflows of stones. However, you're on a peninsula facing the open ocean, which is a completely separate world from the rest of Puerto Vallarta.

The entire northern coastline from Bucerías to Punta de Mita is a succession of sandy coves alternating with rocky inlets. For years the beaches to the north, with their long, clean breaks, have been the favored locale for surfers. The broad, sandy stretches at **Playa Anclote, Playa Piedras Blancas,** and **Playa Destiladeras,** along with their palapa restaurants, have made them favorites with local residents looking for a quick but meaningful getaway from town.

ORGANIZED TOURS

BOAT TOURS   Puerto Vallarta offers a number of different boat trips, including sunset cruises and trips for snorkeling, swimming, and diving. They generally travel one of two routes: to the **Marietas Islands,** which are about a 30- to 45-minute boat ride off the northern shore of Banderas Bay, or to **Yelapa, Las Ánimas,** or **Quimixto** along the southern shore. The trips to the southern beaches make a stop at **Los Arcos,** an island rock formation south of Puerto Vallarta, for snorkeling. When comparing all of these boat cruises, note that some include lunch, while most provide music and an open bar on board. Most leave around 9:30am, stop for 45 minutes of snorkeling, and arrive at the beach destination around noon for a $2^1/_2$-hour stay before returning around 3pm. At Quimixto and Yelapa, visitors can take a half-hour hike to a jungle waterfall or rent a horse for the ride. Prices range from $20 for a sunset cruise or a trip to one of the beaches with open bar to $70 for an all-day outing with open bar and meals.

One boat, the **Marigalante** (☎ 322/3-0309), is an exact replica of Columbus's ship the *Santa Maria,* built in honor of the 500-year anniversary of his voyage to the Americas. It features a daytime "pirate's cruise" complete with picnic barbecue and treasure hunt, or a sunset dinner cruise with folkloric dance and fireworks. Both trips cost $60 per person.

One of the best trips is the new tour to **Caletas,** the cove where John Huston made his home for years. **Vallarta Adventures** (☎ 322/1-0657 or 322/1-0658; www.vallarta-adventures.com; e-mail: info@vallarta-adventures.com) holds the exclusive lease on this private cove, and has done an excellent job of restoring Huston's former home, adding exceptional day-spa facilities and landscaping the beach, which is wonderful for snorkeling. The quality facilities, combined with the relative privacy this excursion offers, has made it one of the most popular, at $55 per person. They also offer an evening cruise, complete with dinner and a spectacular contemporary dance show, "Rhythms of the Night" (see "Puerto Vallarta After Dark," below).

Travel agencies have tickets and information on all cruises. If you prefer to spend a longer time at Yelapa or Las Ánimas without taking time for snorkeling and cruise entertainment, note the information about travel by water taxis in chapter 2, under "Getting Around."

Whale-watching tours are becoming more popular each year, since viewing humpback whales is almost a certainty from mid- to late November through March. The majestic whales have migrated to this bay for centuries (in the 1600s, it was called "Humpback Bay") to reproduce and bear calves. The noted local authorities are **Open Air Expeditions,** Guerrero 339 (☎ and fax **322/2-3310;** e-mail: openair@vivamexico.com), who offer ecologically oriented tours (for up to eight people) in small boats, for $55. They also spearhead a photo-ID project to track returning whales—each one has unique markings on its fluke, or tail. **Vallarta Adventures** (☎ **322/1-0657** or 322/1-0658) offers whale watching on their tours to the Marietas Islands. For $50 you get lunch, time at a private beach, and a more festive than educational ambiance aboard the large catamaran boats.

LAND TOURS   **Tukari Tours** travel agency can arrange bird-watching trips to the fertile birding grounds near **San Blas,** 3 to 4 hours north of Puerto Vallarta in the state of Nayarit; shopping trips to **Tlaquepaque and Tonalá** (6 hr. inland near Guadalajara); or a day-trip to **Rancho Altamira,** a working 50-acre hilltop ranch, for a barbecue lunch and horseback riding, then a stroll through **El Tuito,** a small nearby colonial-era village. They can also arrange an unforgettable morning at **Terra Noble Art & Healing Center** (☎ **322/3-0308;** www.terranoble.com.mx), a mountaintop day spa and center for the arts where participants can get a massage or treatment, work in clay and paint, and have lunch in a heavenly setting overlooking the bay.

Hotel travel desks and travel agencies, including Tukari and American Express, can also book the ever-popular **Tropical Tour** or **Jungle Tour** ($21 each), basically an orientation to the area. These tours are really expanded city tours that include a drive through the workers' village of Pitillal, the posh neighborhood of Conchas Chinas, the cathedral, the market, the Taylor-Burton houses, and lunch at a jungle restaurant. Any stop for shopping usually means the driver picks up commission for what you buy.

The **Sierra Madre Expedition** is another excellent tour offered by **Vallarta Adventures** (☎ **322/1-0657** or 322/1-0658). This daily excursion travels in special Mercedes all-terrain vehicles north of Puerto Vallarta through jungle trails, stopping at a small town, into a forest for a brief nature walk, and winding up on a beach for lunch and swimming. The $60 outing is worthwhile because it takes tourists into scenery that would otherwise be off-limits.

Art Along the *Malecón*

One of the great pleasures of strolling Puerto Vallarta's *malecón* is to take in the fanciful sculptures that line this seaside promenade. Among the notable works on display is *Nostalgia*, across from Carlos O'Brian's restaurant. Created by Ramiz Barquett, it depicts a couple sharing a romantic moment while gazing out to the bay. Further south is the sculpture group *Fantasy by the Sea*, an array of sculpture "chairs" by renowned Mexican artist Alejandro Colunga. This wacky series—one chair is topped by a large octopus head, another bench has two giant ears for backrests—seems to have been inspired by the aliens from *Men In Black*. Closer to the main square is the *Boy on the Sea Horse* sculpture; an image that has come to represent this resort town. Photo ops abound—and don't miss the fountain across from the main square; its three bronze dolphins seem ready to leap right into the bay.

AIR TOURS   Speaking of off-limits, you can explore some of the most remote and undiscovered reaches of the Sierra Madre Mountains in Vallarta Adventures' newest excursion, the **San Sebastian Air Adventure.** A 15-minute flight aboard a 14-seat turbo prop Cessna Caravan takes you into the heart of the Sierra Madre. The plane is equipped with raised wings, which allows you to admire the mountain scenery below. The plane arrives on a gravel landing strip in the old mining town of San Sebastian, a beautiful, antiquated village dating back to 1605. One of the oldest mining towns in Mexico, it reached its peak in the 1700s when it prospered with over 30,000 inhabitants. Today, San Sebastian remains an outstanding example of how people lived and worked in a remote Mexican mountain town—it's a living museum. The half-day adventure costs $130, and includes flight, a walking tour of the town, and brunch at the old Hacienda Jalisco, a favored getaway of John Huston, Liz and Dick and their friends. Reserve by calling ☎ 322/1-0657 or 322/1-0658, or e-mailing info@vallarta-adventures.com.

   Hot-Air Balloon Tours, Morelos 56 at Corona (☎ 322/3-2002), offers two hot-air balloon trips a day at 7am and 5pm (weather permitting) for $120 to $140 per person. The balloons glide along the coast, over beaches, jungle, and farmland; the trip ends with a round of champagne.

TOURS IN TOWN   Every Wednesday and Thursday in high season (from late Nov through Easter), the **International Friendship Club** (☎ 322/2-5466) offers a **Private Home Tour** of four private villas in town for a donation of $25 per person, with proceeds donated to local charities. Tour arrangements begin at 10am at the Hotel Molino de Agua (av. Ignacio L. Vallarta no. 130, adjacent to the southbound bridge over the Río Cuale), where you can buy breakfast while you wait for the group to gather—and arrive early, because this tour sells out quickly! The tour departs at 11am and lasts approximately 2¹/₂ hours.

An **Artist's Studio Tour** starts from Galería Pacífico, 174 Aldama (☎ 322/2-1982), every Monday from 10am to 3pm. Gary Thompson, owner/curator of Galería Pacífico, gives an overview of the Puerto Vallarta and Latin American art scene before guiding the group to the working studios of between four and six artists. The cost is $25; call in advance for reservations.

You can also tour the **Taylor/Burton villas** (Casa Kimberley; ☎ 322/2-1336), located at 445 calle Zaragoza. Tours of the two houses owned by Elizabeth Taylor and Richard Burton cost $6—just ring the bell between 10am and 6pm, and if the manager is available, she will take you through the house.

A TASTY TOUR   There's a new, spirited tour in town—the **Porfidio Tequila Distillery Tour** (☎ 322/1-2543), at Porfidio's facility just 10 minutes north of town. For an entry fee of $10, you can see how agave plants are juiced, fermented, distilled, and bottled for shipping. Hours are 11:30am to 6pm. The entry fee includes a glass of Porfidio, reputed to be one of Mexico's finest tequilas; but in reality, it's just a blend of other premium tequilas with exceptional packaging and marketing.

STAYING ACTIVE

DIVING   Underwater enthusiasts from beginner to expert can arrange scuba diving through **Vallarta Adventures** (☎ 322/1-0657 or 322/1-0658; www.vallarta-adventures.com), a five-star PADI dive

A Spectator Sport

Bullfights are held from December through April beginning at 5pm on Wednesday afternoons, at the bullring "La Paloma," across the highway from the town pier. Tickets can be arranged through travel agencies and cost around $21.

center. Dives take place at Los Arcos, Caletas, Quimixto Coves, the Marietas Islands, or the offshore El Morro and Chimo reefs. A full range of certification courses up through Instructor are also available. **Chico's Dive Shop,** Díaz Ordaz 772–5, near Carlos O'Brian's (☎ **322/2-1895;** www.chicos-diveshop.com), offers similar dive trips and is also a PADI five-star dive center. Chico's is open daily 8am to 10pm, and also has branches at the Marriott, Vidafel, Villa del Palmar, Camino Real, Paradise Village, and Playa Los Arcos hotels.

ECOTOURS & ACTIVITIES   Open Air Expeditions (☎ and fax **322/2-3310;** e-mail: openair@vivamexico.com) offers other nature-oriented trips, including lagoon kayaking and bird watching, and ocean kayaking to Los Arcos. **Ecotours de México,** Ignacio L. Vallarta 243 (☎ and fax **322/2-6606**), has eco-oriented tours including seasonal (August to November) trips to a turtle preservation camp, where you can witness hatching baby Olive Ridley turtles, as well as journeys to the monarch butterfly sanctuary in the neighboring state of Michoacán.

FISHING   A fishing trip can be arranged through travel agencies or through the **Cooperativo de Pescadores** (Fishing Cooperative), on the malecón, north of the Río Cuale, next door to the Rosita Hotel (☎ **322/2-1202** or 322/4-7886). Fishing charters cost $250 to $350 a day for four to eight people; price varies with the size of the boat. Although the posted price at the fishing cooperative is the same as what you'll find through travel agencies, you may be able to negotiate a lower price at the cooperative. Major credit cards are accepted. It's open Monday through Saturday from 7am to 10pm, but make arrangements a day ahead. You can also arrange fishing trips at the Marina Vallarta docks, or by calling **Cheforo's Fleet** (☎ **322/4-7259** or 329/2-2953). Fishing trips generally include equipment and bait, but drinks, snacks, and lunch are optional, so check to see what the price includes.

GOLF   Puerto Vallarta has two long-standing golf courses, with the new Jack Nicklaus–designed **Four Seasons** course open only to guests of the Four Seasons resort. The Joe Finger–designed course at the **Marina Vallarta Golf Club** (☎ **322/1-0073**) is an 18-hole, par-74, private course that winds through the Marina Vallarta peninsula with ocean views. It's for members only, but most of the luxury hotels in Puerto Vallarta have memberships that their guests can use. A bar, restaurant, golf pro, and pro shop are on the premises. The greens fees are $80 to $100 in high season (depending on the type of membership your hotel has) and $60 during low season. Fees include golf cart, caddy, range balls, and tax. Club rentals, lessons, and special packages are also available.

North of town in the state of Nayarit, about 10 miles beyond Puerto Vallarta, is the 18-hole, par-72 **Los Flamingos Club de Golf** (☎ **329/8-0606** or 329/8-0280). The older of the two courses, it's open to the public and has beautiful jungle vegetation, but is not as well maintained. It's open from 7am to 5pm daily, with a snack bar (but no restaurant) and full pro shop. The greens fee is $47; add $25 for use of a golf cart, $9 for a caddy, and $16 for club rental. A free shuttle service is available from downtown Puerto Vallarta; call for pickup times and locations.

HORSEBACK-RIDING TOURS   Guided horseback rides can be arranged through travel agents or directly through one of the local ranches. The two best are **Rancho El Charro,** av. Francisco Villa 895 (☎ **322/4-0114** or 329/2-0122; e-mail: aguirre@pvnet.com. mx), and **Rancho Ojo de Agua,** Cerrado de Cardenal 227, Fracc. Las Aralias (☎ and fax **322/4-0607**). Both of these ranches are located about a 10-minute taxi ride north of downtown, toward the Sierra Madre foothills. The morning or sunset rides last 2 to 3 hours and take you up into the mountains overlooking the ocean and town. The cost is $30. They also have their own comfortable base camp for serious riders who want to stay out overnight.

Rancho El Charro also offers an exclusive **"Fly-away to a Hideaway in San Sebastian"** day-trip from 9:30am to 5pm. A 15-minute flight takes you to this 17th-century mining town (see "Side Trips from Puerto Vallarta," below). A bilingual guide meets you at the airstrip, well-tended horses in tow; after a short ride to the Hacienda Jalisco, you'll get a light breakfast and a tour of the hacienda. The ride continues into town, along a riverside trail used by the locals since mining days. A thorough tour of the town is provided, touching on historical buildings—the church, carpenter shop, and coffee plantation—before heading back to the Hacienda for a gourmet lunch. Overnight stays can be arranged. Prices vary depending on number of participants, and advance reservations are required.

For a unique getaway, try **Horseback on Mexico's Hacienda Trail** from Sea to Sierra Madre, several 3- to 7-day journeys by horseback into the mountains. Trips are offered from November 1 through April 30; there's a 4-person minimum and a 15-person maximum. The cost of $270 per person per day includes food, horses, camping en route, and stays in centuries-old haciendas. They can arrange hotels in Puerto Vallarta and provide complete details on the quality of horses and accommodations. For details, contact Pam Aguirre of Rancho El Charro. No credit cards are accepted.

MOUNTAIN BIKING & HIKING   ✪ **Bike Mex,** calle Guerrero 361 (☎ **322/3-1834** or 322/3-1680; www.bikemex.com), offers expert guided biking and hiking tours up the Río Cuale canyon and to outlying areas. The popular Río Cuale bike trip costs $42 for 4 hours and includes bike, helmet, gloves, shorts, insurance, water, lunch, and an English-speaking guide. Trips take off at either 9am or 2pm, but starting times are flexible; make arrangements a day ahead.

Who says Yelapa is accessible only by boat? I've traveled with Bike Mex on their all-day, advanced-level bike trip to this magical cove (see "Side Trips from Puerto Vallarta," below). Riders depart at 7:30am in a van, traveling to the starting point in the town of El Tuito. The 33-mile ride includes 18^1/2 miles of climbs to a peak elevation of 3,600 feet. The journey consists of switchbacks, fire roads, single tracks, awesome climbs, and steep downhills before ending up at a beachfront palapa restaurant in Yelapa. You have the option of staying the night in Yelapa or returning that afternoon by small boat. This tour costs $120, takes 4 to 6 hours, and includes drinks, lunch, boat transportation, guide, and *ample* encouragement. Other bicycle trips, such as those along the beachfront of Punta Mita, are also available. Guided **hiking tours** are available along the same routes, with prices starting at $30, depending on the route.

SAILING   Sail Vallarta, Club de Tenis Puesta del Sol, Local 7-B, Marina Vallarta (☎ **322/1-0096;** fax 322/1-0097; e-mail: sail@pnet.puerto.net.mx), offers a diverse variety of sailing vessels for hire. A group day-sail, including crew, use of snorkeling equipment, drinks and food, and music, plus a stop at a beach for swimming and lunch, costs $63. Most trips include a crew, but you can make arrangements to sail yourself on one of their smaller boats. Prices vary for full-boat charters, depending on the vessel and amount of time desired.

✪ **SWIMMING WITH DOLPHINS**   Ever been kissed by a dolphin? Take advantage of a unique and absolutely memorable opportunity to swim with Pacific bottlenose dolphins in a clear lagoon. **Dolphin Adventure** (☎ **322/1-0657** or 322/1-0658; www. vallarta-adventures.com) operates an interactive dolphin-research facility, which allows limited numbers of people to swim with their dolphins Monday through Saturday at scheduled times. Cost for the swim is $130, with advanced reservations required—they are generally sold out at least a week in advance. You may prefer the **Dolphin Encounter** ($65), at the same facility, which allows you to touch and learn about these dolphins, in smaller lagoon pools, so you're assured up-close and personal time with them. I give this my highest recommendation. Not only does the experience leave you with an indescribable sensation, but it's a joy to see these dolphins—they are well cared for, happy, and spirited. The program is about education and interaction, not entertainment or amusement, and is especially popular with children 10 and older.

TENNIS   Many hotels in Puerto Vallarta offer excellent tennis facilities, many with clay courts. There are also two full-service tennis clubs. The **Continental Plaza Tennis Club** (☎ 322/4-0123), located at the Continental Plaza hotel in the Hotel Zone, offers indoor and outdoor courts (including a clay court), full pro shop, lessons, clinics, and partner matchups. The **Iguana Tennis Center** (☎ 322/1-0683), located on the main highway just south of the entrance to Marina Vallarta, offers covered courts, clinics, and child care.

WATER-SKIING & PARASAILING   Water-skiing, parasailing, and other water sports are available at many beaches along the Bay of Banderas. The best known for water-sports equipment rental is **Club Bananas Water Sports Center** at the beach of the Las Palmas Hotel, avenida Fco. Medina Ascencio, km 2.5, Hotel Zone (☎ 322/4-0650). Waverunners, banana boats, parasailing, and water-skiing are all available here, for hourly, half-day, or full-day rentals.

A STROLL THROUGH TOWN

Puerto Vallarta's cobblestone streets are a pleasure to explore; they're full of tiny shops, rows of windows edged with curling wrought iron, and vistas of red-tile roofs and the sea. Start with a walk up and down the malecón, the seafront boulevard.

Among the sights you shouldn't miss is the **municipal building,** on the main square (next to the tourism office), which has a large Manuel Lepe mural inside in its stairwell. Nearby, up Independencia, sits the **Parrish of Nuestra Señora de Guadalupe Cathedral,** Hidalgo 370 (☎ 322/2-1326), topped with its curious crown held in place by angels—a replica of the one worn by Empress Carlotta during her brief reign. On its steps, women sell religious mementos and native herbs for curing common ailments. Services in English are held Sunday at 10am. Regular parish hours are 7am until 9:30 or 10pm daily.

Three blocks south of the church, head east on Libertad, lined with small shops and pretty upper windows, to the **municipal market** by the river. After exploring the market, cross the bridge to the island in the river; sometimes a painter is at work on its banks. Walk down the center of the island toward the sea and you'll come to the tiny **Museo Río Cuale** (no phone), which has a small but impressive permanent exhibit of pre-Columbian figurines. It's open Monday through Saturday from 10am to 4pm. Admission is free, and an English-language tour is provided at 2pm.

Retrace your steps back to the market and Libertad and climb calle Miramar to the brightly colored steps up to Zaragoza. Midway is a magnificent view over rooftops to the sea, plus a cute cafe, **Graffiti** (no phone), where you can break for a cappuccino and a snack. Up Zaragoza to the right 1 block is the famous **pink arched bridge** that once connected Richard Burton's and Elizabeth Taylor's houses. This area, known as **"Gringo Gulch,"** is where many Americans have houses.

2 Shopping

Shopping in Puerto Vallarta is generally concentrated in small, eclectic, and independent shops rather than impersonal malls. You can find excellent-quality **folk art,** original **clothing** designs, and fine home accessories at great prices. Vallarta is known for having the most diverse and impressive selection of **contemporary Mexican fine art** available outside of Mexico City. There is also an abundance of tacky T-shirts and the ubiquitous **silver jewelry.**

THE SHOPPING SCENE

There are a few key areas where the best shopping is concentrated: central downtown, the Marina Vallarta malecón, the popular mercados, and on the beach—where the merchandise comes to you. Some of the more attractive shops are found 1 to 2 blocks in **back of the malecón.** Start at the intersection of Corona and Morelos streets—interesting shops are found in all directions from here. **Marina Vallarta** does offer two shopping plazas, but both have a limited selection of shops—Plaza Marina and Neptuno Plaza, both located on the main highway coming from the airport into town. **Neptuno Plaza** has become the better option in the past year, now anchored by a new Radio Shack and Internet cafe. Though still

Downtown Puerto Vallarta

ATTRACTIONS
Catedral ⑪
Gringo Gulch (neighborhood) ⑩
Main Square ⑫
Isla del Río Cuale ⑮
Terra Noble Center for the Arts ①

ACCOMMODATIONS
Hotel Molino de Agua ⑯
Hotel Playa Los Arcos ㉖
Los Cuatro Vientos ⑧

RESTAURANTS
Adobe Café ⑲
Archie's ②
Archie's Wok ㉓
Café San Angel ㉒
Chef Roger ⑭
El Palomar de los Gonzales ⑳
Fajita Republic ⑱
Kit-Kat ㉔
La Bodega de Nina ㉑

La Dolce Vita ④
La Palapa ㉕
Las Palomas ⑥
Ocho Tostadas ⑤
Pane & Vino ⑨
Red Cabbage Café ⑰
Rito's Baci ③
Trio ⑬
Tutifruti ⑦

Bahia de Banderas

Playa Los Muertos
Pier (water taxi)

home to a few interesting shops, the marina boardwalk (*marina malecón*) is dominated by real estate companies, timeshare vendors, restaurants, and boating services.

Puerto Vallarta's **municipal market** is just north of the Río Cuale, where Libertad and A. Rodríguez meet. The mercado sells clothes, jewelry, serapes, shawls, leather accessories and suitcases, papier-mâché parrots, stuffed frogs and armadillos, and, of course, T-shirts. Be sure to do some comparison-shopping, and definitely bargain before buying. The market is open daily from 9am to 7pm. Upstairs, a **food market** serves inexpensive Mexican meals—for more adventurous diners, it's probably the best value and most authentic dining experience in Vallarta. An **outdoor market** is found along Río Cuale Island, between the two bridges. Stalls sell crafts, gifts, folk art, and clothing.

Along any public beach, it's more than likely that you'll be approached by walking **vendors** selling merchandise that ranges from silver jewelry to rugs, T-shirts to masks. "Almost free!" they'll

---

Beware the Silver Scam

Most of the silver sold on the beach is actually alpaca, a lesser-quality silver metal (even though many pieces are still stamped with the designation "9.5," supposedly indicating that it is true silver). The prices for silver on the beach are much lower, as is the quality. If you're looking for a more lasting piece of jewelry, you're better off in a true silver shop.

---

call out, in seemingly relentless efforts to attract your attention. If you're too relaxed to think of shopping in town, this can be an entertaining alternative for picking up a few souvenirs, and remember: bargaining is expected. The most reputable beach vendors are concentrated at Los Muertos beach, in front of the El Dorado and La Palapa restaurants (calle Púlpito).

In most of the better-quality shops and galleries, shipping, packing, and delivery services to Puerto Vallarta hotels are available.

THE LOWDOWN ON HUICHOL INDIAN ART

Puerto Vallarta offers the best selection of Huichol art in Mexico. Descendants of the Aztecs, the Huichol Indians are one of the last remaining indigenous cultures in the world that has remained true to its ancient traditions, customs, language, and habitat. The Huichol live in adobe structures in the high Sierras (4,600 ft. elevation) north and east of Puerto Vallarta. Due to the decreasing fertility (and therefore, productivity) of the land surrounding their villages, they have come to depend more on the sale of their artwork for sustenance.

Huichol art has always been cloaked in a veil of mysticism—probably one of the reasons this form of *artesanía* is so sought after by serious collectors. Huichol art is characterized by colorful, symbolic yarn "paintings," inspired by visions experienced during spiritual ceremonies. In these ceremonies, artists ingest *peyote,* a hallucinogenic cactus, which induces brightly colored visions; these are considered to be messages from their ancestors. The symbolic and mythological imagery seen in these visions is reflected in the art, which encompasses not only yarn paintings but fascinating masks and bowls decorated with tiny colored beads.

The Huichol might be geographically isolated, but they have business savvy, and have adapted their art to meet consumer demand—original Huichol art, therefore, is not necessarily traditional. Iguanas, jaguars, sea turtles, frogs, eclipses, and eggs are a result of popular demand. For more traditional works, look for pieces that depict deer, scorpions, wolves, or snakes.

The Huichol have also had to modify their techniques to create more pieces in less time and meet the increased demand. The detailed designs that used to fill the pieces are sometimes replaced by patterned fill-work that is faster to produce. The same principle applies to yarn paintings. While some are beautiful depictions of landscapes and even abstract pieces, they are not traditional themes. Huichol Indians may also be seen on the streets of Vallarta—they are easy to spot, dressed in white clothing embroidered with colorful designs. A number of fine Huichol galleries are located in downtown Puerto Vallarta (see individual listings under "Decorative & Folk Art," below).

A notable place for learning more about the Huicholes is the **Huichol Collection** (Morelos 490, across from the sea-horse statue on the malecón; ☎ **322/3-2141**). Not only does this shop offer an extensive selection of Huichol art in all price ranges, but it also has a replica of a Huichol adobe hut, informational displays explaining more about their fascinating ways of life and beliefs, and usually, a Huichol Indian at work, creating art. The Huichol Collection donates a portion of all sales proceeds to projects, identified by the village elders, that help them retain their self-sufficiency.

CLOTHING

Vallarta's single true department store is **Lans,** Juárez 867 (☎ **322/3-2899**), offering a wide selection of name-brand clothing, accessories, footwear, cosmetics, and home furnishings. Along with the nationally popular **ACA Joe, Carlos 'n Charlie's,** and **Bye-Bye** brands, Vallarta offers several distinctive shops featuring original designs.

Adriana Gangoiti. Marina las Palmas II, Local 13, Marina Vallarta malecón. ☎ **322/1-2343.** AE.

Elegant, European-style fashions and made-to-order clothing are the specialties of this combination boutique and designer studio. The emphasis is on women's wear, but men's casual clothing is also available, with prices much less than you'd expect to pay for such quality fabrics and workmanship. Open Monday to Saturday, 10am to 2pm, and 6 to 10pm.

✪ **Laura López Labra Designs.** Basilio Badillo 324. ☎ **322/2-3074.**

The most comfortable clothing you'll ever enjoy—LLL is renowned for her trademark all-white (or natural) designs, in 100% cotton or lace. Laura's fine gauze fabrics float in her designs of seductive skirts,

A Huichol Art Primer: Tips for What to Buy

Huichol art falls into two main categories: yarn paintings and beaded pieces. All other items you might find in Huichol art galleries are either ceremonial objects or items used in their everyday lives.

Yarn paintings

Yarn paintings are made on a wooden base covered with wax that is meticulously overlaid with colored yarn. Designs represent the magical vision of the underworld, and each symbol gives meaning to the piece.

Keep these things in mind before you make a purchase:

• Paintings made with wool yarn are more authentic than those made with acrylic; however, acrylic yarn paintings are usually brighter and have more detail, because the threads are thinner. Acrylic was the predominant yarn used from the 1960s to the mid-'90s. Today, the Huicholes have reclaimed their tradition of spinning and dyeing their own wool.

• It is normal to find empty spaces where the wax base shows. Usually the artist starts with a central motif and works around it, but it's common to have several independent motifs that, when combined, take on a different meaning.

• A painting with many small designs tells a more complicated story than one with only one design and fill-work on the background.

romantic dresses, blouses, beachwear, and baby-dolls. Men's offerings include cotton drawstring pants and lightweight shirts. New designs include a line of precious children's clothing, and some pieces with elaborate embroidery based on Huichol Indian designs. Personalized wedding dresses are also available. It's open Monday through Saturday from 10am to 2pm and 5 to 9pm. No credit cards.

CONTEMPORARY ART

Known for sustaining one of the stronger art communities in Latin America, Puerto Vallarta has an impressive selection of fine galleries featuring quality original works of art. The several dozen galleries get together to offer art walks almost every week between November and April, alternating between galleries located in Marina Vallarta and those in central downtown. These are a social highlight of Vallarta during high season.

- Most Huichol artists write the story of the piece on the back of the painting. Usually it is written in pencil in Huichol and Spanish.

Beaded work

Beaded pieces are made on carved wooden shapes depicting different animals, wooden eggs, or small bowls made from gourds. The pieces are covered with wax, and tiny *chaquira* beads are applied one by one to form different designs. Usually the beaded designs represent animals; plants; the elements of fire, water, or air; and certain symbols that give a special meaning to the whole.

Some tips when shopping for beaded pieces:

- Deer, snakes, wolves, and scorpions are traditional elements; other pieces such as iguanas, frogs, and any animals not endemic to Huichol territory are a result of popular demand.
- Beadwork with many small designs that do not exactly fit into one another is more time-consuming and has a more complex symbolic meaning. This kind of work will have empty spaces where the wax shows.
- In many occasions the figure, whether it be a jaguar head or a snake, is not as important as the beaded designs covering the piece.

Galería AL (Arte Latinoamericano). Josefa Ortiz Dominguez 155. ☎ and fax **322/2-4406.** AE, MC, V.

The newest gallery success in town is a showcase of contemporary works created by young, primarily Latin American artists, as well as Vallarta favorite Marta Gilbert. Feature exhibitions take place every 2 weeks during high season. The historic building (one of Vallarta's original structures) has exposed brick walls; small rooms of exhibition spaces on the second and third floors surround an open courtyard. It's also rumored to have a friendly resident ghost, who partner Susan Burger says has been quite welcoming to this new, cultured environment. Open Monday through Saturday 10am to 9pm.

Galería Dante. Basilio Badillo 269. ☎ **322/2-2477.** Fax 322/2-6284. E-mail: dante@acnet.net. MC, V.

This gallery-in-a-villa showcases contemporary sculptures and classical reproductions of Italian, Greek, and art-deco bronzes—all set against a backdrop of gardens and fountains. Located on the "calle de los cafés," the gallery is open daily during the winter from 10am to 2pm and from 6 to 9pm. Viewings by appointment are also welcome.

☼ **Galería Pacífico.** Aldama 174, 2nd floor. ☎ **322/2-1982.** www.artmexico.com. E-mail: gary@artmexico.com. AE, MC, V.

Since opening in 1987, Galería Pacífico has been considered one of the finest galleries in Puerto Vallarta, and in Mexico. On display is a wide selection of sculptures and paintings in various media by midrange masters and up-and-comers alike. The gallery expanded and changed locations in the fall of 1998; it's now 1¹/₂ blocks inland from the fantasy sculptures on the malecón. Among the artists whose careers they have influenced are rising international sensation Rogelio Díaz, Ramiz Barquet, Evelyne Boren, Javier Fernandez, and Patrick Denoun. The gallery is open Monday through Saturday from 10am to 3pm and from 5 to 9pm, and Sundays by appointment only. Between May and October, check for reduced hours or vacation closings. This gallery also organizes the Artist's Studio Tour (see "Tours in Town," above).

Galería Rosas Blancas. Juárez 523. ☎ **322/2-1168.** AE, MC, V.

This notable recent addition to Puerto Vallarta's gallery community features contemporary painters from throughout Mexico. The downstairs courtyard exhibition space showcases a featured artist, while the upstairs offers a sampling of the artists that regularly exhibit here. A shop next door sells art supplies and books on Mexican art in English and Spanish. Owner Marcella Alegría also runs the adjacent folk-art store, Querubines (see "Decorative & Folk Art," below). Open Monday through Saturday from 9am to 9pm, Sundays from 10am to 6pm.

Galería Uno. Morelos 561 at Corona. ☎ **322/2-0908.** AE, MC, V.

One of Vallarta's first galleries, this features an excellent selection of contemporary paintings by Latin American artists, plus a variety of posters and prints. During high season, featured exhibitions change every 2 weeks. Set in a classic adobe building with open courtyard, it's also a casual, *salón*-styled gathering place for friends of owner Jan Lavender and her partner Martina Goldberg. Open Monday through Saturday from 10am to 8pm.

    Arte de las Americas (☎ **322/1-1985**) at the Marina Vallarta (between La Taberna and the Yacht Club) is an arm of Galería Uno; it exhibits some of the same artists, but has a decidedly more abstract orientation. Open Monday through Saturday from 10am to 10pm.

CRAFTS & GIFTS

Alfarería Tlaquepaque. av. México 1100. ☎ **322/3-2121.**
www.at.com.mx.

Opened in 1953, this is Vallarta's original source for Mexican ceramics and decorative crafts, all at excellent prices. Talavera pottery and dishware, colored glassware, bird cages, baskets, and wood furniture are just a few of the many items found in this warehouse-style store. Open Monday through Sunday from 9am to 9pm.

El Vuelo. Morelos 676, ¹/₂ block from American Express. ☎ **322/2-1822.** AE, MC, V.

You'll find a collection of ethnic and contemporary gifts here, including world music (the Cuban music recordings are outstanding), woven fabrics, jewelry, and decorative objects for the home. This is part of a larger studio where dance classes are taught and musical performances featured. There's even a small cafe next door. It's open Monday through Saturday from 10am to 10pm.

✪ **Safari Accents.** Olas Altas 224, Local 4. ☎ **322/3-2660.**

Flickering candles glowing from within colored-glass holders welcome you into this highly original shop overflowing with creative gifts, one-of-a-kind furnishings, and reproductions of paintings by Frida Kahlo and Botero.

DECORATIVE & FOLK ART

Azul Siempre Azul. Ignacio L. Vallarta 228. ☎ **322/3-0060.** MC, V.

Religious figurative pieces, antique *retablos* (painted scenes on tin backgrounds depicting the granting of a miracle), artistic jewelry, and beeswax candles in grand sizes all come together in this tiny store brimming with captivating treasures. Open Monday through Saturday from 10am to 2pm and 5 to 10pm. Located across from Club Roxy, just across the southbound bridge.

✪ **La Tienda.** Rodolfo Gómez 122, near Los Muertos beach. ☎ **322/2-1535.** AE, MC, V.

Fine antiques and decorative objects for the home, including unique furniture, religious-themed items (including *retablos*), glassware, and pewter. Outstanding selection of rustic candlesticks and beeswax candles, both in a variety of sizes. It's open Monday through Saturday from 10am to 2pm and 4 to 8pm. A second, smaller location is on "restaurant row," Basilio Badillo 276 (☎ **322/3-0692**), with the same hours.

✪ **Lucy's CuCu Cabaña and Zoo.** Basilio Badillo 295. No phone. MC, V.

Owners Lucy and Gil Givens have assembled one of the most entertaining, eclectic, and memorable collections of Mexican folk art—about 70% of which is animal-themed. Each summer they travel and personally select the handmade works, created by over 100 indigenous artists and artisans. Items include metal sculptures, Oaxacan wooden animals, *retablos* (commemorations of miracles), and fine Talavera ceramics. Five percent of all sales goes to benefit the Puerto Vallarta Animal Protection Association, organized by the Givenses. It's open Monday through Saturday from 10am to 10pm. Closed May 15 to October 15.

Olinala. Cárdenas 274. ☎ **322/2-4995.** MC, V.

Two floors of fine indigenous Mexican crafts and folk art, including an impressive collection of museum-quality masks and original contemporary art by Brewster Brockman, the gallery owner. It's open Monday through Friday from 10am to 2pm and 5 to 8pm, and Saturday 10am to 2pm.

✪ **Querubines.** Juárez 501A (corner of Galena, behind Planet Hollywood). ☎ **322/2-2988.**

My personal favorite for the finest-quality artisan works from throughout Mexico. Owner Marcella García Alegría personally travels across the country to hand-select items for this shop, which include exceptional artistic silver jewelry, embroidered and handwoven clothing, bolts of loomed fabrics, tin mirrors and lamps, glassware, pewter frames and trays, high-quality wool rugs, straw bags, and Panama hats. It's open Monday through Sunday from 9am to 9pm.

JEWELRY

Pladi. Púlpito 116. ☎ **322/2-3732.** AE.

These pieces of jewelry made from silver and semiprecious gemstones are more accurately works of art, created by the owners and other local designers exclusively for this avant garde jewelry shop. This location also features a small collection of original clothing. Found next door to the Kit Kat Martini Lounge, it's open from 10am to 3pm and 5 to 10pm. They have a second location around the corner from Restaurant Chef Roger, calle Hidalgo 168 (☎ **322/2-5606**), open Monday to Saturday from 10am to 3pm and 4 to 9pm.

Viva. Basilio Badillo 274. ☎ **322/2-4078.** AE, MC, V.

At Viva, a new addition to Vallarta's shopping scene, both the shop and the jewelry are stunning. You enter through a long corridor lined with displays showcasing exquisite jewelry from 72 international designers. The main room has a large glass pyramid-shaped skylight as its roof, with comfy couches surrounded by more memorable jewelry displays. Open 10am to 10pm daily.

TEQUILA & CIGARS

La Casa del Tequila. Morelos 589. ☎ **322/2-2000.** AE, MC, V.

An extensive selection of premium tequilas, plus information and tastings to help guide you to an informed selection. Also, cigars from Cuba and Veracruz, regional bulk coffees, books, tequila glassware, humidors, and other tequila-drinking and cigar-smoking accessories. In the back, there's a garden patio with cafe and bar for enjoying espresso drinks and tequila drinks. Open Monday to Friday from 9:30am to 11pm. They feature a happy hour daily from 5 to 7pm, and have live music Friday evenings from 8 to 11pm.

Sir Walter Raleigh. Morelos 210, Local 5, near the Río Cuale. ☎ **322/3-0244.** AE, MC, V.

This fine tobacco shop has certified quality cigars from Cuba, Mexico, and the Dominican Republic, along with humidors, cutters, elegant lighters, and other smoking accessories. They're open Monday to Saturday 10am to 9pm, and Sunday noon to 6pm.

3 Puerto Vallarta After Dark

Puerto Vallarta's spirited nightlife reflects the town's dual nature: part resort, part colonial Mexican town. In the past 2 years, Vallarta's nightlife has seen an expansion of live music, especially in clubs along calle Ignacio L. Vallarta (the extension of the main southbound road), after it crosses the Cuale River. Along one 3-block stretch you'll find a live blues club, a sports bar, a Harley Davidson–themed bar with live rock 'n' roll, live mariachi music, a gay dance club, a steamy-hot live salsa dance club, and the obligatory, newly opened, **Señor Frogs.** Walk from place to place and take in a bit of it all!

The **malecón,** which used to be lined with restaurants, is now known more for its selection of hip dance clubs and a few more relaxed options, all of which look out over the ocean. You can first walk along the broad walkway by the water's edge and check out the action at the various clubs, which extend from **Carlos O'Brian's** on the north end to **Star's** and **Hooters** just off the central plaza.

Marina Vallarta has its own array of clubs, with a more upscale, indoor, air-conditioned atmosphere. Also south of the Cuale River, the Olas Altas zone literally buzzes with action pouring out of its wide selection of small cafes and martini bars. In this zone, there's also an active gay and lesbian club scene.

PERFORMING ARTS & CULTURAL EVENTS

Truth be told, there's a limited selection of cultural nightlife beyond the **Mexican Fiesta.** Culture in Vallarta centers around the visual arts, so here the opening of an exhibition has great social and cultural significance. Puerto Vallarta's gallery community comes together to present almost weekly **art walks** where new exhibits are presented, feature artists are in attendance, and complimentary cocktails are served. These social events alternate between the galleries located along the Marina Vallarta malecón and those in the central downtown area. Check listings in the daily English-language newspaper, *Vallarta Today,* upon arrival, to see what may be on the schedule during your stay.

FIESTA NIGHTS

Major hotels in Puerto Vallarta feature frequent fiestas for tourists— open-bar, Mexican buffet dinner, and live-entertainment extravaganzas. Some are fairly authentic and good introductions for first-time travelers to Mexico; others can be a bit cheesy. Shows are usually held outdoors but move indoors when necessary.

Krystal Vallarta Hotel. av. de las Palmas, north of downtown off the airport road. ☎ **322/4-1041.** Cover $35.

One of the best Fiesta Nights is hosted by the Krystal Vallarta on Tuesday and Saturday at 7pm. These things are difficult to quantify, but Krystal's program is probably less tacky than most of its hotel counterparts.

✪ **Rhythms of the Night (Cruise to Caletas).** Departs from Terminal Marítima. ☎ **322/1-0657** or 322/1-0658. www.vallarta-adventures.com. $60, includes boat cruise, dinner, open bar, and entertainment.

An unforgettable evening under the stars at John Huston's former home at the pristine cove called Las Caletas. The smooth, fast Vallarta Adventure catamaran travels here, entertaining guests along the way, until you're greeted at the dock by tiki torches and native drummers. There's no electricity here—you'll dine by the light of the multitude of candles, the stars, and the moon. The buffet dinner is delicious—steak, seafood, and generous vegetarian options. Everything is first class. The show, set to the music of native bamboo flutes and guitars, showcases the indigenous dances of the region, in a contemporary style. Departs at 6pm and returns by 11pm.

THE CLUB & MUSIC SCENE
RESTAURANT/BARS

Carlos O'Brian's. paseo Díaz Ordaz 786 (the malecón), at Pípila. ☎ **322/ 2-1444** or 322/2-4065. No cover. AE, DISC, MC, V.

Vallarta's original nightspot, it was once the only place you'd think of going for an evening of revelry. Although the competition is stiffer, COB's still packs them in—especially the 20-something set. Late at night, the scene resembles a college party. It's open daily from noon to 2am. Happy hour is from 6 to 8pm.

✪ **La Cantina.** Morelos 709, downtown. ☎ **322/2-1734.** No cover. No credit cards.

It's a Mexican classic gone contemporary—*cantinas* have been a centuries-old tradition in Mexico, and this one has retained the fundamentals while updating the concept to a hip club. Cantinas serve little complimentary plates of food as your table continues to order drinks. This is done here from 1 to 5pm, and might include carne con chile (meat in a chile sauce), soup of the day, or quesadillas. In the evenings, enjoy a romantic, clubby atmosphere with recorded music alternating between sultry boleros and the hottest in Mexican rock, at levels that still permit conversation. If you require more stimulation, board games are available to play in one of the brightly colored, smaller rooms or on the larger, open-air patio. Beers cost $1.30, with bar drinks priced at $2. Open Sunday through Wednesday noon to 2am, Thursday through Saturday noon to 4am.

La Casa del Tequila. Morelos 589. ☎ **322/2-2000.** No cover. AE, MC, V.

It's primarily known as a tequila specialty store (see "Shopping," above), but don't overlook the patio-bar in this former hacienda for a daytime break or a romantic evening. You can order a sampler of premium tequilas for a do-it-yourself tasting, or try one of their exceptional fresh-fruit tequila daiquiris (strawberry, peach, mango, pineapple, or guava). And there's always the best-selling margarita. Just don't slam your tequila; sip it slowly, and educate yourself about Mexico's most famous beverage. They feature a happy hour daily from 5 to 7pm, and have live music Friday evenings from 8 to 11pm. Open daily 9:30am to 11pm.

ROCK, JAZZ & BLUES

✪ **Club Roxy.** Ignacio Vallarta 217. ☎ **322/3-2404.** No cover. AE, MC, V.

Currently the most popular live-music club in Vallarta, Club Roxy features a hot house band led by club owner Pico, playing a mix of reggae, blues, rock, and anything by Santana. Live music jams between

10pm and 2am Monday through Saturday nights. It's south of the river between Madero and Cárdenas. Hours are nightly from 6pm to 2am.

Cuiza. Isla Río Cuale no. 3, below the southbound bridge. ☎ **322/2-5646.** www.cuiza.com. No cover. AE, MC, V.

Although a notable restaurant in its own right, Cuiza has gathered a following for its nightly live jazz, performed by locally popular Beverly and Willow from 9pm to 1am. The large bar serves infused vodkas and other innovative cocktails. Open daily noon to 1am.

✪ **El Faro Lighthouse Bar.** Royal Pacific Yacht Club, Marina Vallarta. ☎ **322/1-0541** or 322/1-0542. No cover. AE, MC, V.

El Faro is a circular cocktail lounge at the top of the Marina lighthouse and one of Vallarta's most romantic nightspots. Live or recorded jazz plays, and conversation is manageable. Drop by at twilight for the magnificent panoramic views. Open every evening 5pm to 2am.

Mariachi Loco. Lázaro Cárdenas 254, at Ignacio Vallarta. ☎ **322/3-2205.** No cover. AE, DC, MC, V.

OK, so it's not rock, jazz, or blues, but this live and lively mariachi club also features singers belting out boleros and ranchero classics. By 10pm it gets going, with the mariachi show beginning at 9pm—the mariachis stroll and play as guests join in impromptu singing. After midnight the mariachis play for pay, which is around $3.50 for each song. They also serve Mexican food until 1am. The club itself is open daily from 11am to 4am.

DANCE CLUBS & DISCOS

A few of Vallarta's clubs or discos charge admission, but generally you'll just pay for drinks—$3 for a margarita, $2 for a beer, more for a whiskey and mixed drinks. Keep an eye out for the discount passes that are frequently available in hotels, restaurants, and other tourist spots. Most clubs are open from 10pm to 4am.

Christine. In the Krystal Vallarta Hotel, north of downtown off av. Fco. Medina Ascencio. ☎ **322/4-0202.** Cover $6. AE, DC, MC, V.

Proving that disco is alive and well, this dazzling club still packs a crowd with an opening laser-light show, pumped-in dry ice and oxygen, flashing lights, and a dozen large-screen video panels. The sound system is truly amazing, and the mix of music can get almost anyone dancing. Open nightly from 10pm to 4am; the light show begins at 11pm. *Note:* No shorts (for men, of course), tennis shoes, or thongs.

Collage. calle Proa s/n, Marina Vallarta. ☎ **322/1-0505** or 322/1-0861. Cover varies with entertainment. AE, MC, V.

A multilevel monster of nighttime entertainment, including Champs pool salon, Captain America's video arcade, Bowl Vallarta, and the always-packed Crazy Worm Disco Bar, with frequent live entertainment. Open daily 10am to 6am, it's easily visible from the main highway, just past the entrance to Marina Vallarta, and is very popular with a young and mainly local crowd.

✪ **J&B Salsa Club.** av. Fco. Medina Ascencio, km 2.5 (Hotel Zone). ☎ **322/4-4616.** Cover $5. MC, V.

This is the locally popular place to go for dancing to Latin music—from salsa to samba, the dancing here is hot! Fridays, Saturdays, and holidays they feature live bands. Open from 9pm to 6am.

✪ **Señor Frogs.** Ignacio L. Vallarta and Venustiano Carranza. ☎ **322/2-5171** or 322/2-5177. Up to $5 cover, depending on the night. AE, MC, V.

The sheer size of this hot new outpost of the famed Carlos 'n Charlie's chain is daunting, but it still fills up and rocks until the early morning hours. Those cute waiters remain a signature trait of the chain, and one never knows when they'll assemble on stage and call on a bevy of beauties to join them in a tequila-drinking contest. Occasionally guest live bands appear. Though mainly popular with the 20s set, all ages will find it fun. There's food service as well, but it's better known for its dance-club atmosphere. Open noon to 4am.

Zoo. paseo Díaz Ordaz 630 (the malecón). ☎ **322/2-4945.** No cover (except peak weeks). AE, MC, V.

Your chance to be an animal and get wild in the night. The Zoo even has cages to dance in if you're feeling unleashed. This popular club has a terrific sound system and a great variety of dance music, including techno, reggae, and rap. Every hour's a happy hour here with two-for-one drinks. Open 11:30am until the wee hours.

A SPORTS BAR & A STRIP JOINT

Micky's No Name Cafe. Morelos 460 (the malecón) at Mina. ☎ **322/3-2508.** No cover. MC, V.

With a multitude of TVs and enough sports memorabilia to start a minimuseum, Micky's offers a great venue for catching your favorite game, with all NBA, NHL, NFL, MLB, and PPV sporting events broadcast. He also serves great barbecue ribs and USDA imported steaks. Open daily 11am to midnight.

Q'eros. búlevar Fco. Medina Ascencio, in front of Plaza Genovesa. ☎ **322/ 2-4367.** $5 cover. MC, V.

An adult nightclub featuring exotic dancers, private shows, and strip-tease. Open nightly 9pm to 6am.

GAY & LESBIAN CLUBS

Vallarta has a vibrant gay community with a wide variety of clubs and nightlife options, including special bay cruises and evening excursions to nearby ranches. The free **Southside PV Guide,** Amapas 325 (☎ **322/2-2517;** e-mail: pvguide@hotmail.com), specializes in gay-friendly listings.

The two top clubs are:

Club Paco Paco. Ignacio L. Vallarta 278. ☎ **322/2-1899.** Cover $4, which includes a drink. (Cover applies at 10pm or before the first show, whichever is first.)

This combination disco, cantina, and rooftop bar also hosts a spectacular "Trasvesty" transvestite show every Friday, Saturday, and Sunday night at 1:30am. The club is open from noon to 6am daily and is air-conditioned. **Paco's Ranch,** located around the corner at V. Carranza 239, has nightly specials including Western night on Tuesdays and Leather night on Thursdays. A nightly "Ranch Hand's Show" performs at 9pm and 12:30 and 3am. This club, which can be accessed from Club Paco Paco, is open from 8pm to 6am. Cover is the same at both clubs.

Los Balcones. Juárez 182. ☎ **322/2-4671.** No cover. MC, V.

One of the original gay clubs in town, this bilevel club with several dance floors and an excellent sound system earned a few chuckles when it was listed as one of the most romantic spots in Vallarta by *Brides* magazine. Air-conditioned, it's open from 9pm to 4am and posts nightly specials, including exotic male dancers.

4 Side Trips from Puerto Vallarta

YELAPA: ROBINSON CRUSOE MEETS JACK KEROUAC

It's a cove straight out of a tropical fantasy, and only a 45-minute trip by boat from Puerto Vallarta. Yelapa has no electricity, no cars, and just had its first paved (pedestrian-only) road put in last year—it remains accessible only by boat. Its tranquillity, natural beauty, and seclusion have made it a popular home for hippies, hipsters, artists, and writers (looking for inspiration) and a few ex-pats (looking to escape the stress of the rest of the world, or perhaps the law). A seemingly strange mix, but you're unlikely to ever meet a stranger there—Yelapa remains casual and friendly.

To get there, travel either by excursion boat or inexpensive water taxi (see "Getting Around," in chapter 2). Of course, there's also a challenging mountain-bike trip with Bike Mex (see "Mountain Biking & Hiking," above). You can spend an enjoyable day, but a longer stay is recommended—and provides a completely different perspective of the place.

Once you're in Yelapa, you can lie in the sun, swim, snorkel, eat fresh grilled seafood at a beachfront restaurant, or sample the local moonshine, *raicilla*. The local beach vendors specialize in the most amazing pies you've ever tasted (coconut, lemon, or chocolate); they also sell crocheted swimsuits. You can also have your picture taken with an iguana (for $1 a shot), tour this tiny town, or hike up a river to see one of two waterfalls. The closest to town is about a 30-minute walk from the beach. *Note:* If you use a local guide, agree on a price before you start out. Horseback riding, guided bird watching, fishing trips, and paragliding are also available.

For overnight accommodations, local residents frequently rent rooms, and there's also the very clean, rustic ✪ **Hotel Lagunita** (☎ **329/8-0554;** e-mail: lagunita@pnet.puerto.net.mx). With 27 cabañas (all with private bathroom, and a few hours of power daily), plus a saltwater pool and an amicable restaurant/bar, this is the most accommodating place for most visitors. Rates run $35 to $45 per night, depending on the cabaña and the time of year.

If you stay over on a Wednesday or Saturday night, don't miss the regular dance at the ✪ **Yelapa Yacht Club.** Typically tongue-in-cheek for Yelapa, the "yacht club" consists of a cement dance floor and a disco ball, but the DJ spins a great range of tunes from Glenn Miller to the Beastie Boys, attracting all ages and types to the dance. Dinner is a bonus—the food may be the best anywhere in the bay. The menu changes depending on what's fresh. Ask for directions; it's located in the main village, on the beach.

NUEVO VALLARTA: ALL-INCLUSIVE

Many people assume Nuevo Vallarta is simply a suburb of Puerto Vallarta, but it's really a stand-alone destination, located in Nayarit, a different state. Original plans called for a megaresort development—complete with marina, golf course, and luxury hotels—but much of this remains to be built. Currently, it's a collection of mostly all-inclusive hotels, located on one of the widest, most attractive beaches in the bay. The lengthy entrance road from the highway passes by fields that are great for birding, and nearby lagoons are great for kayaking. Although the marina exists, the draft is so shallow that larger boats still head for Marina Vallarta. There are a few convenience shops, but little in the way of dining or nightlife outside of the hotels. A trip into downtown Puerto Vallarta takes about 30 minutes by taxi, costing about $12 and available 24 hours a day. The ride is slightly longer by public bus, which costs 50¢ and operates from 7am to 11pm.

Paradise Village. paseo de los Cocoteros 001, 63731 Nuevo Vallarta, Nay. ☎ **800/995-5714** or 322/6-6770. Fax 322/6-6713. www.paradisevillage.com. 475 Junior 1- and 2-bedroom suites. A/C TV TEL. High season $175–$350 double, low season $140–$280 double. AE, DC, MC, V.

Truly a village, this self-contained resort has a full array of guest services from an on-site disco to a full-service European spa and health club. Styled in a Mayan-influenced design, the collection of pyramid-shaped buildings houses all-suite accommodations in studio, one-bedroom, and two-bedroom configurations. All are well-designed, with a muted color scheme, sitting areas, and kitchenettes—making it ideal for families or groups of friends. The Mayan theme extends to both oceanfront pools, with mythical creatures forming water slides and waterfalls. The exceptional spa is reason enough to book a vacation here, with treatments, hydrotherapy, massage (including massage on the beach), and fitness and yoga classes. Special spa packages are always available.

Dining/Diversions: Two beachfront snack bars and two full-service restaurants offer a variety of international and Mexican cuisine, plus seafood specialties, with a variety of meal plans. The hotel also offers special theme nights—Mexican, Barbecue, Casino Night, and '50s Flashback. The Los Arcos open-air theatre features regular performances, and their glass pyramid–topped Xcaret nightclub has a dance floor with a view of the ocean and city lights of Vallarta.

Amenities: Four tennis courts, two oceanfront swimming pools, lap pool, European spa and complete fitness center, basketball court, beach volleyball, water-sports center, meeting facilities, petting zoo, even a Kid's Club. They have their own travel services desk for tours and excursions, plus a fleet of rental cars for guests only.

BUCERÍAS: A COASTAL VILLAGE WITH CHARM

Only 11 miles north of the Puerto Vallarta airport, Bucerías (boo-sayr-*ee*-ahs, meaning "place of the divers") is a small coastal fishing village of 10,000 people in Nayarit State on Banderas Bay. It's caught on as an alternative to Puerto Vallarta for those who find the pace of life there too invasive. Bucerías offers a seemingly contradictory mix of accommodations—trailer-park spaces and exclusive villa rentals tend to dominate, although there's a small selection of hotels as well.

To reach the town center by car, drive down the shaded, divided street that leads to the beach and turn left when you see the line of minivans and taxis that service Bucerías and Vallarta. Go straight ahead 1 block to the main plaza. The beach, with a lineup of restaurants, is half a block farther. You'll see cobblestone streets leading from the highway to the beach and hints of the villas and town homes behind high walls. Bucerías has already been discovered by second-home owners and by about 1,500 transplanted Americans as a peaceful getaway; tourists have discovered its relaxed pace as well.

If you are taking the bus to Bucerías, get off the bus when you see the minivans and taxis to and from Bucerías lining up on the shaded, divided street that leads to the beach. To get here from Puerto Vallarta via public transportation, take a minivan or bus marked BUCERÍAS (they run from 6am to 9pm). The last minivan stop is Bucerías's town square. There's also 24-hour taxi service.

EXPLORING BUCERÍAS

Come here for a day-trip from Puerto Vallarta just to enjoy the long, wide, and uncrowded beach, along with the fresh seafood served at the beachfront restaurants or at one of the unusually great cafes listed below. If you are inclined to stay a few days, you can relax inexpensively and explore more of Bucerías. Sunday is street-market day, but it doesn't get going until around noon, in keeping with the town's casual pace.

A PLACE TO STAY

Several small hotels and condominiums rent rooms here. For advanced planning, check out the Bucerías villa rental bulletin board at **www.sunworx.com**. Locally, **Las Palmas** in Bucerías (☎ **329/8-0060;** fax 329/8-1100), will book accommodations, including villas, houses, and condos. Call ahead, or when you get to Bucerías, ask for directions to their office, open Monday through Friday from 9am to 2pm and 4 to 6pm, and Saturday from 9am to 2pm.

Posada Olas Altas. calle Héroes de Nacozari s/n, 63732 Bucerías, Nay. ☎ **329/8-0407.** 28 units. FAN. $11–$22 double. No credit cards. Free parking on the street.

Fronting the highway and just down (left) from the roadside food stands, this is the ideal inexpensive place to stay while getting to know the area. Owners Arnulfo Sánchez and his wife Rosalina Ortega have created cheery and clean rooms with concrete floors and blue-iron doors and window frames. Bathrooms have doors and walls but no ceiling separating them from the rest of the room. Most rooms have a single and double bed or two doubles, and one room on the roof has both a king-size bed and a double bed. There's no hot water unless you ask for it (the room price is the same with or without it). An inexpensive lobby restaurant is open Monday through Saturday from 7am to 7pm and Sunday (high season only) from 7am to 2pm.

GREAT PLACES TO EAT

Besides those mentioned below, there are many seafood restaurants fronting the beach. The local specialty is *pescado sarandeado,* a whole fish smothered in tasty sauce and slow-grilled.

Cafe Magaña. Lázaro Cárdenas 500. ☎ **329/8-1091.** Main courses $4–$10. No credit cards. Daily 5–11pm. BARBECUE RIBS.

Famous for its barbecue ribs and chicken, Cafe Magaña gives you a choice of 10 original sauces, all homemade. Flavors have mythological names and contain creative ingredients like ginger, garlic, oranges, apples, cinnamon, and chiles. The sauces have been such a hit that British owner Jeff Rafferty now offers them bottled and for sale. This casual, colorful cafe and takeout restaurant also features TV sports and an occasional live band. It's located directly across from the Bucerías Trailer Park.

✪ **Mark's.** Lázaro Cárdenas 56. ☎ **329/8-0303.** Pasta $6.50–$11.50, main courses $9–$16. MC, V. High season Wed–Mon noon–11pm. Low Season Wed–Mon 5:30–11pm. ITALIAN/STEAK/SEAFOOD.

It's worth a special trip to Bucerías just to eat at this covered-patio restaurant. The most popular American hangout in town, Mark's offers a great assortment of thin-crust pizzas and flat bread, baked in their brick oven and seasoned with fresh herbs grown in the garden. In fact, everything from the shrimp in the angel-hair pasta to the pesto-crusted fish fillet and grilled pork tenderloin with mango basil sauce has a wonderfully fresh taste. The multitalented Chef Jan Marie (Mark's charming wife and partner) runs an adjacent boutique, with the nicest selection of women's resort wear in town. All major sporting events are televised in the bar. Mark's is only half a block from the beach. From the highway, turn left just after the bridge where there's a small sign for Mark's. Then double-back left at the next street (it's immediately after you turn left) and turn right at the next corner. Mark's is on the right, the block before the ocean.

SAN SEBASTIAN: AN AUTHENTIC MOUNTAIN HIDEAWAY

If you haven't heard about San Sebastian yet, it probably won't be long—its remote location and historic appeal have made it the media's new darling destination in Mexico. Originally discovered in the late 1500s, it peaked as a center of mining operations, swelling to a population of over 30,000 by the mid-1800s. Today, with roughly 800 year-round residents, San Sebastian retains all the charm of a village locked in time, with an old church, a coffee plantation, and an underground tunnel system—and without a T-shirt shop to be found.

GETTING THERE   You can arrive by car—it's a 2¹/₂-hour drive up the Sierra Madre from Puerto Vallarta on an improved road, but this can be difficult during the summer rainy season, as the road washes out frequently. **Vallarta Adventures** (☎ 322/1-0657) runs a daily plane service there for half-day tours, but can occasionally accommodate overnight visitors. The small private airport can arrange flights, for about $100 round trip, depending on the type of plane and number of passengers traveling.

WHERE TO STAY

There are two places to stay in San Sebastian. The first is the very basic **El Pabellon de San Sebastian,** which faces the town square. Its eight rooms are clean and simply furnished, surrounding a central patio. Don't expect extras here, but the rates run $12 per double, or $7.50 for singles. Reservations are handled through the town's central phone lines—you call and leave a message or send a fax, and hopefully the hotel will receive it. On any given day, any of the following can serve as the fax line: ☎ **329/7-0416,** 329/7-0418, or 329/7-0332. More secure is by e-mail: ssb@pvnet.com.mx. Excepting holidays, there is generally room at this inn.

A more enjoyable option is the stately **Hacienda Jalsico** (reserve through e-mail at ssb@pvnet.com.mx, or through the town telephones listed above), built in 1850 and once the center of mining operations in this mining town. Located near the airstrip, a 15-minute walk from town, the beautifully landscaped, rambling old Hacienda has walls that seem to whisper stories of its past. If proprietor Bud Acord is feeling social, his stories will probably outshine any the hacienda has to tell. He's welcomed John Huston, Liz Taylor, Richard Burton, Peter O'Toole, and a cast of local characters as his guests.

The extra-clean rooms have wood floors, rustic furnishings and antiques, and working fireplaces; some are decorated with pre-Columbian reproductions. The ample baths are beautifully tiled with skylights. Hammocks grace the upstairs terrace, while a sort-of museum on the lower level attests to the celebrity guests and prior importance this Hacienda has enjoyed over the years. Because of its remote location, all meals are included. Rates are $120 per couple per night, including meals; alcoholic beverages are extra. Group rates are available, and discounts can be had for longer stays. Guided horseback, walking, or mine tours can be arranged through the Hacienda.

SAN BLAS: FOR BIRD WATCHERS & SURFERS

San Blas is a rather nondescript Pacific Coast fishing village of 10,000 people in Nayarit State, but it's one of the country's premier birding spots. Birding enthusiasts come often and stay long. Surfers do too, since some of Mexico's best surfing waters are at Las Islitas Beach.

Only 150 miles from Puerto Vallarta, San Blas is an easy 3½-hour trip, along a new, two-lane, paved highway that starts at Las Varas off Highway 200 (a sign announces Las Varas), goes through the villages of Santa Cruz and Aticama, then connects with the two-lane highway into San Blas. Signs are few, so if you're driving, keep asking directions. Buses depart from Puerto Vallarta's new central bus station (1km north of Puerto Vallarta's airport) and travel regularly to San Blas. Day-trips and bird-watching excursions run regularly from Puerto Vallarta, available through most hotel tour desks.

As you enter the village, you'll be on avenida Juárez, the principal street, which leads to the main plaza on the right. At its far end sits the old church, with a new church next to it. Across the street from the church is the bus station, and on the other side of the churches is the market. After you pass the square, the first one-way street to your left is Batallón, an important street that passes a bakery, a medical clinic, several hotels, and Los Cocos Trailer Park and ends up at Borrego Beach, with its many outdoor fish restaurants. Nearly everything is within walking distance, and there are public buses that go to the farther beaches—Matanchen and Los Cocos—on their way to Santa Cruz, the next village to the south.

EXPLORING SAN BLAS

Like Acapulco, San Blas was once a very important port for New Spain's trade with the Philippines, and the town was fortified against pirates. Ruins of the fortifications, complete with cannons, the old church, and houses all overgrown with jungle, are still visible atop La Contadura Hill. The fort settlement was destroyed during the struggle for independence in 1811 and has been in ruins ever since. Also, it was from San Blas that Father Junípero Serra set out to establish missions in California in the 18th century.

The view from La Contadura is definitely worth the walk there—a panorama of coconut plantations, coastline, town, and the lighthouse at Playa del Rey. To reach the ruins from San Blas, head east on avenida Juárez about half a mile, as if going out of town. Just before the bridge, take the stone path that winds up the hill to your right.

BEACHES & WATER SPORTS   One of the closest beaches is **Borrego Beach;** to reach it, head south from the town plaza on Batallón until it ends. Half a mile past the settlement is a dirt road to **Las Islitas Beach,** a magnificent stretch of sand extending for miles with a few beach-shack restaurants. This is a famous surfing beach with mile-long waves, especially during September and October, when storms create the biggest swells. If you don't have a surfboard, you can usually rent one from one of the local surfers. The bodysurfing at Islitas is good, too. A taxi to Islitas will cost about $5 from downtown San Blas.

JUNGLE CRUISE TO TOVARA SPRINGS   Almost the moment you hit San Blas, you'll be approached by a guide offering a boat ride into the jungle. This is one of Mexico's unique tropical experiences. To make the most of it, find a guide who will leave at 6:30 or 7am, since the first boat on the river encounters the most birds and the Tovara River is like glass early in the morning, unruffled by breezes. Around 9am, boatloads of groups start arriving, and the serenity evaporates like the morning mist.

The cost is about $40 for a boatload of one to four people for the 3- to 4-hour trip from the bridge at the edge of town on Juárez. It's less (about $30) for the shorter, 2-hour trip from the embarcadero near Matanchen Bay, out of town. Either way, you won't regret taking the early-morning cruise through shady mangrove mazes and tunnels, past tropical birds and cane fields to the beautiful natural springs, **La Tovara,** where you can swim. There's a restaurant here, too, but it's much more costly than what's available in town. *Note:* The guide may also offer to take you to "The Plantation," which refers to pineapple and banana plantations on a hill outside of town. The additional cost of this trip is not worth it for most people.

BIRD WATCHING   As many as 300 species of birds have been sighted around San Blas, one of the highest counts in the Western

Hemisphere. Birding is best from mid-October through April. Birders and hikers should go to the **Hotel Garza Canela** (☎ **328/5-0307** or 328/5-0480) in San Blas (see "A Place to Stay & Dine," below) to buy a copy of the booklet *Where to Find Birds in San Blas, Nayarit,* by Rosalind Novick and Lan Sing Wu. With maps and directions, it details all the best birding spots and walks, including hikes to some lovely waterfalls where you can swim. Ask the staff at Hotel Garza Canela to put you in touch with the bilingual guide they currently recommend. A half-day tour will cost around $100 for up to four persons, with an extra charge of $5 for additional people.

A PLACE TO STAY & DINE

There aren't many good accommodations and dining options in San Blas. The ✪ **Hotel Garza Canela** (☎ **328/5-0307,** 328/5-0480, or 328/5-0112) is still one of the most comfortable places to stay on the coast. A block inland from the waterfront and nestled among pretty gardens of palms, hibiscus, and other tropical plants are the cottagelike fourplexes and other buildings of this resort. You'll find a tranquil ambiance, two pools (one for toddlers), and the best restaurant/bar in town. Pets are welcome. The 45 rooms and minisuites ($70 double, $152 suite, breakfast included; AE, MC, V) are modern, bright, airy, and immaculate, with well-screened windows, fans, and air-conditioning. Several rooms have kitchens and come with king-size beds; otherwise, most have two double beds, and a few have an extra single bed. Each room has satellite TV, an in-room safe-deposit box, and air-conditioning. The hotel's **El Delfín** restaurant (main courses $6 to $12; open daily 8 to 10am and 1 to 9pm) serves the best food in San Blas in an air-conditioned dining room with soft lights, soft music, and comfortable captain's chairs. Try the exquisite shrimp with creamy chipotle pepper sauce. The spaghetti dishes include pasta with shrimp in lime, roasted garlic, and basil sauce. The homemade soups and desserts are also quite good. Find the hotel and restaurant on calle Paredes Sur 106. To get here, walk south from the square on Batallón about 6 blocks, turn right on Campeche across from the Marino Inn, then turn left on the next street, Paredes Sur. The hotel, which accepts major credit cards, has a fax (328/5-0308) and toll-free telephone number from within Mexico (☎ **800/71-32313**).

4

The Costa Alegre: From Puerto Vallarta to Barra de Navidad

*C*osta Alegre, translates as the "happy coast," but driving along this 145-mile stretch of road that connects tropical forests with a series of dramatic cliff-lined coves, I don't think the term does the area justice. I am left with more a feeling of awe, inspired by the sheer beauty of it all. I am drawn to every road that trails down to another magical cove with a pristine beach. Some of these feel like extensions of small-town *rancheros;* others are steeped in privileged exclusivity. Considered one of Mexico's great undiscovered treasures, this area is becoming a favored hideaway for publicity-fatigued celebrities and those in search of natural seclusion. The area is also referred to as **Costa Careyes** (Turtle Coast), after the first deluxe resort to be located here. Today, it is home to an eclectic array of the most unique, captivating, and exclusive places to stay in Mexico, with a selective choice of activities that includes championship golf and polo. Stops along Highway 200, as it meanders between Puerto Vallarta to the north and Manzanillo to the south, can be an enjoyable day-trip or an ultimate destination in themselves.

EXPLORING THE COSTA ALEGRE   Renting a car and driving is the best way to see this region. Highway 200 is safe along this route, but has no lighting, and curves through the mountains, so it's recommended for travel only during the day. A few buses travel this route, but stop only at the towns that line the highway, and many of these are several miles inland from the resorts tucked in along the coast.

1 Along the Costa Alegre (from North to South)

CRUZ DE LORETO AND ITS LUXURY ECO-RETREAT

✪ **Hotelito Desconocido.** Playa de Mismaloya sin numero, 48360 Cruz de Loreto, Tomatlán, Jal. ☎ **877/486-3372** in the U.S. and Canada, or 322/2-2526. Fax 322/3-0293. www.hotelito.com. E-mail: hotelito@pvnet.com.mx. 21 rooms, 9 suites. High season $500 room, $600 suite. Low season $390 room, $470 single or double suite. All meals and activities are included; drinks extra. AE, MC, V.

The fact that the *Hotelito Desconocido* (little, unknown hotel) is ecologically minded is a bonus in my opinion, but it's not the principal appeal. A cross between *Out of Africa* and *The Blue Lagoon,* it is quite simply my favorite place to stay in all of Mexico. Think camping out with luxury linens, the romance of candles everywhere, and a symphony performed by cicadas, birds, and frogs.

The rooms, called *palafitos,* are located in cottages perched on stilts over a lagoon. The rustic, open-air rooms seem to extend out beyond the bamboo-planked doors and wooden terraces. A new grouping of suites—with inviting daybeds that practically cry out *"siesta"*—has been added on the ample sandbar that separates the tranquil estuary from the rousing Pacific Ocean. Their ingenious saltwater pool (refilled daily) is also located here, a clever diversion since the ocean is generally too aggressive for even seasoned swimmers.

Inside each of the 30 rooms you'll find weighty white cotton sheets, thick oversized bath towels, and gauzy mosquito nets draped seductively over the beds—needed or not. The housekeeper performs a ritualistic turn down and light up (candles, that is) service each evening at sundown. They also have an inventive system for morning room service —from the comfort of your bed, pull a rope and a flag is hoisted, signaling that you're ready for coffee. The air is cooled by ceiling fans, and water is solar-heated. Everything used here is either biodegradable or recycled, most of the produce is organically grown on the property, and the hotel encourages you to use only their handmade soaps, shampoos, and natural bath oils.

It's easy to disconnect here, in fact it's mandatory; there's no electricity, no phones, no neighboring restaurants, nightclubs, or shopping—only delicious tranquillity for those in search of seclusion. What service lacks in polished professionalism is made up for in enthusiasm.

Part Polynesia and *muy* Mexicano, each room revels in singular style. The Italian designer who owns the place traveled throughout Mexico to assemble an admirable collection of antiques, curios, and "so tacky they're classy" knick-knacks. With a generous creative dash, this *hotelito* is a conscious respite from an overly revved-up world.

To get there, take Highway 200 south for 1 hour, then turn off at the exit for Cruz de Loreto and continue on the unpaved road for about 25 minutes to the Hotelito Desconocido. The signs are clearly marked.

Dining: The hotelito has one palapa-topped restaurant and bar, where gourmet meals are prepared three times daily.

Amenities: Daytime activities include beach volleyball, bird-watching tours, windsurfing, billiards, kayaking, mountain biking,

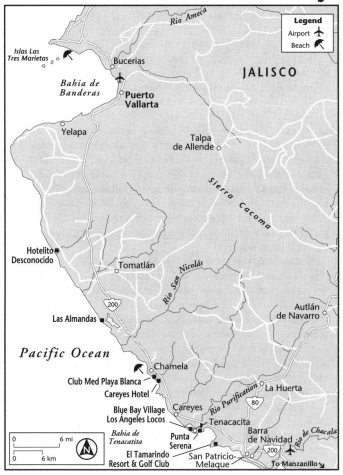

The Costa Alegre

Legend
Airport ✈
Beach ⚓

Islas Las Tres Marietas

Bucerías

Bahía de Banderas

Puerto Vallarta

JALISCO

Yelapa

Talpa de Allende

Sierra Cacoma

Hotelito Desconocido

Tomatlán

Rio San Nicolás

200

Autlán de Navarro

Las Almandas

Pacific Ocean

Chamela

Club Med Playa Blanca
Careyes Hotel

Blue Bay Village
Los Ángeles Locos

Careyes

Rio Purificación

La Huerta

80

Tenacacita

Bahía de Tenacatita

Punta Serena

Barra de Navidad

Rio de Chacala

0   6 mi
0   6 km

El Tamarindo Resort & Golf Club

San Patricio–Melaque

200

To Manzanillo

hiking, and riding well-kept horses down the long stretch of beach—all included in your room price. There's also a primitive-luxury spa that offers massage, sauna and whirlpool, plus hammocks for hanging out in, post-therapy.

LAS ALAMANDAS: AN EXCLUSIVE LUXURY RESORT

✪ **Las Alamandas.** Hwy. 200, 48800 Manzanillo–Puerto Vallarta, Jal. ☎ **888/882-9616** or 800/223-6510 in the U.S. and Canada, or 328/5-5500. Fax 328/5-5027. E-mail: alamada@zonavirtual.com.mx. 6 villas. High-season $390–$680 room, $1,050–$2,248 villa. Low-season $290–$680 room, $420–$1,520 villa. AE, MC, V.

Almost equidistant between Manzanillo ($1^1/2$ hr.) and Puerto Vallarta ($1^3/4$ hr.), a small sign points in the direction of the ocean to Las Alamandas. A dirt road winds for about a mile through a poor village to the guard house of Las Alamandas, part of a 1,500-acre estate, and itself set on 70 acres against low hills. The small cluster of buildings that make up this resort almost spreads to the wide, clean beach. The resort is one of the most exclusive in Mexico, and its architecture, a blend of Mediterranean, Mexican, and Southwestern United States, has been featured in *Architectural Digest, Condé Nast Traveler,* and *Vogue.* The furnishings are a stunning blend of Mexican handcrafted furniture, pottery and folk art, and sofa beds and pillows covered in bright textiles from Mexico and Guatemala. While exquisite, the furnishings still exude a relaxed feel. Only 20 guests can be accommodated at any one time, so the threat of crowds is nonexistent.

All the villas are spacious and have high-pitched tiled roofs, cool tiled floors, and tiled verandas with ocean views. The six villas have several bedrooms (each with its own bathroom) and can be rented separately or as a whole house; preference for reservations is given to guests who rent whole villas. Some villas are on the beach, while others are set back from the beach across a cobblestone plaza. Transportation in the hotel's van to and from Manzanillo ($180 one way) and Puerto Vallarta ($180 one way) can be arranged when you reserve your room.

Dining: One restaurant serves all meals.

Amenities: All rooms have TVs with VCRs, but there's no television reception from the outside. There's also a weight room, 60-foot swimming pool, lighted tennis court, horses, hiking trails, boat tours to Río San Nicolás for birding, mountain bikes, and boogie boards. A private 3,000-foot paved landing strip capable of accommodating a King Air turbo prop is on the premises; make advance arrangements for landing.

CAREYES

The resorts **Club Med Playa Blanca** and **The Careyes Hotel** are roughly 100 miles south of Puerto Vallarta. They're about a 2-hour drive north of Manzanillo on Highway 200 but only about a 1-hour drive from the Manzanillo airport. If you haven't arranged for transportation through either hotel, taxis from the Manzanillo airport charge around $100 one way for the trip. There are also car rentals at both the Manzanillo and Puerto Vallarta airports. While these resorts are completely self-contained, a car is useful for exploring the coast—Barra de Navidad and other resorts, for example—although the hotels can also make such touring arrangements.

Club Med Playa Blanca. Cihuatlán, 48980 Careyes, Jal. ☎ **800/CLUBMED** in the U.S. and Canada, 335/1-0001, or 335/1-0002. Fax 335/1-0004. www.clubmed.com. 295 units. A/C. Weekly all-inclusive $965 single (no roommate), $800 per person double. Air-inclusive rates also available. AE, MC, V. Closed May–Nov.

On a beautiful cove separated by grand bluffs from The Careyes Hotel, this sienna-colored resort climbs up, around, and down a lovely, lushly landscaped hillside to the beach. Accommodations are in comfortable adobe brick *casitas*, with large, bright rooms with a choice of two full beds or one king bed.

This Club Med has always been popular with active singles and young couples, as the extensive, innovative program of activities would indicate. No facilities are available for children. Numerous special-interest activities are included in the prices. You can avail yourself of the circus workshop and learn to fly from a high trapeze, jump on a trampoline, juggle, and walk the high wire. There is a PADI scuba-certification class for beginning divers (extra charge), but no exploration dives. Usually there are twice-daily boat excursions that include snorkeling and a picnic at a nearby, secluded beach.

Other special-interest activities are offered at an additional charge, including an intensive horseback-riding program and a rock-climbing wall. There are daily excursions to nearby Bird Island (a natural habitat for nesting boobies), out into the ocean for deep-sea fishing, and to nearby Manzanillo, Barra de Navidad, and more. Massages are available, as well as arts-and-crafts workshops, with a small charge for materials.

Dining/Diversions: The main dining room, above the bar and pool, is open for all three buffet-style meals and features Mexican and continental food. **El Pelicano,** on the beach, serves extended breakfast and lunch buffets; for two people or more, seafood dinners are served at the table. **El Zapata,** on the beach, serves steaks. Bars include one by the pool, a disco bar, and a beach bar. The staff provides evening entertainment in a combination of shows and games that involve guests. There's disco dancing every night.

Amenities: One Olympic-size pool; six tennis courts (four lit for night play); equipment for sailing, kayaking, snorkeling, archery, volleyball, basketball, Ping-Pong, bocce, and billiards; fitness center with aerobics and calisthenics; in-room safes; irons and ironing boards available; token-operated washers and dryers; infirmary; telephone messages are posted.

The Careyes Hotel. Hwy. 200, km 53.5, Careyes, Jal. (Apdo. Postal 24; 48970 Cihuatlán, Jal.). ☎ **800/525-4800** in the U.S. and Canada, or 335/1-0000. Fax 335/1-0100. www.grupoplan.com. 51 units and suites. A/C MINIBAR TV TEL. High season $230 double, $415 suite. Low season $195 double, $355 suite. AE, MC, V.

The former Bel-Air Costa Careyes has returned to private operation as The Careyes, but still offers pampered accommodations in a secluded setting facing the ocean. Although guests come here for its isolation, you can still enjoy many services, including a full European spa and polo. It's both rustic and sophisticated, with the room facades awash in scrubbed pastels forming a U around the center lawn and free-form pool. Earthy but elegant Mexican tiles and decorative accents give each room a dramatic feel, from the colony shutters and white-tile floors to the handsome loomed bedspreads and colorful pillows. Some rooms have balconies; all have ocean views, robes and hair dryers, and small refrigerators. Twenty rooms have private pools, and affiliated full villas are also available for rent through the hotel. The hotel is a member of the Small Luxury Hotels of the World group, and has become popular for small corporate retreats.

The hotel offers a number of special-interest activities for guests. Named after the hawksbill turtle ("carey" in Spanish), the hotel sponsors a "save the turtle" program in which guests can participate between July and December. You can also arrange horseback excursions and riding lessons at the equestrian center. Polo clubs from around the world converge here for polo season, December through April.

Dining/Diversions: The Bistro Terrace restaurant/bar features international menus with light fare options. All meals are served in a casual, open setting beside the beach and pool. There's also a deli bordering the pool, for sandwiches and snacks, plus pool service for drinks. "Just for Kids" is a program of activities for children. There's a movie theater and a library, well stocked with reading material and videos for in-room viewing.

Amenities: The resort has a large pool fronting the ocean and a fully equipped, state-of-the-art spa with massage, loofah scrub, wax, hot and cold plunge, steam and sauna, and weight equipment. There are two tennis courts, plus a paddle court, and on the beach the hotel has kayaks, windsurf boards, and Aquafins available for guest use. Guests also have privileges at the superexclusive El Tamarindo

Resort, 25 miles south, where there's a fabulous 18-hole mountaintop golf course overlooking the ocean. Laundry, purified tap water, room service, boutique, tobacco shop.

TENACATITA BAY

Located 60 minutes (33 miles) north of the Manzanillo airport, this jewel of a bay is accessed by a 5-mile dirt road, passing through a small village set among banana plants and coconut palms. Sandy, serene beaches are tucked into coves around the bay, and dolphins playing along the beachfront are a common sight; a coastal lagoon is filled with exotic birds. Swimming and snorkeling are good here, and the bay is a popular stop for luxury yachts cruising down the coast. Just south of the entrance to Tenacatita is a sign directing you to the area's accommodations: the all-inclusive **Blue Bay Los Ángeles Locos** and **Punta Serena** resorts, as well as the exclusive **El Tamarindo Resort and Golf Club.** There is no commercial or shopping area, and dining options outside of your hotel are limited to a restaurant or two that may emerge during the winter months (high season). Relax, that's what you're here for.

Blue Bay Village Los Ángeles Locos. carr. Federal 200, km 20, Tenacatita, 48989 Municipio de la Huerta, Jal. ☎ **800/BLUE BAY** in the U.S., 335/1-5020, or 335/1-5100. Fax 335/1-5050. www.BlueBayResorts.com. E-mail: LAL@bluebayresorts.com. 200 units. A/C TV TEL. High season $85 double. Low season $75 double. Rates are all-inclusive. AE, DC, MC, V.

Set on a 3-mile stretch of sandy beach, Blue Bay Village Los Ángeles Locos offers an abundance of activities and entertainment in the midst of the seclusion of Tenacatita Bay. Water sports, tennis, horseback riding, an extensive activities program, and an ample selection of dining and entertainment options offer guests excellent value. It's a good choice for families and groups of friends. All rooms have ocean views, with either balconies or terraces. The three-story hotel is basic in its decor and amenities, but clean and comfortable. The attraction here is the wide array of activities on-site.

Two restaurants and a snack bar offer the option of ample buffets or a la carte dining. **Arrecife,** set into a bluff overlooking the beach and bay, features specialty Italian cuisine. Three bars mean unlimited drinks almost anytime you feel the urge. There are nightly shows and entertainment. La Largata Disco is a little on the dark and smoky side, but can really rock, depending on the crowd—it's basically the only option on the bay.

A large pool for adults and one for kids are adjacent to the beach. Also included in the price of your stay are a Jungle River–cruise excursion, basketball court, exercise room, activities program, kids' club, horseback riding, windsurfing, kayaks, Hobie cats, and pool tables. Tennis (three courts) is available for an extra charge, as are laundry, massage, and baby-sitting services.

✪ **Punta Serena.** carr. Federal 200, km 20, Tenacatita, 48989 Municipio de la Huerta, Jal. ☎ **800/551-2558** in the U.S., or 335/1-5100. Fax 335/1-5013. www.puntaserena.com. E-mail: info@puntaserena.com. 21 smoke-free units. A/C. High season $85–$110. Low season $65–$110 double. Rates are all-inclusive. AE, DC, MC, V.

Punta Serena is a refuge for relaxation and renewal. Set on a mountain overlooking this virgin bay, it's an adults-only holistic resort with a complete offering of services aimed at either putting you into a total state of relaxation or awakening new energy inside.

Punta Serena is one of the only resorts in Mexico truly geared for spiritual renewal, and does an excellent job of offering enough without making nonenthusiasts feel uncomfortable. Yoga, tai chi, and chi kung classes, native Aztec *Temazcal* (sweat lodge) ceremonies, and guided meditation sessions are offered over a daily-changing schedule. Too much introspection for your taste? It's also perfectly OK to simply immerse yourself in a mindless read while lolling in one of the two hot tubs that are nestled into the side of the cliff overlooking the Pacific blue below.

All rooms and suites are set in two-story bungalows, with ocean views and either balconies or large terraces with hammocks. Smoke-free and spacious, the rooms are very basic but both comforting and comfortable. One open-air restaurant serves three meals daily featuring excellent buffets of healthful selections, fresh juices, and vegetarian cuisine—it's the one buffet that I've ever really enjoyed. Palapa-topped, it has a stunning view of the bay and a constant breeze. Yes, drinks are served with meals, also included in your stay.

There are cliff-side hot tubs, a small but striking pool, and a private beach—one of the only allowable nude (optional) beaches in Mexico. Take a massage in the open-air massage area, or in a more private room. A library and video corner are part of the common areas, and there's a sauna and small but well-equipped gym. Guests have access to the facilities at the neighboring Blue Bay Village, if things get too quiet.

2 Barra de Navidad & Melaque

Only 30 minutes north of Manzanillo's airport by car, or 65 miles north of downtown, this pair of rustic beach villages (only 3 miles apart) has been attracting longtime travelers to Mexico for decades. Barra has a few bricked or cobblestone streets, good budget hotels and restaurants, and funky beach charm, all next to the superluxurious Grand Bay Hotel, which sits on a bluff across the inlet from Barra. Melaque offers a lineup of budget hotels both on and off the beach, fewer restaurants, and no funky charm, although the beach is as wide and more beautiful than Barra's. Both villages appeal to those looking for a quaint, quiet, and inexpensive retreat, rather than a modern, sophisticated destination. The Grand Bay Hotel, with its five-star quality and 27-hole golf course, provides a whole new dimension to vacationing in Barra.

In the 17th century, Barra de Navidad was a harbor for the Spanish fleet, and it was from here that galleons first set off in 1564 to find China. Located on a gorgeous crescent-shaped bay with curious rock outcroppings, Barra de Navidad and neighboring Melaque are connected by a continuous beach on the same wide bay and enjoy a very relaxed pace. It's safe to say that the only time Barra and Melaque hotels are full is during Easter and Christmas weeks. **Barra de Navidad** has the most charm, most tree-shaded streets, best restaurants, most stores, and the best conviviality between locals and tourists. Barra is very laid-back; faithful returnees adore its lack of flash. Other than the new Grand Bay Hotel, on the cliff across the waterway in what is called Isla Navidad (although it's not on an island), nothing is new or modern. But there's a bright edge to Barra now, with more good restaurants, a small, growing nightlife, and streets that are being bricked little by little. **Melaque,** on the other hand, is larger, rather sun-baked, treeless, and lacking in attractions. It does, however, have plenty of cheap hotels available for longer stays and a few restaurants. Although the beach between the two is continuous, Melaque's beach, with deep sand, is more beautiful than Barra's, where the sand is more packed down by the wave action.

Although the long-awaited **Isla de Navidad Resort** is mostly finished, with its fabulous 27-hole golf course and the superluxurious Grand Bay Hotel, the area's pace hasn't quickened as fast as expected. The golf is not only fabulous, it's also uncrowded, with another exceptional course at nearby Tamarindo. Simply put, it's become a serious golfer's dream.

ESSENTIALS

GETTING THERE   Buses from Manzanillo frequently run the route up the coast along Highway 200 on their way to Puerto Vallarta and Guadalajara. Most stop in the central villages of both

Barra de Navidad and Melaque. From the Manzanillo airport, it's only around 30 minutes to Barra, and taxis are available to take you there. Puerto Vallarta is a 3-hour (by car) to 5-hour (by bus) ride north on Highway 200 from Barra. From Manzanillo, the highway twists through some of the Pacific Coast's most beautiful mountains covered in oak and coconut palm and acres of banana plantations.

VISITOR INFORMATION   The **tourism office** for both Barra de Navidad and Melaque is in Barra on Jalisco 67 between Veracruz and Mazatlán (☎ and fax **335/5-5100**). The office is open Monday through Friday from 9am to 5pm. The **Travel Agency Isla Navidad Tours** at Veracruz 204-A (☎ **335/5-5665** or 335/5-5666; fax 335/5-5667) can handle arrangements for plane tickets and sells bus tickets from Manzanillo to Puerto Vallarta and Guadalajara. It's open Monday through Saturday from 10am to 8pm. American Express, MasterCard, and Visa are accepted.

ORIENTATION   In Barra, the main beachfront street, **Legazpi,** is lined with hotels and restaurants. From the bus station, beachfront hotels are 2 blocks straight ahead across the central plaza. Two blocks behind the bus station and to the right is the lagoon side. More hotels and restaurants are located on its main street, **Morelos/ Veracruz.** Few streets are marked, but 10 minutes of wandering will acquaint you with the village's entire layout.

ACTIVITIES ON & OFF THE BEACH

Swimming and enjoying the attractive beach and views of the bay take up most tourists' time. Hiring a small boat for a coastal ride or to go fishing can be done in two ways. Go toward the malecón on calle Veracruz until you reach the tiny boatmen's cooperative with fixed prices posted on the wall. You can also walk two buildings farther to the water-taxi ramp. The inexpensive water taxi is the best option for going to Colimilla (5 min. away) or across the inlet (3 min.) to the Grand Bay Hotel. The water taxis make the rounds regularly, so if you're at Colimilla, all you have to do is wait and a water taxi will be along shortly. At the Cooperative, a 30-minute **tour around the lagoon** costs $15, and a tour out on the sea costs $18. **Sportfishing** is $75 for up to four people for half a day in a small *panga* (open fiberglass boat like they use for the water taxis).

Unusual **area tours; house, condo, and apartment rentals;** and **sports-equipment rental** can be arranged through **The Crazy Cactus,** Jalisco 8 (☎ and fax **335/5-6099**), operated by Trayce Ross and located half a block inland from the town church on Legazpi. She

Barra de Navidad Bay Area

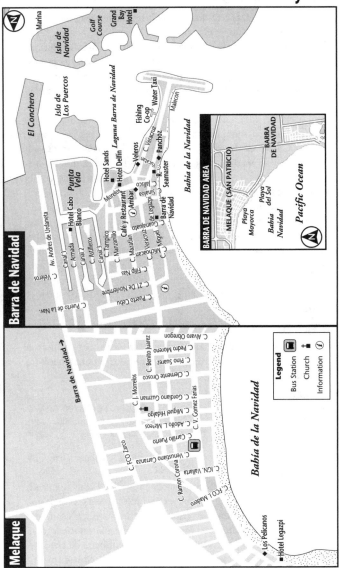

Barra de Navidad

Melaque

Marina
Isla de Navidad
Golf Course
Grand Bay Hotel
Isla de Los Puercos
El Conchero
Laguna Barra de Navidad
Av. Andres de Urdaneta
Canal 1
C. Armada
Hotel Cabo Blanco
Punta Vela
Canal 2
C. Astilleros
Canal 3
C. Tampico
C. Manzanillo
C. Mazatlan
Hotel Sands
Hotel Delfin
Morelos
C. Sinaloa
C. Jalisco
Café y Restaurant Ambar
Tucxan
Veleros
Pancho'z
Fishing Co-op
Water Taxi
Malecon
C. Veracruz
Seamaster
Barra de Navidad
C. Guanajuato
C. Michoacan
C. Miguel Legazpi
C. Veracruz
C. 21 De Noviembre
Filip Nas
C. Veleros
C. Puerto de la Nav.
C. Puerto Cebu
Bahia de la Navidad

Barra de Navidad →
C. FCO Zarco
C. J. Morelos
C. Clemente Orosco
C. Benito Juarez
C. Alvaro Obregon
C. Pedro Moreno
C. Pino Suarez
C. Cordiano Guzman
C. Miguel Hidalgo
C. Adolfo L. Mateos
C. V. Gomez Farias
C. Camillo Puerto
C. Venustiano Carranza
C. Ramon Corona
C. IGN. Vallarta
C. FCO.I. Madero
Los Pelicanos
Hotel Legazpi
Bahia de la Navidad

BARRA DE NAVIDAD AREA

MELAQUE (SAN PATRICIO)
Playa Mayorca
Playa del Sol
Bahia Navidad
BARRA DE NAVIDAD
Pacific Ocean

Legend
Bus Station
Church
Information

113

rents cars, bicycles, boogie boards, snorkeling equipment, life jackets, and kayaks. (The store may be closed from May through Oct.) **Paraíso Pacífico Tours** (☎ 335/5-5122; fax 335/5-5303), located in the lobby of the Hotel Barra de Navidad (see below) and operated by Mari Blanca Pérez, offers up-to-date maps of both Barra and Melaque; a good lineup of nearby boat excursions for snorkeling, diving, and sunning at beaches north near Tenacatita; horseback riding near Melaque; an interesting trip to Bird Island near Chamela to see nesting boobies; shopping tours to Manzanillo; a daylong trip to Colima City to see the town's volcanoes and shop; a day-trip to a village devoted to marble mining and making huaraches (leather sandals); a very long day-trip to Guadalajara and Tlaquepaque; sunset cruises; and fishing (a half day for $128 in a *panga* or $300 in a yacht).

For **golf,** the Grand Bay Hotel's beautiful and challenging 27-hole, 7,053-yard, par-72 course is open to the public. Hotel guests pay greens fees of $95 for 18 holes, or $115 for 27 holes, while nonguests pay $115 and $140, respectively; the prices include a motorized cart. Caddies are available, as are rental clubs. The Crazy Cactus (mentioned above) can also arrange golf at El Tamarindo's gorgeous, mountaintop 18-hole course about 20 miles north of Barra.

WHERE TO STAY

Low season is considered any time except Christmas and Easter weeks in Barra. Except for those 2 weeks, it doesn't hurt to ask for a discount at the inexpensive hotels.

VERY EXPENSIVE

✪ **Grand Bay Hotel.** 45110 Puerto de la Navidad, Col. ☎ **888/80-GRAND** in the U.S., 335/5-5050, or 335/5-6390. Fax 335/5-6070. www.grandbay.com. E-mail: grandbay@mail.udg.mx. 191 units. A/C MINIBAR TV TEL. High season $381–$498 double, $585–$848 parlour and executive suites. Low season $263–$321 double, $468–$614 parlour and executive suites. Ask about tennis, golf, fishing, and honeymoon packages. AE, DC, MC, V.

Across the yacht channel from Barra de Navidad, this luxurious hotel opened in 1997 on 1,200 acres next to the hotel's 27-hole golf course. It overlooks the village, the bay, the Pacific Ocean, and Navidad's lagoon. The hotel's beach is narrow and on the lagoon. A better beach is opposite the hotel on the bay in Barra de Navidad. The hotel's spacious rooms are sumptuously outfitted with marble floors, large bathrooms, and beautiful hand-carved wood furnishings. Prices vary according to view and size of room, but even the more modest rooms are large. Each room comes with a king-size or two double beds, glass-top desk, in-room security box, bathrobes, hair dryers, magnified makeup mirrors, cable TV with remote control, ceiling fans plus air-conditioning, and balcony. Executive suites are enormous and include a separate shower and bathtub, living room, dining room table, bar with butler's kitchen and separate entry, and an enormous bedroom. Junior suites lack the dining area. All suites have a steam sauna and telephones in the bathroom as well as a sound system. The hotel is a short water-taxi ride across the inlet from Barra de Navidad; it can also be reached by paved road from Highway 200. Although the hotel bills itself as being on the Island of Navidad at Port Navidad, the port is the marina, and the hotel is on a peninsula, not an island.

Dining/Diversions: Dining options are convenient dining by the pool, in a casual restaurant overlooking the lagoon, or fine dining. **Alfonso's,** the fine-dining restaurant, features Mexican cuisine with European preparation, as well as international and vegetarian dishes. There's a lobby bar and swim-up pool bar—hours vary by season. There is a full restaurant at the golf club, along with a convenient snack hut on the course serving snacks and drinks. The **Club de Niños** (Children's Club) is a specially outfitted, brightly colored area on the ground floor set aside just for children up to age 11. A special staff entertains children with crafts, games, and other activities between 9am and 6pm.

Amenities: One main swimming pool with swim-up bar; 27-hole, par-72 golf course designed by Robert Von Hagge; golf club with pro shop, driving range, and restaurant; 150-slip marina with private yacht club; three lighted, grass tennis courts with stadium seating. 24-hour concierge, room service, boutique, laundry, dry cleaning, business center, beauty salon, baby-sitting, high chairs, cribs, and complimentary round-trip transportation between the Manzanillo airport and the hotel. Fishing, boat tours, and other excursions can be arranged.

MODERATE

✪ **Hotel Cabo Blanco.** Armada y Bahía de la Navidad s/n, 48987 Barra de Navidad, Jal. ☎ **335/5-5103** or 335/5-5136. Fax 335/5-6494. E-mail: caboblan@guadalajara.net. 101 units. A/C TV TEL. $75 double, $144 suites with kitchenette. All-inclusive option, add $49 per person. AE, MC, V.

Located on the point where you cross over to Isla Navidad, the Cabo Blanco reigns as an outstanding option for family vacations or longer-term stays. There are four pools spread out among the gardens, and hacienda-style buildings, two reserved for adults only.

Rooms are pleasantly rustic, with tile floors, large tile tub, separate dressing area, and stucco walls. Views overlook the bay, but it's a mere 5-minute walk to the beach. The beamed-ceiling lobby is housed in its own building, and the resort also offers two tennis courts and two restaurants, one featuring seafood specialties. The atmosphere is generally tranquil, except for weekends and Mexican holidays, when this hotel tends to fill up.

INEXPENSIVE

✪ **Hotel Barra de Navidad.** Legazpi 250, 48987 Barra de Navidad, Jal. ☎ **335/5-5122.** Fax 335/5-5303. E-mail: hot-barra@acnet.net. 60 units. A/C FAN. $43 double. MC, V.

At the northern end of Legazpi, this popular and comfortable beachfront hotel has friendly management and some rooms with balconies overlooking the beach and bay. Other, less-expensive rooms afford only a street view. A nice swimming pool is on the street level to the right of the lobby.

Hotel Delfín. Morelos 23, 48987 Barra de Navidad, Jal. ☎ **335/5-5068.** Fax 335/5-6020. 22 units, 2 apts. FAN. High season $29 double. Ask about low-season discounts. MC, V. Free parking in the front.

One of Barra's better-maintained hotels, the four-story (no elevator) Delfín is on the landward side of the lagoon. It offers pleasant, basic, well-maintained, and well-lit rooms. Each has red-tile floors and either one double, two double, or two single beds. The tiny courtyard, with a small pool and lounge chairs, is shaded by an enormous rubber tree. From the fourth floor there's a view of the lagoon. A breakfast buffet is served from 8:30 to 10:30am (see "Where to Dine," below).

Hotel Sands. Morelos 24, 48987 Barra de Navidad, Jal. ☎ and fax **335/5-5018,** or 36/16-2859. 42 units. FAN. High season $48 double. Low season $38 double. Rates include breakfast and parking. Discounts for stays of 1 week or more. MC, V.

The colonial-style Sands, across from the Hotel Delfín (see above) on the lagoon side at Jalisco, offers small but homey rooms with red-tile floors and windows with both screens and glass. Bathrooms have just been remodeled with new tiles and fixtures. Lower rooms look onto a public walkway and wide courtyard; upstairs rooms are brighter. Twelve rooms (suites or bungalows) have air-conditioning and kitchenette facilities. In back there is a pool with a Jacuzzi overlooking the lagoon beach. The hotel is known for its high-season happy hour from 2 to 6pm at the pool terrace bar beside the lagoon. On weekends from

9pm to 4am, an adjacent patio "disco" has recorded music for dancing. Breakfast is served from 7:30am to noon. Fishing trips can be arranged, and tours are available to nearby beaches.

WHERE TO DINE

✪ **El Manglito.** Veracruz, near the Fishing Cooperative. No phone. Main courses $4–$8. Daily 9am–11pm. SEAFOOD/INTERNATIONAL.

Located on the placid lagoon, with a view of the palatial Grand Bay Hotel, El Manglito serves home-style Mexican food to a growing number of repeat diners. The whole fried fish accompanied by drawn garlic butter, boiled vegetables, rice, and french fries is a crowd-pleaser. Other enticements include boiled shrimp, chicken in orange sauce, and shrimp salad.

Hotel Delfín. Morelos 23. ☎ **335/5-5068.** Breakfast buffet $2.50–$3. Daily 8:30am–10:30am. INTERNATIONAL.

The second-story terrace of this small hotel is a pleasant place to begin the day in Barra. The self-serve buffet offers an assortment of fresh fruit, juices, granola, yogurt, milk, pastries, and unlimited coffee. Eggs, and the delicious banana pancakes—for which the restaurant is known—are made to order and included in the buffet price.

Restaurant Bar Ambar. av. Veracruz 101-A. No phone. Crepes $4–$12, main courses $4–$12. Daily 12am–12pm (happy hour 1pm–midnight). Closed July through Oct. CREPES/SPANISH/FRENCH.

At the corner of Veracruz and Jalisco, you'll find this cozy thatched-roof, upstairs restaurant open to the breezes. The crepes are named after towns in France; the delicious crepe Paris, for example, is filled with chicken, potatoes, spinach, and green sauce; sweet desert crepes are their desert. International main dishes include imported rib-eye steak in a Dijon mustard sauce, mixed brochettes, quiche, and Caesar salad. Ambar serves Spanish-style Tapas from noon until 6pm, with French specialties added for dinner service.

✪ **Restaurant Bar Ramón.** Legazpi 260. ☎ **335/5-6435.** Main courses $4–$6.50. Daily 7am–11pm. SEAFOOD/MEXICAN.

Ramón ran the excellent restaurant in the Hotel Barra de Navidad until the rent went up. Then he staked out a new place under two giant, peaked, thatched-palapa roofs across the street from the hotel. Now it seems like everybody eats at Ramón's, where the chips and fresh salsa arrive unbidden, service is prompt and friendly, and the food is especially good. Try the fresh fish with french fries or any of the daily specials that might feature vegetable soup or chicken-fried steak.

Seamaster. Legazpi at Yucatán. No phone. Main courses $4–$12. Daily noon–11pm. SEAFOOD/INTERNATIONAL.

This cheery and colorful restaurant on the beach facing the ocean is a great place for sunsets and margaritas or a meal anytime. Specialties include steamed shrimp (peeled or unpeeled); fried calamari; barbecued chicken, ribs, and steak; plus chicken wings, hamburgers, and other sandwiches.

BARRA DE NAVIDAD AFTER DARK

When dusk arrives, visitors and locals alike find a cool spot to sit outside, sip cocktails, and chat. Many outdoor restaurants and stores in Barra fill the bill for this relaxing way to end the day, adding extra tables and chairs to accommodate drop-ins. It's very friendly.

During high season there is always happy hour from 2 to 6pm at the **Hotel Sands** poolside/lagoon-side bar. **Sunset Bar and Restaurant,** facing the bay, at the corner of Legazpi and Jalisco, is a favorite for sunset watching, and afterwards for dancing to live or taped music. In the same vein, **Chips Restaurant,** on the second floor facing the ocean at the corner of Yucatán and Legazpi near the southern end of the malecón, has an excellent sunset vista. Live music follows the last rays of light, and patrons stay for hours.

At the **Disco El Galleón,** in the Hotel Sands on calle Morelos, cushioned benches and cement tables encircle the round dance floor. It's all open-air, but garden walls restrict air flow and there are a few fans. It serves drinks only. Admission is $4, and it's open on Friday and Saturday from 9pm to 4am.

A VISIT TO MELAQUE (SAN PATRICIO)

For a change of scenery, you may want to wander over to Melaque (also known as San Patricio), 3 miles from Barra on the same bay. You can walk on the beach from Barra or take one of the frequent local buses from the bus station near the main square in Barra. The bus is marked MELAQUE. To return to Barra, take the bus marked CIHUATLÁN.

Melaque's pace is even more laid-back than Barra's, and though it's a larger village, it seems smaller. It has fewer restaurants and less to do. Although there are more hotels or "bungalows," as they are usually called here, few manage the charm of those in Barra. If Barra hotels are full on a holiday weekend, then Melaque would be a second choice for accommodations. The paved road ends where the town begins. A few yachts bob in the harbor, and the palm-lined beach is gorgeous.

If you come by bus from Barra, you can exit the bus anywhere in town or stay on until the last stop, which is the bus station in the middle of town, a block from the beach. Restaurants and hotels line the beach; it's impossible to get lost, but some orientation will help. Coming into town from the main road, you'll be on the town's main street, **avenida López Mateos.** You'll pass the main square on the way to the waterfront, where there's a trailer park. The street going left (southeast) along the bay is **avenida Gómez Farías;** the one going right (northwest) is **avenida Miguel Ochoa López.**

WHERE TO EAT   At the north end of Melaque beach is **Los Pelicanos,** serving the usual seafood specialties; the tender fried squid is delectable. In addition, you can find burritos, nachos, and hamburgers. Many Barra guests come here to stake a place on the beach and use the restaurant as headquarters for sipping and nipping. It's peaceful to watch the pelicans bobbing just in front. The restaurant is at the far end of the bay before the **Hotel Legazpi** (☎ **335/5-5397**), which, by the way, is a pleasant place to stay. The restaurant is open daily from 9am to 10pm.

In addition to the Los Pelicanos, there are many rustic **palapa restaurants** both in town on the beach and farther along the bay at the end of the beach. You can settle in on the beach and use one of the restaurants as your base for drinking and dining.

5

Manzanillo

*O*ne of Mexico's most active commercial ports has also developed, somewhat paradoxically, into a serene resort. Luxury properties, a diversity of sporting activities, and several interesting side trips within a few hours' drive have made Manzanillo an attractive spot for travelers looking for a mix of seclusion and exploration.

The geography surrounding Manzanillo is its principal attraction: emerald tropical mountains and the cobalt blue of the Pacific Ocean. The two most popular pastimes are golf, with courses that showcase the view, and sportfishing. Sailfish run almost year-round and are the featured catch in a pair of annual tournaments held each November.

Manzanillo is at the southern end of the unspoiled Costa Alegre, which begins in Puerto Vallarta to the north. This stretch of coast, with tropical-fruit plantations and jungle landscape bordering the coastal highway, is in the process of being discovered as one of Mexico's seaside treasures. Within an hour or two's drive north from Manzanillo, pristine beaches are tucked into isolated bays sprinkled with a handful of exclusive, secluded, and very unique resorts. (See chapter 4 for more information on Costa Alegre.) In addition to the Costa Alegre beaches, excellent, well-maintained roads connect Manzanillo to the colonial cities of Guadalajara and Colima.

Manzanillo itself is fairly neatly divided into two zones: the downtown commercial port and the luxury Santiago Peninsula resort zone to the north. The downtown zone is dominated by its busy harbor and rail connections to Mexico's interior. A visit to the town's waterfront zócalo provides a glimpse into local life. The Santiago Peninsula, home to the resorts and golf course, separates two golden-sand bays.

1 Manzanillo Essentials

160 miles (256km) SE of Puerto Vallarta; 167 miles (267km) SW of Guadalajara; 40 miles (64km) SE of Barra de Navidad

GETTING THERE & DEPARTING

BY PLANE **Aeromexico** and its sister airline **Aerolitoral** (☎ 800/237-6639 in the U.S., or 333/4-1990 at the airport), as well as

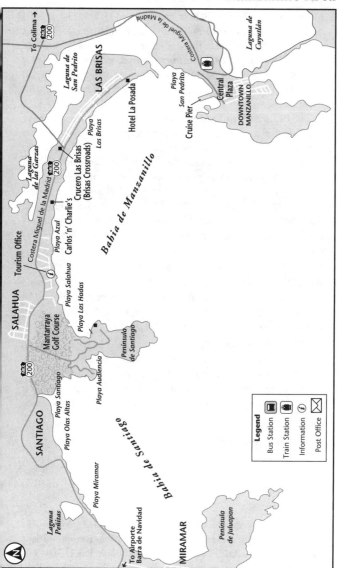

Legend

- Bus Station
- Train Station
- Information
- Post Office

Mexicana (☎ **800/531-7921** in the U.S., or 333/3-2323 at the airport) offer flights to and from Mexico City, Guadalajara, Monterrey, and to connecting cities in the United States and Canada. **America West** (☎ **800/235-9292**) flies from Phoenix, and **Aero California** (☎ **800/685-5500** or 333/4-1414) has flights from Los Angeles. Ask a travel agent about the numerous charters that operate in winter from the States.

The **Playa de Oro International Airport** is 25 miles (45 min.) northwest of town. The colectivo-van airport service is available from the airport, with returns arranged by your hotel. Reservations for return trips should be arranged 1 day in advance. The colectivo fare is based on zones and ranges from $6 to $8 to most hotels. Private taxi service between the airport and the downtown area is around $20. **Budget** (☎ **800/527-0700** or 333/3-1445) and **AutoRent** (☎ **333/3-2580**) have counters in the airport open during flight arrivals; they will also deliver a car to your hotel. Daily rates run $45 to $75, desirable only if you plan on exploring surrounding cities and the Costa Alegre beaches.

BY CAR   Coastal Highway 200 leads from Acapulco (south) and Puerto Vallarta (north). From Guadalajara, take Highway 54 through Colima (outside Colima you can switch to a toll road, which is faster but less scenic, into Manzanillo).

BY BUS   Buses run to Barra de Navidad (1¹/₂ hr. north), Puerto Vallarta (5 hr. north), Colima (1¹/₂ hr.), and Guadalajara (4¹/₂ hr.), with deluxe service and numerous daily departures. Manzanillo's Central Camionera (bus station) is about 12 long blocks east of town. If you follow Hidalgo east, the Camionera will be on your right.

ORIENTATION
VISITOR INFORMATION

The tourism office (☎ **333/3-2277** or 333/3-2264; fax 333/3-1426) in Manzanillo is on the costero Miguel de la Madrid 4960, km 8.5. It's open Monday through Friday from 9am to 3:30pm.

CITY LAYOUT

The town lies at one end of a 7-mile-long beach facing Manzanillo Bay and its commercial harbor. The beach has four sections—**Playa Las Brisas, Playa Azul, Playa Salahua,** and **Playa Las Hadas.** The northern terminus of the beaches is the high, rocky **Santiago Peninsula.** Santiago is 7 miles from downtown; it's the site of many beautiful homes and the best hotel in the area, Las Hadas, as well as the Mantarraya Golf Course owned by Las Hadas. The peninsula juts out into the bay, separating Manzanillo Bay from Santiago Bay. The beach, Playa Las Hadas, is on the south side of the peninsula facing Manzanillo Bay, and **Playa Audiencia** is on the north side facing Santiago Bay. There's also the inland town of **Santiago,** which is opposite the turnoff to Las Hadas.

Activity in downtown Manzanillo centers around the **central plaza,** officially known as the Jardín Álvaro Obregón, which is separated from the waterfront by a railroad and shipyards. The plaza has flowering trees, a fountain, a kiosk, and a view of the bay. Large ships dock at the pier nearby. **Avenida México,** the street leading out from the plaza's central gazebo, is the town's principal commercial thoroughfare. Walking along here you will find a few shops, small restaurants, and juice stands.

Once you leave downtown, the highway (the costero Miguel de la Madrid, or the costero Madrid, for short) runs through the neighborhoods of Las Brisas, Salahua, and Santiago to the **hotel zones** on the Santiago Peninsula and at Miramar. Shell shops, minimalls, and several restaurants are located along the way.

There are two main lagoons: One, **Laguna de Cuyutlán,** almost behind the city, stretches for miles south paralleling the coast. The other, **Laguna de San Pedrito,** north of the city, parallels the costero Miguel de la Madrid; it's behind Playa Las Brisas beach. Both are good sites for bird watching. There are also two bays: **Manzanillo Bay** encompasses the harbor, town, and beaches; the Santiago Peninsula separates it from the second bay—**Santiago.** Between downtown and the Santiago Peninsula is **Las Brisas,** a flat peninsula with a good beach, a lineup of inexpensive but run-down hotels, and a few very good restaurants.

GETTING AROUND

BY TAXI   Taxis in Manzanillo are plentiful. Fares are fixed by zones; rates for trips within town, as well as to more distant points, should be posted at your hotel. Daily rates can be negotiated for longer drives outside of the Manzanillo area.

Motorist Advisory: Car-jackings

Motorists planning to follow Highway 200 south from Manzanillo toward Lázaro Cárdenas and Ixtapa should be aware of reports of random bus and motorist hijackings on that route, especially around Playa Azul. Before heading in that direction, ask locals and the tourism office about the current state of affairs.

BY BUS The local buses (camionetas) make a circuit from downtown in front of the train station, along the Bay of Manzanillo, to the Santiago Peninsula and the Bay of Santiago to the north; the cost is 25¢. The ones marked LAS BRISAS go to the Las Brisas crossroads, then to the Las Brisas Peninsula, and back to town; "Miramar," "Santiago," and "Salahua" buses go to outlying settlements along the bays and to most restaurants mentioned below. Buses marked LAS HADAS go to Santiago Peninsula and make a circuit past the Las Hadas resort and the Sierra Manzanillo and Plaza Las Glorias hotels. This is an inexpensive way to see the coast as far as Santiago and to tour the Santiago Peninsula.

FAST FACTS: Manzanillo

American Express The local representative is **Bahías Gemelas Travel Agency,** Costero M. Madrid, km 10 (☎ **333/3-1000** or 333/3-1053; fax 333/3-0649).

Area Code The telephone area code is **333.**

Bank Banamex downtown is just off the plaza on avenida México; it's open Monday through Friday from 9:30am to 5pm, but changes foreign currency only until 12:30pm.

Internet Access The air-conditioned **Net Café** (☎ **333/2-2660;** e-mail: mayocomp@bay.net.mx) is located one-half block from the central plaza at calle Benito Juárez 115, Int. 7-B. They charge $2.50 per hour, and are open from 10am to 2pm, and from 4:30pm to 8:30pm, Monday through Friday. Saturdays, they're open 10am to 2pm, and they are closed Sundays.

2 Activities On & Off the Beach

Activities in Manzanillo revolve around its golden-sand beaches, which frequently have a film of black residue accumulate on them. Most of the resort hotels here are completely self-contained, with restaurants and sports on the premises. Manzanillo's public beaches provide an opportunity to see more local color and scenery, and are the daytime playground for those staying off the beach or without pools.

STAYING ACTIVE

BEACHES Playa Audiencia, on the Santiago Peninsula, offers the best swimming as well as snorkeling, but **Playa San Pedrito,** shallow for a long way out, is the most popular beach for its proximity to the downtown area. **Playa Las Brisas** is an optimal combination of location and good swimming. **Playa Miramar,** on the Bahía de Santiago past the Santiago Peninsula, is popular with bodysurfers, windsurfers, and boogie boarders, and is accessible by local bus from town. The major part of **Playa Azul** drops off sharply, but is noted for its wide stretch of golden sand.

BIRD WATCHING   There are several lagoons along the coast good for bird watching. As you go from Manzanillo up past Las Brisas to Santiago, you'll pass **Laguna de Las Garzas** (Lagoon of the Herons), also known as Laguna de San Pedrito, where you can see many white pelicans and huge herons fishing in the water. They nest here in December and January. Directly behind downtown is the **Laguna de Cuyutlán** (follow the signs to Cuyutlán), where birds can usually be found in abundance; species vary between summer and winter.

DIVING   Susan Dearing, who conducts diving expeditions and classes, pioneered diving in Manzanillo and has come up with some unusually intriguing underwater scenery. Many locations are so close to shore that there's no need for a boat. Close-in dives include the jetty with coral growing on the rocks at 45 feet, and a nearby sunken frigate downed in 1959 at 28 feet. Divers can see abundant sea life, including coral reefs, sea horses, giant puffer fish, and moray eels. A one-tank dive requiring a boat costs $50 per person with a three-person minimum, or two tanks for $80. Offshore dives cost $50 per person for one tank. Dearing is certified in scuba (YMCA and CMAS) and lifesaving and CPR by the Red Cross, and offers divers' certification (PADI, YMCA, NAUI, CMAS, and SSI) in very intensive courses of various durations. She offers a 10% discount on your certification when you mention you read about her in a Frommer's guide. Students who dive with her after her certification course are entitled to discounted dive prices. For reservations, contact her directly at ☎ and fax **333/3-0642** or cellular 335/8-0327; e-mail: scubamex@bay.net.mx. MasterCard and Visa are accepted.

ESCORTED TOURS   Because Manzanillo is so spread out, you might consider a city tour. Reputable local tour companies include **Hectours** (☎ **333/3-1707**) and **Bahías Gemelas Travel Agency,** an American Express representative (☎ **333/3-1000;** fax 333/3-0649). Tours can be scheduled at flexible times, with a half-day city tour costing around $15. Other tours include the daylong Colima Colonial Tour ($38), which includes a stop at a sugar-cane plantation, Colima's Archeological Museum, principal colonial buildings, and past the active volcano.

FISHING Manzanillo is famous for its fishing, particularly sailfish. Marlin and sailfish are abundant year-round. Winter is best for dolphin fish and dorado (mahimahi), and in summer wahoo and rooster fish are in greater supply. The international sailfish competition is held around the November-20 holiday and the national sailfish competition is in February. Fishing can be arranged through travel agencies or directly at the fishermen's cooperative (☎ **333/2-1031**), located downtown where the fishing boats are moored. You can call from 7am to 5pm. A fishing boat is approximately $240 for a 5-hour fishing trip.

GOLF The 18-hole **La Mantarraya Golf Course** is now also open to nonguests as well as guests of Las Hadas. Greens fees are $50 for 18 holes, cart and gear extra. Reserve in advance. In addition, the fabulous Von Hagge–designed, 27-hole golf course associated with the **Grand Bay Hotel** in Barra de Navidad is open to the public. The greens fees are $95/$115 for 18/27 holes for guests of Grand Bay, $140 for nonguests, including a motorized cart. Barra is about a 1- to 1$^{1}/_{2}$-hour drive north of Manzanillo on Highway 200. (See chapter 4.)

OTHER DIVERSIONS

SUNSET CRUISES For a sunset cruise, buy tickets from a travel agent or downtown at La Perlita Dock (across from the train station) fronting the harbor. Tickets are on sale at La Perlita daily from 8:30am to 2pm and cost around $19. The trips vary in their combinations of drinks, music, and entertainment and last 1$^{1}/_{2}$ to 2 hours.

A WORTHY MUSEUM In 1996, the **Museum of Archeology and History** opened, a small but impressive structure that houses exhibits depicting the region's history, plus rotating exhibitions of contemporary Mexican art. It's located on avenida Niños Heroes where it intersects with avenida Teniente Azueta, on the road leading between the downtown and Las Brisas areas.

SHOPPING

There is a selection of shops that carry Mexican crafts and clothing, mainly from nearby Guadalajara, one of Mexico's artisan centers. Almost all are downtown on the streets near the central plaza. Shopping in downtown Manzanillo is an experience—for example, you won't want to miss the shop bordering the plaza that sells a combination of shells, religious items (including shell-framed Virgin of Guadalupe nightlights), and orthopedic supplies. The Plaza Manzanillo is an American-style mall on the road to Santiago, and

Downtown Manzanillo

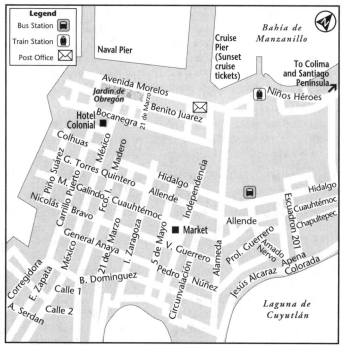

there's a traditional "tianguis" market in front of the entrance to Club Maeva with touristy items from around Mexico. Most resort hotels also have boutiques or shopping arcades.

3 Where to Stay

The strip of coastline on which Manzanillo is located can be divided into three areas: downtown, with its shops, markets, and commercial activity; Las Brisas, the hotel-lined beach area immediately to the north of the city; and Santiago, the town and peninsula, now virtually a suburb to the north at the end of Playa Azul. Transportation by either bus or taxi makes all three areas fairly convenient to each other. Reservations are recommended for hotels during the Easter, Christmas, and New Year's holidays.

DOWNTOWN

Hotel Colonial. av. México 100 and González Bocanegra, 28200 Manzanillo, Col. ☎ **333/2-1080** or 333/2-1134. 37 units. A/C TV TEL. $20–$25 double. MC, V.

An old favorite, this three-story colonial-style hotel is very consistent. It still offers the same beautiful blue-and-yellow tile, colonial-style carved doors, and windows in the lobby and restaurant. Rooms are decorated with minimal furniture, red-tile floors, and basic comforts. A restaurant/ bar is located in the central courtyard. The hotel is 1 block inland from the main plaza at the corner of Juárez and Galindo.

LAS BRISAS

The Las Brisas area has yet to be repaired from earthquake damage suffered in 1995, and is looking run-down, with numerous buildings in various states of disrepair.

Hotel La Posada. av. Lázaro Cárdenas 201, Las Brisas (Apdo. Postal 135), 28200 Manzanillo, Col. ☎ and fax **333/3-1899.** www.mexonline/ laposada.htm. E-mail: posada@bay.net.mx. 24 units. FAN. High season $72 double. Low season $48 double. Rates include breakfast. AE, MC, V.

This small inn has a shocking-pink stucco facade with a large arch that leads to a broad tiled patio right on the beach. The rooms have exposed-brick walls and simple furnishings with Mexican decorative accents. Mattresses are beginning to sag, and the place could use a general round of upkeep, but it still remains popular with longtime travelers to Manzanillo. The atmosphere here is casual and informal—you can help yourself to beer and soft drinks all day long, and at the end of your stay, owner Bart Varelmann (a native of Ohio) counts the bottle caps you deposited in a bowl labeled with your room number. All three meals are served in the dining room or out by the pool. If a nonguest wants to come for a meal, breakfast is served between 8 and 11am and costs around $7; lunch and dinner (sandwiches) are served between 1:30 and 8pm and cost about the same. During low season the restaurant is open only from 8am to 3pm. Stop by for a drink at sunset; the bar's open until 9pm all year. It's located at the end of Las Brisas Peninsula, closest to downtown; on the local "Las Brisas" bus route.

SANTIAGO

Three miles north of Las Brisas is the wide Santiago Peninsula. The settlement of Salahua is on the highway at one end, where you enter the peninsula to reach the hotels Las Hadas, Plaza Las Glorias, and Sierra Manzanillo, as well as the Mantarraya Golf Course. Buses from town marked LAS HADAS pass by these hotels every 20 minutes. Past the Salahua turnoff and at the end of the settlement of Santiago, an obscure road on the left is marked ZONA DE PLAYAS and leads to the hotels on the other side of the peninsula and Playa de Santiago.

✪ **Camino Real Las Hadas.** av. de los Riscos s/n, Santiago Peninsula, 28200 Manzanillo, Col. ☎ **800/722-6466** in the U.S. and Canada, or 333/4-0000. 233 units, including 30 Fantasy Suites, 5 Magic Suites, and 1 Presidential Suite. A/C MINIBAR TV TEL. High season $250–$300 double, $385–$440 Fantasy Suite, $350–$400 Camino Real Club. Low season $190–$232 double, $309–$400 Fantasy Suite, $278–$319 Camino Real Club. AE, DC, MC, V.

For me, Las Hadas is the most compelling reason to visit Manzanillo, and for many people the two are synonymous. The signature property of Manzanillo, Las Hadas was featured in the movie *10*—along with Bo Derek, of course. Featuring Moorish-style architecture, this elegant white resort is built on the beach and into the side of the rocky peninsula. A member of the exclusive "Leading Hotels of the World" group, it was the creation of the Bolivian millionaire Antenor Patino. The service at Las Hadas is on par with the finest resorts in the world—gracious, warm, and unobtrusive but always at hand. The rooms are built around the hillside overlooking the bay, and are connected by cobbled lanes lined with colorful flowers and palms. Covered, motorized carts are on call for transportation within the property. Though it's a large resort, it maintains an air of seclusion since rooms are spread out over the meticulously landscaped grounds. Views, room size, and extra amenities categorize the six types of accommodations. Understated, elegant, and spacious, the units have white-marble floors, sitting areas, and large, comfortably furnished balconies. Robes and in-room security boxes are standard. Camino Real Club rooms are on the upper tier and have great bay views; nine Club rooms have private pools. The exquisite lobby is a popular place for curling up for a good read in one of the numerous overstuffed seating areas or, at night, for enjoying a drink while live music entertains.

Dining/Diversions: Of this resort's four restaurants, the most famous is elegant Legazpi, open in high season from 4pm to midnight (see "Where to Dine," below). Arab, Mexican, and White Gala–themed nights, featuring patio dining, are available at a cost of $45 per person. There are four lounges and bars with live entertainment somewhere on the property almost every evening. Hours and restaurants may vary during low season.

Amenities: Club Las Hadas includes La Mantarraya, the hotel's 18-hole, par-71 golf course designed by Pete and Roy Dye; two pools; shade tents on the beach; 10 tennis courts (eight hard-surface, two clay); marina for 70 vessels; and water sports—scuba diving, snorkeling, sailing, and trimaran cruises. Camino Real Club guests have an exclusive pool and reserved lounge chairs at the pool and beach. Laundry, room service, shopping arcade, travel agency, safe-deposit box, workout room, beauty and barber shops. Camino Real Club guests have rapid check-in, continental breakfast, cocktails, concierge, preferred restaurant reservations, and late checkout.

Hotel Plaza Las Glorias. av. de Tesoro s/n, Santiago Peninsula, 28200 Manzanillo, Col. ☎ **333/4-1098.** Fax 333/3-1395. E-mail: lasglorias @delfincolimanet.com. 103 units. A/C TV TEL. $89 double. AE, MC, V.

The sunset-colored walls of this pueblolike hotel ramble over a hill-side on Santiago Peninsula. From the restaurant on top and from most rooms is a broad vista of other red-tiled rooftops and either the palm-filled golf course or the bay. It's one of Manzanillo's undiscovered resorts, known more to wealthy Mexicans than to Americans. Originally conceived as private condominiums, the quarters were designed for living; each accommodation is spacious, stylishly furnished, and very comfortable. Each unit has a huge living room; a small kitchen/bar; one, two, or three large bedrooms with tile or brick floors; large Mexican-tiled bathrooms; huge closets; and large, furnished private patios with views. Some units have en-suite Jacuzzis and a few rooms can be partitioned off and rented by the bedroom only. Water is purified in the tap and each room has a key-locked security box. Rooms can be a long walk from the main entrance, through a succession of stairways and paths. If stair climbing bothers you, try to get a room by the restaurant and pool—you'll have a great view, and a hillside rail elevator goes from top to bottom, but doesn't stop in between. Package rates are available.

Dining: La Plazuela, a casual and informal restaurant shaped like a half moon, adjoins the pool and fronts the bay, capturing both the views and breezes. It's open for all three meals. Live musicians often serenade diners.

Amenities: One pool on the restaurant level and game area; beach club on Las Brisas beach, where there's a pool and small restaurant; transportation to the beach club from the main hotel in the morning with return transportation in the afternoon. Laundry, room service, boutique, elevator from bottom of property to top; baby-sitters arranged with advance notice.

Hotel Sierra Manzanillo. av. La Audiencia 1, Los Riscos, 28200 Manzanillo, Col. ☎ **800/448-5028** in the U.S., or 333/3-2000. Fax 333/3-2611. 317 units. A/C MINIBAR TV TEL. High season $292 double, $342–$362 suite. Low season $128–$218 double, $218–$268 suite. AE, MC, V.

Opened in 1990, this all-inclusive hotel has 21 floors overlooking La Audiencia beach and a full program of activities, dining, and entertainment. Its excellent kids program makes it a top choice for families. Architecturally, it mimics the white Moorish style of Las Hadas that has become so popular in Manzanillo. Inside, it's palatial in scale and covered in a sea of pale-gray marble. Room decor picks up the pale-gray theme with washed gray armoires that conceal the TV and minibar. Most standard rooms have two double beds or a king-size bed, plus a small table, chairs, and desk. Several rooms at the end of most floors are small, with one double bed, small porthole-sized windows, no balcony, and no view. Most rooms, however, have balconies and either ocean or hillside views. The 10 honeymoon suites are carpeted and have sculpted shell-shaped headboards, king-size beds, and chaise lounges. Junior suites have a sitting area with couch, and large bathrooms.

Dining/Diversions: Three restaurants and four bar areas cover all meals and styles from casual to elegant, and take turns offering nightly music and entertainment.

Amenities: Grand pool on the beach plus children's pool; four lit tennis courts; health club with exercise equipment, scheduled aerobics, hot tub, and separate sauna and steam rooms for men and women. Scuba-diving lessons are given in the pool and excellent scuba-diving sites are within swimming distance of the shore. Laundry, room service, hair dryers, beauty salon with massage, travel agency, 24-hour currency exchange.

4 Where to Dine

DOWNTOWN

Roca del Mar. 21 de Marzo 204 (across from the plaza). ☎ **333/2-0302.** Main courses $2–$5. No credit cards. Daily 7am–10:30pm. MEXICAN/INTERNATIONAL.

Join locals at this informal cafe facing the plaza. The large menu includes club sandwiches, hamburgers, *carne asada a la tampiqueña* (thin grilled steak served with rice, poblano pepper, an enchilada, and refried beans), fajitas, fish, shrimp, and vegetable salads. A specialty is their paella, and the economical pibíl tacos are outstanding. This spot is very clean, with sidewalk dining available.

LAS BRISAS

In addition to Willy's, below, the Hotel La Posada (see "Where to Stay," above) offers breakfast to nonguests at its beachside restaurant; it's also a great place to mingle with other tourists and enjoy the sunset and cocktails.

✪ **Willy's.** Las Brisas crossroads. ☎ **333/3-1794.** Reservations required. Main courses $8–$15. MC, V. Daily 7pm–midnight. SEAFOOD/INTERNATIONAL.

You're in for a treat at Willy's, one of Manzanillo's most popular restaurants. It's homey, casual, and small, with perhaps 13 tables inside and 10 more on the narrow balcony over the bay. Among the grilled specialties are shrimp imperial wrapped in bacon, red-snapper tarragon, dorado basil, sea bass with mango and ginger, homemade pâté, and coconut flan. The food has flair and wins over locals and tourists alike.

If you double back left at the Las Brisas crossroads, you'll find Willy's on the right, down a short side street that leads to the ocean.

SANTIAGO ROAD

The restaurants below are on the costero Madrid between downtown and the Santiago Peninsula, and include the Salahua area.

Benedetti's Pizza. av. del Mar 1, Crucero Las Brisas. ☎ **333/4-0141.** Pizza $9–$12; main courses $2–$5.55. AE, MC, V. Daily 12am–11:30pm. PIZZA.

Since there are several branches in town, you'll probably find a Benedetti's not far from where you are staying. The variety isn't extensive, but the pies are quite good; add some chimichurri sauce to enhance the flavor. They specialize in seafood pizzas such as smoked oyster and anchovy pizza. In addition to pizza, you can select from pastas, sandwiches, burgers, fajitas, salads, Mexican soups, cheesecake, and apple pie. This branch is on the costero Madrid, on the left, just after the Las Brisas turnoff; across from the Coca-Cola plant.

Bigotes III. Puesta del Sol 3. ☎ **333/3-1236.** Main courses $6–$16. MC, V. Daily noon–10pm. SEAFOOD.

Locals flock to this large, breezy restaurant (named "Mustache") by the water for the good food and festive atmosphere. Strolling singers serenade diners, who are rewarded with large portions of grilled seafood. To find Bigotes, follow the costero de la Madrid from downtown past the Las Brisas turnoff. It's behind the Penas Coloradas Social Club across from the beach.

Manolo's Norteño Campestre. Costero Miguel de la Madrid, km 11.5. ☎ **333/3-0475.** Main courses $5–$20. AE, MC, V. Mon–Sat 5pm–11pm. INTERNATIONAL/STEAK/SEAFOOD.

Owners Manuel and Juanita López and family offer excellent dining in a tropical garden setting. They cater to American tastes with a "safe" salad that is included with dinner. Among the popular entrees are Fillet of Fish Manolo on a bed of spinach with melted cheese Florentine-style and frogs' legs in brandy batter. Most people can't leave without first being tempted by the fresh coconut or homemade pecan pie. Coming from downtown, Manolo's is on the right, about 3 blocks before the turn to Las Hadas.

SANTIAGO PENINSULA

✪ **Legazpi.** Camino Real Las Hadas hotel, Santiago Peninsula. ☎ **333/ 4-0000.** Main courses $8–$12. AE, MC, V. High season daily 7pm–11:30pm. Low season open only Tues, Thurs, and Sat. INTERNATIONAL.

This is a top choice in Manzanillo for sheer elegance, gracious service, and outstanding food. The candlelit tables, covered in pale-pink and white, are set with silver and flowers. Enormous bell-shaped windows on two sides show off the sparkling bay below. The sophisticated menu includes prosciutto with melon marinated in port wine, crayfish bisque, broiled salmon, roast duck, lobster, or veal, and flaming desserts from crepes to Irish coffee.

5 Manzanillo After Dark

Nightlife in Manzanillo is much more exuberant than you might expect, but then Manzanillo is not only a resort town—it's a thriving commercial center. Clubs and bars tend to change from year to year, so check with your concierge for current hot spots. Perennial favorites include **Carlos 'n Charlie's,** avenida Audiencia Cocoteros s/n (☎ **333/4-1272**), always a good choice for both food and fun. In the evening during high season, there may be a required minimum order/cover if you come just to drink and dance, but the "cover" includes three drinks. **El Bar de Felix** (☎ **333/4-1444**), between Salahua and Las Brisas by the Avis rental-car office, is open Tuesday through Sunday from 9pm to 2am and doesn't charge a cover. The new **Vog Disco** (☎ **333/3-1875;** km. 9.2, blvd. Costero Miguel de la Madrid) features alternative music in a cavernous setting; it's Manzanillo's current late-night hot spot, open until 5am. They feature an early happy hour, from 9pm to 11pm, and waive the $4 cover for ladies on Friday nights. Also very popular—with a built-in crowd—is the nightclub at the **Club Maeva Hotel & Resort,** located on the inland side of the main highway, north of the Santiago Peninsula. Nonguests are welcome, but must pay a $10 to $15 entrance fee, after which all drinks are included. The fee varies depending on the night of the week and the time of year. Some area clubs have a dress code prohibiting shorts or sandals, principally applying to men.

6 A Side Trip to Colima & Its Volcano

The city of Colima makes for an interesting and accessible day-trip from Manzanillo. It's just about an hour's drive along a well-maintained, four-lane highway to this charming, colonial city and the capital of Colima State. Well-preserved colonial buildings, such as the city's **cathedral,** originally built in 1527, and the **Palacio de Gobierno,** with its murals depicting Mexican history, are key attractions in the city's center.

Colima has several interesting museums, including the **Museo de las Culturas del Occidente,** which displays an impressive permanent collection of pre-Columbian pottery and artifacts. The **Casa de la Cultura** hosts changing exhibitions of contemporary art and offers free art, music, and dance classes.

Two imposing volcanoes (one still active) border the town. The Volcán de Fuego is located 15 miles to the north, next to the taller, extinct Nevado de Colima. Through early 1999, the Volcán de Fuego has been more active than ever, sometimes blowing smoke and ash up to 3 miles high. Popular day-tours to Colima will often include a visit to two newly opened archaeological sites, El Chanal and La Campana.

6

Settling into Guadalajara

*G*uadalajara is the second-largest city in Mexico (with five million people, it's a very distant second to Mexico City), but as the homeland of mariachi music, the *jarabe tapatío* (the Mexican hat dance), and tequila, it is considered by many to be the most Mexican of cities. Despite its size, Guadalajara is easy to navigate, and the people are friendly and helpful. And unlike in Mexico City, visitors here can enjoy big-city pleasures without the metropolis-size hassles.

The handcrafts and decorative arts here are perhaps the best in Mexico. Shoppers can browse through the very sophisticated shops of Tlaquepaque, which offer an immense variety of merchandise. Or they can pay a visit to Tonalá, which has hundreds of workshops and is a bargain-hunter's paradise.

Guadalajara is the capital of the state of Jalisco and, in Mexico's stormy history, has functioned on occasion as the nation's capital. The historic center of Guadalajara is a wonderful place to wander among plazas, fountains, churches, and old convents. The relatively new Plaza Tapatía, which doubled the amount of public space in the downtown area, has helped enliven this part of town. With its history and architecture, its shopping, its restaurants and cultural life, and its mild climate, Guadalajara is a great side trip into the interior from Puerto Vallarta or Manzanillo.

While in Guadalajara, you will undoubtedly come across the word *tapatío* (or *tapatía*). In the early days, people from the area were known to trade in threes, called tapatíos. Gradually the locals came to be called tapatíos too, and the word now signifies "Guadalajaran" when referring to a thing, a person, or a manner of doing something.

1 Guadalajara Essentials

GETTING THERE

BY PLANE   Guadalajara's international airport is a 25- to 45-minute ride from the city. Taxi and colectivo (shared ride) tickets to Guadalajara or Chapala are sold in front of the airport and are priced by zone. Local taxis are the only transport from town to the airport (around $10 to the center of town; $8 going the other way).

If you're flying out of Guadalajara, you'll be required to check in at least 1¹/₂ hours before takeoff for international flights, and at least 1 hour before takeoff for domestic flights.

The Major Airlines   See chapter 1, "Planning a Trip to Mid-Pacific Mexico," for a list of toll-free numbers of international airlines serving Mexico. Numbers to call in Guadalajara for international airlines are: **Aeromar** (☎ 3/615-8509), **Aeromexico** (☎ 3/669-0202), **American Airlines** (☎ 3/616-4090), **Continental Airlines** (☎ 01-800/900-5000), **Delta Air Lines** (☎ 3/630-3530), **Mexicana** (☎ 01-800/366-5400), **Taesa** (☎ 3/615-9761), and **United** (☎ 3/616-9489).

Aero California (☎ 3/616-2525) serves Guadalajara from Tijuana, Mexico City, Los Mochis, La Paz, and Puebla; **Aeromexico** (☎ 3/669-0202) and **Mexicana** (☎ 01-800/366-5400) have flights and connections to all points in Mexico; **Taesa** (☎ 3/615-9761) has nonstop flights to and from Mexico City, Chicago, and Oakland.

BY CAR   Guadalajara is at the hub of several four-lane toll roads (called *cuotas* or *autopistas*) that can cut travel time considerably, but are expensive. From Nogales on the **U.S. border,** follow Highway 15 south (21 hr.). From **Tepic,** you can decrease this time by taking toll road 15D to Guadalajara (5 hr, $18). From **Puerto Vallarta,** go north on Highway 200 to Compostela and the toll road 68D that heads east to join the Tepic toll road. Total time is 5¹/₂ hours and the tolls add up to $17. From **Barra de Navidad,** on the coast southeast of Puerto Vallarta, take Highway 80 northeast (4¹/₂ hr.). From **Manzanillo,** you might also take this road, but it would be faster to take the toll road 54D through Colima to Guadalajara (3¹/₂ hr., $11). From **Mexico City,** take toll road 15D (7 hr., $30).

BY BUS   Two bus stations serve Guadalajara: the old one near downtown has buses to Lake Chapala and other nearby areas; and the new one 6 miles southeast of the city's center has buses to more distant destinations.

The Old Bus Station   For bus trips within a 60-mile radius of Guadalajara, including to Lake Chapala, Ajijic, Jocotepec, Mazamitla, and San Juan Cosalá, go to the old bus terminal on Niños Héroes off calzada Independencia Sur. To go to any towns in the Lake Chapala region, try **Transportes Guadalajara-Chapala,**

Greater Guadalajara

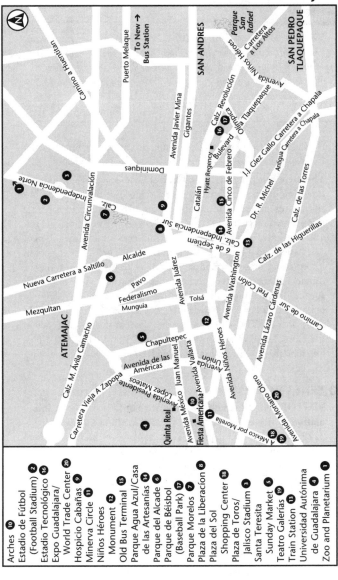

Arches **10**
Estadio de Fútbol
(Football Stadium) **2**
Estadio Tecnológico **16**
Expo Guadalajara/
World Trade Center **20**
Hospicio Cabañas **9**
Minerva Circle **11**
Niños Héroes
Monument **12**
Old Bus Terminal **15**
Parque Agua Azul/Casa
de las Artesanías **14**
Parque del Alcade **6**
Parque de Béisbol
(Baseball Park) **17**
Parque Morelos **7**
Plaza de la Liberación **8**
Plaza del Sol
Shopping Center **18**
Plaza de Toros/
Jalisco Stadium **3**
Santa Teresita
Sunday Market **5**
Teatro Galerías **19**
Train Station **13**
Universidad Autónima
de Guadalajara **4**
Zoo and Planetarium **1**

137

The men [of Guadalajara] are handsome and cling to their attractive charro outfits and extremely large sombreros. At one time the brims of their hats were so wide that they were declared a public nuisance. Any man caught wearing a sombrero with a brim that extended much beyond his shoulders was arrested and fined.
——Burton Holmes, *Mexico,* 1939

which has frequent bus and *combi* (minivan) service beginning at 6am to Chapala (see also "Side Trips from Guadalajara," in chapter 7).

The New Bus Station   The **Central Camionera** is a 35-minute ride from downtown. Taxis charge about $4 for the trip. This bus station resembles an international airport, with seven separate terminals connected by a covered walkway. Each building contains different lines, offering first- and second-class service, for different destinations, so it can be a little confusing. The best place to get bus information, make reservations, or buy tickets is downtown at the **Agencia Plaza Tapatía,** calzada Independencia 254, a "bus-ticket agency" located under Plaza Tapatía. They work with all six main bus lines that connect Guadalajara to the rest of Mexico. One of those lines is **ETN,** which has a ticket agent at the travel agency in the Hotel Misión Carlton (☎ **3/614-8875** or 3/614-2479). This line specializes in deluxe bus travel with large seats and plenty of leg and elbow room.

ORIENTATION

VISITOR INFORMATION   The **State of Jalisco Tourist Information Office** is at calle Morelos 102 (☎ **3/658-0049** or 3/658-2222; fax 3/613-0335) in the Plaza Tapatía, at the crossroads of paseo Degollado and Paraje del Rincón del Diablo. It's open Monday through Friday from 9am to 8pm; and Saturday, Sunday, and festival days from 9am to 1pm. They have a supply of maps as well as a monthly calendar of cultural events in the city.

GETTING AROUND   By Taxi   Taxis are the best and easiest way to get around town. Though the price of gas in Mexico is at press time twice that of the United States, taxis still remain incredibly cheap. I don't know how they do it. Cab fares for most of town run between $3 and $5. A lot of hotels post cab prices for specific locations. Or you can simply ask at the desk before you take a cab ride. Of course, you still need to agree on a price with the driver before setting out.

By Car Keep in mind several main arteries. The **Periférico** is a loop around the city that connects with most other highways entering the city. Traffic on the Periférico is slow, filled with trucks, and has only two lanes. Several important freeway-style thoroughfares crisscross the city. **González Gallo** leads south from the town center and connects with the road to Tonalá and Tlaquepaque; it also leads straight to Lake Chapala. **Highway 15** to Tepic is a continuation of **avenida Vallarta** and **calzada Lázaro Cárdenas.** Traffic on Vallarta heads west from downtown. The eastbound avenues are **Mexico** and **Hidalgo** (both of which are north of Vallarta). **Cárdenas** is the best way to get from the west side of town to Tlaquepaque and Tonalá or to the highway to Chapala.

By Bus & Colectivo There is an electric bus known as the *Par Vial* that is quite handy for going from downtown to the west side and back again. It bears the sign "PAR VIAL" and runs east-west along Hidalgo and Independencia streets (on the north side of the cathedral). It goes as far east as Mercado Libertad, and as far west as Minerva Circle.

There are six varieties of city buses that run along many of the same routes but offer different grades of service. The best are **Línea Turquesa buses,** which are colored pale turquoise and have the distinguishing letters "TUR" on the side. These are air-conditioned, have padded seats, and best of all, carry only as many passengers as there are seats; they are worth the additional price (about 50¢ for most destinations). Once they've picked up passengers in the Centro Histórico, only a few stops remain until they reach their final destination, making them a relatively fast mode of public transportation. Frequent **TUR** buses run between the Centro Histórico, Tlaquepaque, Central Camionera (new bus station), and Tonalá. Some of these go to Tonalá and not Tlaquepaque, or Tlaquepaque but not Tonalá. For more information on Tlaquepaque and Tonalá, see "Shopping," in chapter 7.

Many buses run north-south along the calzada Independencia (not to be confused with calle Independencia), but the **"San Juan de Dios–Estación"** bus goes between the points you are likely to want—San Juan de Dios church, next to the Mercado Libertad, and the railroad station (*estación*) past Parque Agua Azul. Other buses on calzada Independencia have longer routes (out to the suburbs, for instance), and thus tend to be heavily crowded at all times. Fares are generally 40¢; exact change is not necessary. The city also has a rapid-transit system called *Tren Ligero,* but it doesn't serve areas that are of interest to visitors.

Colectivos are minivans that run throughout the city day and night, picking up and dropping off passengers at fixed and unfixed points. There are no printed schedules, and routes and fixed pickup points change frequently. However, locals know the routes by heart and can tell you where and how to use these minivans if you tell them where you want to go. Fares are generally 40¢.

CITY LAYOUT

Obviously, the **downtown area (centro histórico),** with all its attractions, will be of great interest to the visitor. Due west of downtown is the fashionable part of Guadalajara, where many of the top hotels and restaurants are located. The main artery connecting this area with downtown is **avenida Vallarta,** which intersects another major artery, **avenida Adolfo López Mateos** at Minerva Circle (*Fuente Minerva* or simply *La Minerva*). Minerva Circle, only a 15-minute drive from downtown, is the hub and central point of reference for this part of town. North of Minerva and northwest of downtown lies Zapopan, the home of the Virgin of Zapopan, the patron saint of Guadalajara. The main artery to Zapopan from the center of town is avenida Ávila Camacho; it takes about 20 minutes by car. Completely across town from Zapopan, on the southeast side, are Tlaquepaque and Tonalá, which offer the best shopping in Mexico. The main artery to the southeast is calzada Revolución. Tlaquepaque is 5 miles from downtown and takes 15 to 20 minutes by car; Tonalá is 10 minutes farther.

GUADALAJARA'S NEIGHBORHOODS IN BRIEF

Centro Histórico   The heart of the city contains the five main plazas, the cathedral, and several museums and public buildings. Two of those buildings hold several spectacular murals by Orozco, who, in my opinion, was the best of the Mexican muralists. Theaters, restaurants, shops, and clubs dot the area around the largest covered market in Latin America. All of this is located in a space that is roughly 12 blocks by 12 blocks, an easy area for a good walker to explore on foot. Amid the plazas and pedestrian-only streets, walking can be quite pleasant.

Parque Agua Azul   This is a large inner-city green space 20 blocks south of the Centro Histórico. It has a children's area and miniature train. Nearby are the state-run craft shops (worth the short trip), performing-arts theaters, and the anthropology museum.

Chapultepec/Minerva Circle/Plaza del Sol   These areas constitute the fashionable west side of the city. Avenida Chapultepec runs north-south and intersects avenida Vallarta between downtown and Minerva. Southwest of Minerva along avenida López Mateos is the Plaza del Sol area. The west side holds most of the fine dining spots, luxury hotels, boutiques, galleries, etc., as well as the American, British, and Canadian consulates.

Zapopan   Founded in 1542 as a separate village, Zapopan is now a de facto suburb of Guadalajara. It's noted for its 18th-century basilica, the home of Guadalajara's patron saint, the revered 16th-century image of the Virgin of Zapopan. Made of corn paste, the image is honored by enormous throngs of people every October 12. Zapopan's main square and basilica are quite lovely, and next to the basilica is a small museum about the life and customs of the Huichol Indians, who live in a remote region of the state. It has a museum shop whose proceeds go to aid these Indians.

Tlaquepaque   This was a village of artisans (especially potters) that grew into a market center which, in the last 30 years, has attracted designers from all over Mexico. Almost every form of art and craft is for sale here: furniture, pottery, glass, jewelry, wood carvings, leather goods, sculpture, and painting. And these shops are quite sophisticated; in contrast, the town's center has retained a certain small-town feel, making door-to-door browsing most enjoyable.

Tonalá   This has remained a town of artisans. There are plenty of stores selling mostly local products from the town's more than 400 workshops. The materials worked in this town are metal, clay, glass, and paper. A huge street market is held each Thursday and Sunday.

FAST FACTS: Guadalajara

American Express   The local office is at avenida Vallarta 2440, Plaza los Arcos (☎ **3/615-8910**); it's open Monday through Friday from 9am to 6pm and Saturday from 9am to noon.

Area Code   The telephone area code is **3.**

Books/Newspapers/Magazines   **Gonvil,** a popular chain of bookstores, but with few English selections, has a branch across from Plaza de los Hombres Ilustres on avenida Hidalgo, and another a few blocks south at av. 16 de Septiembre 118 (Alcalde becomes 16 de Septiembre south of the cathedral). **Sanborn's,** at the corner of Juárez and 16 de Septiembre, does a good job of keeping

English-language periodicals in stock, but most of these are specialty magazines. Also many newsstands sell the two English local papers: the *Guadalajara Reporter* and the *Guadalajara Weekly*.

Business Hours   Store hours are generally 10am to 2pm and 4 to 8pm Monday through Saturday.

Climate & Dress   Guadalajara is mild, pleasant, and dry year-round. From November through March you'll need a sweater in the evening. The warmest months, April and May, are hot and dry. From June through September, the city gets afternoon and evening showers that keep the temperature a bit cooler. Dress in Guadalajara is conservative; attention-getting sportswear (short shorts, halters, and the like) is out of place here.

Consulates   The largest **American consular offices** in the world are here, at Progreso 175 (☎ **3/825-2998** or 3/825-2700). The offices are open Monday through Friday from 8am to 4:30pm. Other consulates include the **Canadian consulate,** Hotel Fiesta Americana, Local 31 (☎ **3/615-6215**); the **British consulate,** Eulogio Parra 2539, Oficina 12 (☎ **3/616-0629**); and the **Australian consulate,** López Cotilla 2030 (☎ **3/615-7418**).

Currency Exchange   The best rates are found 3 blocks south of the cathedral on López Cotilla street, between the streets Corona and Degollado. There are more than 20 casas de cambio on these 2 blocks. Almost all have their rates posted, which are better than what the banks offer and without the long lines.

Hospitals   For medical emergencies, there's the **Hospital México-Americano,** Cólomos 2110 (☎ **3/642-7152**).

Luggage Storage/Lockers   You can store luggage in the main bus station, the Central Camionera, and at the Guadalajara airport.

Police   Tourists should first try to contact the Jalisco tourist information office in Plaza Tapatía, listed under "Visitor Information," above (☎ **3/658-0049**). If you can't reach this office, call the municipal police at ☎ 3/617-6060.

Post Office   The main post office (correo) is at the corner of Carranza and calle Independencia, about 4 blocks northeast of the cathedral. Standing in the plaza behind the cathedral and facing the Degollado Theater, walk to the left and turn left on Carranza; walk past the Hotel Mendoza, cross calle Independencia, and look for the post office on the left side.

Safety   Guadalajara doesn't have the violent crime that exists in Mexico City. Crimes against tourists and foreign students are infrequent and most often take the form of pick-pocketing and purse-snatching. Criminals usually work in teams and target travelers in busy places, such as outdoor restaurants: one will create a distraction while the other slips off with whatever the tourist may have set down. There have been reports of purse-snatching, usually against unaccompanied women at night, and rarely in places with crowds. The same can be said of necklace-snatching, where the assailant will grab hold of a necklace, especially if it has a gold chain, and pull hard, hoping it will break.

Spanish Classes   Foreigners can study Spanish at the **Foreign Student Study Center,** University of Guadalajara, calle Guanajuato 1047 (Apdo. Postal 12130), 44100 Guadalajara, Jalisco (☎ **3/853-2150;** fax 3/653-0040).

2 Where to Stay

All of the luxury hotels in Guadalajara are in the modern west side. Listed here are the Presidente Inter-Continental, the Quinta Real, and the Fiesta Americana. Other chain hotels include a Hilton, a Camino Real, and a Holiday Inn Crowne Plaza. There are no luxury hotels in the centro histórico, but there are several moderate-to-inexpensive hotels that are quite comfortable. These include the Calinda Roma, the Cervantes, the Mendoza, and the San Francisco Plaza. I have also included one moderate hotel in the Parque Agua Azul area close to downtown, and a bed-and-breakfast in Tlaquepaque.

VERY EXPENSIVE

✪ **Hotel Presidente Inter-Continental.** av. López Mateos Sur y Moctezuma, 45050 Guadalajara, Jal. ☎ **800/327-0200** in the U.S. and Canada, or 3/678-1234. Fax 3/678-1222. www.interconti.com. 411 units. A/C MINIBAR TV TEL. $224 double, $368 suite, $299 Club floors. AE, DC, MC, V. Free guarded parking.

Housed in a 14-story glass building that suggests a pyramid, this smart-looking hotel has a cavernous atrium-lobby with glass elevators. What separates it from the rest of the hotels in this genre is the quality of its services and amenities. The well-managed hotel has little turnover in staff, and the concierge proved more capable and knowledgeable than any other in the city. Rooms are comfortable and quiet. The furnishings are modern, and all rooms have a small desk with a modem/phone outlet, a small table, and two chairs. To the side of the main lobby entrance is a separate, discreet check-in area and elevator entrance for those staying in club rooms. The club rooms are like the regular rooms, but they are on limited-access hallways, and include a free continental breakfast and newspaper, and evening cocktails. The extra privacy is perfect for Mexican soap opera stars and for regular business travelers who want the concierge to be familiar with their preferences. If you're neither of those, opt for a regular room. Nonsmoking rooms are on the 11th floor. The hotel is across the street from the Plaza del Sol shopping center.

Dining/Diversions: There are three restaurants that offer international, Mexican, and cafe food. The breakfast buffet is large and very good. The lobby bar is a popular night spot.

Amenities: Laundry; dry cleaning; room service; beauty shop; travel agency; car rental; business center with bilingual secretarial services; 24-hour doctor; safe; Tane jewelry store; extremely good fitness center that offers massages and has separate saunas, steam rooms, and whirlpools for men and women, as well as an outdoor heated swimming pool.

✪ **Quinta Real.** av. Mexico 2727, 44680 Guadalajara, Jal. ☎ **800/445-4565** in the U.S. and Canada, or 3/615-0000. Fax 3/630-1797. www.quinta-real.com. 78 suites. A/C MINIBAR TV TEL. $236 master suite, $259 grand-class suite. AE, DC, MC, V. Free secured parking.

This chain hotel specializes in creating extremely elegant settings that are suggestive of Mexico's past. You won't find a glass skyscraper here—the hotel occupies two four-story buildings made of stone, plaster, wood beam, and tile, situated amidst the hotel's lush grounds. Rooms vary quite a bit: Eight have brick cupolas, most are split-level, some have balconies, several have scallop-shaped headboards, and four are equipped with a whirlpool bathtub in the bathroom. All the rooms are large, have antique decorative touches, and come with large, fully equipped bathrooms with tub/shower combinations and excellent water pressure. The hotel is 2 blocks from the Minerva Circle on avenida Mexico at López Mateos. Ask for a room that doesn't face López Mateos.

Dining/Diversions: The casual but sophisticated restaurant, just off the lobby, has indoor and outdoor dining. The adjacent bar is open until 2am.

Amenities: Concierge, laundry and dry cleaning, massage by reservation, rental video players, travel agency. There's also a small heated pool.

EXPENSIVE

✪ **Fiesta Americana.** Aurelio Aceves 225, Glorieta Minerva, 44100 Guadalajara, Jal. ☎ **800/343-7821** in the U.S., or 3/825-3434. Fax

3/630-3671. www.fiestamexico.com. 399 units. A/C MINIBAR TV TEL. $144 double, $170 Fiesta Club. AE, DC, MC, V. Free secured parking.

A 22-story luxury hotel on a grand scale, the Fiesta Americana caters to the exacting demands of business and holiday travelers. Located 40 blocks from the Centro Histórico, it's a bustling hotel with a 14-story lobby and spacious rooms. All have TVs with U.S. channels. The 27 exclusive Fiesta Club rooms and three suites on the 12th and 14th floors come with special amenities (see below). One room is equipped for guests with disabilities.

Dining/Diversions: There are two restaurants and a popular lobby bar that features occasional live entertainment.

Amenities: Laundry, dry cleaning, room service, travel agency, heated rooftop swimming pool, two lighted tennis courts, fitness room, business center, purified tap water. Fiesta Club guests have access to club floors, separate check-in and checkout, concierge, remote-control TV, continental breakfast and afternoon wine and hors d'oeuvres daily, as well as business services such as secretaries, fax, copy machine, and conference room.

Hotel Misión Carlton. av. Niños Héroes 125 and 16 de Septiembre, 44190 Guadalajara, Jal. ☎ **800/448-8355** in the U.S. and Canada, or 3/614-7272. Fax 3/613-5539. www.misionpark.com.mx. 215 units. A/C MINIBAR TV TEL. $121 double. Weekend discounts. AE, DC, MC, V. Parking $1 daily.

The Misión Carlton is a 20-story hotel near Agua Azul Park, a short cab or bus ride from the historic center. Remodeled this year, it offers well-furnished rooms that are spacious and have large bathrooms with hair dryers and make-up mirrors. The 10th floor is reserved for nonsmokers. Ask for a room with a view well away from the club and the ballrooms.

Dining/Diversions: There is a lovely indoor/outdoor restaurant facing beautifully groomed grounds, and a cafe by the pool. There are also two bars and a disco.

Amenities: A small fitness center with whirlpool, a large swimming pool, and a business center.

MODERATE

Calinda Roma. Juárez 170, 44100 Guadalajara, Jal. ☎ **800/228-5151** in the U.S., 01-800/900-0000 in Mexico, or 3/614-8650. Fax 3/614-2629. 174 units. A/C MINIBAR TV TEL. $74–$84 double. AE, DC, MC, V. Free secured parking.

This is a comfortable, modern hotel in the Centro Histórico. Although there are a number of hotels on avenida Juárez, this one has plenty of rooms that don't face the very noisy street. The only rooms you should ask for are the remodeled ones that don't face

Juárez. These well-lit units have carpeting, modern furniture, and good mattresses. Bathrooms come with hair dryers and make-up mirrors. Unremodeled rooms are dismal. The hotel offers a small section of remodeled rooms for women travelers only. There's a small pool and sunning area on the roof. The hotel is at the corner of Juárez and Degollado.

Hotel de Mendoza. Carranza 16, 44100 Guadalajara, Jal. ☎ **800/221-6509** in the U.S., or 3/613-4646. Fax 3/613-7310. mexplaza.com.mx/dmendoza. 110 units. A/C TV TEL. $82 double. AE, DC, MC, V. Secured parking $1.25 daily.

On a quiet street next to the Degollado Theater and Plaza Tapatía, and only 2 blocks from the cathedral, the Mendoza has the best location by far of any downtown hotel. The decor would best be described as old Spanish with wood paneling and exposed ceiling beams. Rooms are slightly smaller than the other hotels in this price range, but are comfortable, although the TV has less English-language programming. The big decision here is deciding between a room facing the street or one facing an interior courtyard with a swimming pool. One note: the bath towels are the narrowest I've ever seen—obviously the brainchild of a demented cost-cutting expert. If the hotel hasn't changed these, you might as well ask for a couple extra when you get your room.

✪ **La Villa del Ensueño.** Florida 305, 45500 Tlaquepaque, Jal. ☎ **800/ 220-8689** in the U.S., or 3/635-8792. Fax 3/659-6152. 12 units. TEL. $76 double, $87 deluxe double. Rates include continental breakfast. DISC, MC, V. Free parking for 2 cars at hotel; more free parking 5 min. away.

This B&B in central Tlaquepaque is a lovely alternative to big-city hotels. Built in the traditional style of Mexican architecture, it is a delight to the eye—small courtyards and beautiful gardens bordered by old stucco walls, which have been painted in muted shades of orange oxide or covered in carefully trimmed ivy, with an occasional wrought iron balcony or stone staircase. The rooms are individually decorated and have much more character than any hotel room. All come with ceiling fans. Doubles have either twin or double beds. There is a small pool.

INEXPENSIVE

Hotel Cervantes. Prisciliano Sánchez 442. Col. Centro Histórico, 44100 Guadalajara, Jal. ☎ and fax **3/613-6686.** 100 units. A/C TV TEL. $42–$47 double. AE, MC, V. Free secured parking.

This six-story, modern downtown hotel, brought to you by the same people who brought you the San Francisco Plaza (see below), is slightly more upscale, but still a bargain. The rooms have wall-to-wall carpeting, tile bathrooms with ample sink areas and shower/tub combinations, and TVs with English-language channels. There is a large, heated, outdoor pool, a rooftop sunning area, a small fitness room, and a lobby bar and restaurant. The best rooms are on the upper floors and face towards the back. It's 6 blocks south and 3 blocks west of the cathedral.

✪ **Hotel San Francisco Plaza.** Degollado 267, 44100 Guadalajara, Jal. ☎ **3/613-8954** or 3/613-8971. Fax 3/613-3257. 76 units. A/C TV TEL. $26–$32 double. AE, CB, MC, V. Free parking.

This downtown hotel is the best bargain in Guadalajara. What you get is a big, clean, comfortably furnished room with good beds that cost two to three times as much at most hotels. All rooms have rugs or carpeting, and most have tall ceilings except for the remodeled area behind the reception desk. Rooms along Sánchez street can be noisy and have small bathrooms. The hotel is built in colonial style around four courtyards, which are decorated with fountains and potted plants. A small plaza out front gives the hotel its name. It is 6 blocks south of the cathedral and 2 blocks east.

3 Where to Dine

Guadalajara has many excellent restaurants for either fine dining or taking in some of the local fare. Most of the great restaurants are on the west side. Those in the centro histórico are uniformly bad, with two exceptions: La Fonda de San Miguel, and Siglo XV. Tlaquepaque has some good choices: Mariscos Progreso, Restaurant with No Name, and Casa Fuerte. Popular eateries serving good local fare are abundant, especially in the centro histórico. Local dishes worth trying include *birria*, which is meat (goat, lamb, or pork) that has been covered in maguey leaves and roasted. It can be served either in a tomato-based broth or with the broth on the side. To get it right, go to one of the many birrierías, where it is the specialty. Another local favorite is the *torta ahogada*, something similar to a sub sandwich with a spicy pork filling. Also, there is the Jalisco-style *pozole*, a chicken-and-hominy soup to which you add lime juice, onion, and chile.

EXPENSIVE

"**Restaurant with No Name.**" Madero 80, Tlaquepaque. ☎ **3/635-4520** or 3/635-9677. Breakfast $4–$7; main courses $11–$20. AE, DISC, MC, V. Daily 8:30am–10pm. HAUTE MEXICAN.

The food and service here are excellent, in a cool, shaded patio that has the informal feel of a Mexican country house. Vegetation is allowed to grow pretty much at will, with a little coaxing to get it to form green canopies; peacocks strut around unruffled by the goings-on. This place could also be called Restaurant with No Menu; the waiters will recite the full list of dishes in English or Spanish and you can interrupt with questions at any time. I don't feel comfortable without text on a page, but the waiter's impressive knowledge of how dishes were prepared was reassuring. If you like something rich and strong-flavored, try the pork in a three-chile sauce (rich, dried chiles, not hot ones). I also liked the seafood dishes. It's 1 1/2 blocks north of Tlaquepaque's Parián.

Suéhiro. La Paz 1701 (west side). ☎ **3/826-0094** or 3/826-3122. Reservations recommended. Main courses $12–$20. AE, MC, V. Mon–Sat 1:30–5:30pm and 7:30–11:30pm, Sun 1:30–7:30pm. JAPANESE.

Guadalajarans love having this Japanese gem in their city, and have made it a popular place. Dishes are wonderfully flavored and expertly cooked. Teppanyaki is the specialty, but the menu also offers a wide selection of tempura. If you want just sushi, you can dine in the separate sushi bar, where the selection is large, fresh, delicious, and prepared right in front of you. The restaurant is about 13 blocks beyond the Parque de la Revolución and avenida Enrique Díaz de León.

MODERATE

Casa Fuerte. 224-A Independencia, Tlaquepaque. ☎ **3/639-6481.** Reservations recommended. Main courses $5–$9. AE, DISC, MC, V. Daily noon–8pm. MEXICAN/INTERNATIONAL.

Clothing designer Irene Pulos has turned her former showroom into this popular and charming patio restaurant. The setting says colorful Mexico: pastel walls and waiters sporting bold Pulos-designed vests. Imaginatively prepared dishes include shrimp in tamarindo juice, grilled brochette with banana, fresh vegetable salads, steaks, and fajitas. The restaurant is tucked in a town house among the row of shops on Independencia.

✪ **El Sacromonte.** Pedro Moreno 1398 (west side). ☎ **3/825-5447.** Reservations recommended. Main courses $4.50–$9. AE, MC, V. Mon–Sat 1:30pm–midnight. NOUVELLE MEXICAN.

The food here is so exquisite that I try to dine here every time I'm in Guadalajara. Great emphasis is placed on presentation and artful design, from the menu in verse to "Queen Isabel's crown," a dish of shrimp woven together in the shape of a crown and covered in a divine lobster and orange sauce. The appetizers are also things of beauty, such as quesadillas with rose petals. My favorite soup, "el viejo progreso," is a cream soup of Roquefort and chipotle. The dining area is a pleasant, shaded, open-air patio. This place is popular, so make reservations.

Hostería del Ángel. 5 de Mayo 295 (Zapopan, west side). ☎ and fax **3/656-9516.** Breakfast $2–$3.50; comida corrida $4; deli specialties and tapas $2–$4. AE, MC, V. Tues–Sat 9am–11pm, Sun 10am–8pm. TAPAS/SPANISH-ITALIAN DELI.

This is a difficult restaurant to categorize. The owner-chef cooked for years in Spain and Italy, where he became fascinated with the making of cheeses and deli meats such as *prosciutto* and the Spanish *jamón serrano*. Now he has returned and opened a restaurant where he can combine his specialties with Mexican ingredients. He serves different tapas every day and a large variety of wines. This is a wonderful place to go in the evening for a glass of wine and some tapas, a sandwich, or a rotolata of cheese, meats, and vegetables. The restaurant is 4 blocks from the basilica of the virgin of Zapopan.

✪ **La Destilería.** av. México 2916, corner of Nelson; Fracc. Terranova (west side). ☎ **3/640-3440** or 3/640-3110. Main courses $6–$15. AE, DISC, MC, V. Mon–Sat 1pm–midnight, Sun 1–6pm. MEXICAN.

You know that with a name like "The Distillery," tequila will somehow be involved. Although this museum-restaurant is filled with artifacts, photos, and curios thoughtfully organized to depict every stage of the tequila-making process, it's the food that really brings Guadalajarans back. Specialties include *molcajete de la casa*—steaming fajitas, *rajas* (chile strips), cheese, onion, and avocado in a large, sizzling molcajete (three-legged stone mortar). The spicy steak dish "*medallones Tenochtitlán*" is memorable, as is the delicately flavored fish in parsley sauce. This is one of those places that is almost sure to please everyone. You can order salads here without hesitation (all greens are washed in an antimicrobial solution), and the desert menu has such favorites as "pastel de tres leches". And, with its vast selection of tequilas, it's the perfect place to do a little tasting. It's 5 blocks northwest of the Fuente Minerva and about 2^{1}/$_{2}$ miles west of the Centro Histórico.

✪ **La Fonda de San Miguel.** Donato Guerra 25 (downtown). ☎ **3/613-0809.** Breakfast $5, main courses $7–$12. AE, MC, V. Sun–Tues 8am–6pm, Wed–Sat 8am–midnight. MEXICAN.

My favorite way to enjoy a good meal in Mexico is to have it in the beautiful courtyard of a colonial building. I love the wonderful contrast between the bright and noisy street outside, and the quiet and shaded courtyard inside. This particular restaurant is in a former convent with stone arches and plaster walls painted in muted tones of orange and yellow. (Check out the shops and galleries as you enter.) Waiters will bring you little crisp tacos, pumpkin bread, and mildly spiced butter to awaken your appetite. For main courses, try the chile en nogada if it's in season (a little spicy and a little sweet), or perhaps a traditional mole poblano. The restaurant is 4 blocks west and 1 block south of the cathedral in the old convent of Santa Teresa de Jesús.

La Trattoría Pomodoro Ristorante. Niños Héroes 3051 (west side). ☎ **3/ 122-1817.** Pasta $3–$5; chicken, beef, and seafood $5–$7. AE, MC, V. Daily 1pm–midnight. Free parking. ITALIAN.

Sooner or later, visitors to Guadalajara learn about the good food at this popular restaurant. Service is friendly and swift, and the newly decorated restaurant is refreshing, with natural wood chairs, cushioned seats, and linen-clad tables. A large span of windows looks out onto Niños Héroes. There's separate seating for smokers and nonsmokers. For starters, you might want to sample the antipasto bar or the shrimp in white-wine cream sauce with chiles. As a main course, the fettuccine Alfredo is excellent. The superb salad bar and garlic bread are included in the price of main courses.

✪ **Mariscos Progreso.** Progreso 80, Tlaquepaque. ☎ **3/657-4995.** Main courses $6–$12. AE, MC, V. Daily 11am–7pm. SEAFOOD/MEXICAN.

In a large, open patio shaded by trees and tile roofs, waiters navigate among the tables carrying large platters of delicious seafood. Mexicans do a wonderful job with seafood, and this popular restaurant does the tradition proud. Charcoal-grilled, Mexican-style, is the specialty here (for a sampling of grilled favorites, try the *parrillada* for two), but they'll cook it in a variety of ways. Sometimes there can be quite a bit of *ambiente*, with mariachis adding to the commotion. At other times, the crowd thins and one can rest from the exertions of shopping with a cold, peaceful drink. It's ¹/₂ block from the Parián, in Tlaquepaque.

✪ **Modern Art Café.** av. Américas 1939, corner av. Patria (Zapopan–west side). ☎ **3/636-6141** or 3/636-2999. Breakfast $3.75–$6, main courses $9–$12. AE, MC, V. Mon–Fri 8am–12:30am, Sat–Sun 9am–1am. Valet parking. CONTINENTAL.

This perennially popular but unpretentious restaurant offers good food in an artsy atmosphere. Pass the small gift shop on the left as you enter and step down to the light and airy restaurant with a wood-burning pizza oven at one end and walls lined with paintings.

House specialties include pizza, delicious gazpacho, and several wonderful seafood dishes. They have a version of shrimp alambres that is simply delicious. The large portions are carefully presented. It's at the corner of avenida Patria, diagonally across from the Plaza Patria shopping center. Take a taxi.

Siglo XV. Colón 383 (downtown). ☎ **3/614-4278.** Main courses $8–$11. AE, MC, V. Mon–Sat 1pm–1am. SPANISH.

Chef Antonio Ruíz and his partners have gone to great lengths to create a dining hall suggestive of 15th-century Spain—stone walls, tables and benches made of thick wooden planks, torches, etc. The end result is impressive, and the food is excellent. Mr. Ruíz is a blue-ribbon chef who has championed the cooking of his native Spain in many culinary festivals around the world. Popular favorites include his scallops "cayos a la madrileña", the paella, and roasted pig "cochinillo asado a la segoviana." From Wednesday to Saturday there are flamenco performances, and every night there is live acoustic music. If you want to go on a weekend, make reservations. The restaurant is in the downtown area known as "nueve esquinas."

INEXPENSIVE

✪ **Café Madrid.** Juárez 264 (downtown). ☎ **3/614-9504.** Breakfast $2–$4, main courses $3–$6. No credit cards. Daily 7:30am–10:30pm. MEXICAN.

This little cafe is like many cafes used to be—a kind of social institution where people come in, greet each other and the staff by name, and chat over breakfast or coffee and cigarettes. Change comes slowly here: despite being very informal, the waiters wear white jackets with black bow ties, as they did 20 years ago. The coffee and Mexican breakfasts are good, as is the standard Mexican fare served in the afternoon. There's a room open to the street in front with a small lunch counter and another in the back. From the Plaza de Armas, walk 1 block on Corona to Juárez and turn right; the cafe is on the right.

La Chata Restaurant. Corona 126 (downtown). ☎ **3/613-0588.** Breakfast $2–$4, main courses $2–$5. AE, CB, DC, MC, V. Daily 8am–11:30pm. REGIONAL/MEXICAN.

At this popular downtown spot, tasty Mexican standards are offered at reasonable prices. Aromas waft into the street from the kitchen in front, where women with bandannas on their heads busily stir, chop, and fry. Past this is a large dining area. Local dishes include *pozole* (chicken-and-hominy soup) or a *torta ahogada* (a spicy pork sandwich), or if you're very hungry, the *platillo jaliciense* (sampler platter)

will fit the bill. To find La Chata from the Plaza de Armas, walk
1¹/₂ blocks south on Corona; it's on the right between Juárez and
López Cotilla.

☢ Los Itacates Restaurant. Chapultepec Nte. 110 (west side). ☎ **3/
825-1106** or 3/825-9551. Breakfast buffet $4, tacos 50¢, main courses $3–$5.
MC, V. Mon–Sat 8am–11pm, Sun 8am–7pm. MEXICAN.

This is the Mexican equivalent to down-home cooking—nothing
exotic or unheard-of, just well-prepared traditional food. This place,
very popular with office workers, is packed during the afternoon dinner hour (2 to 4pm), but at other times it's easy to find a table. The
atmosphere is festive, with colorfully painted chairs and table cov-
erings. You can choose to dine outdoors at sidewalk tables or in one
of the three interior rooms. Specialties include pozole, *lomo adobado*
(baked pork), and chiles rellenos. The *pollo Itacates* is a quarter of a
chicken, two cheese enchiladas, potatoes, and rice. To find the restaurant, take the Par Vial west on Independencia/Hidalgo. Get off
at Chapultepec and walk to the right (north) on Chapultepec about
3 blocks. It's on the right.

Sanborn's. Juárez at 16 de Septiembre (downtown). ☎ **3/613-6264.** Breakfast $3–$4; main courses $4–$8. AE, MC, V. Daily 7:30am–1am.
INTERNATIONAL.

On one side of the intersection is Sanborn's restaurant and on the
other is its coffee shop sibling, which offers a more limited menu.
Both places are popular and can be crowded almost any time of day.
Like other branches of the Mexican chain, this restaurant has wait-
resses in festive dresses. The varied menu features everything from
tacos and hotcakes to steaks and sandwiches, but the traditional
thing to order here is the enchiladas suizas. After eating, check out
the section filled with drugstore items, English-language books and
magazines, and gifts. To find it from the Plaza de Armas, walk 1
block south on 16 de Septiembre to Juárez; it's on the left corner.

7

Exploring Guadalajara & Beyond

*G*uadalajara is one of the most Mexican of Mexico's cities. Spend a few days exploring its historic downtown area, with all its cultural and architectural highlights, parks, and attractions, and even the most hard-core resort tourist will realize there is much more to Mexico than sandy beaches and souvenir shops. Several outlying towns also merit a visit, including Tequila (for those who like to imbibe), and the villages surrounding Lake Chapala, a popular vacation spot.

1 What to See & Do in Guadalajara

DOWNTOWN GUADALAJARA

The most easily recognized building downtown is the ✪ **cathedral,** around which four open plazas make the shape of a Latin cross. Later, a long swath of land was cleared to extend the open area from the cathedral to the Hospicio Cabañas, creating **Plaza Tapatía.** Most of the downtown attractions are adjacent to this area.

The cathedral was begun in 1561 and was an ongoing project into the 18th century. With such a long time span, it was inevitable that remodeling would take place before the building was ever completed. The result is an unusual facade that is actually an amalgam of several architectural styles, including baroque, neoclassical, and gothic. An 1818 earthquake destroyed the original large towers; their replacements were built in the 1850s, inspired by designs on the bishop's dinner china. The colors on the towers—blue and yellow—are the symbolic colors of Guadalajara, and match the city's coat of arms. Inside, the cathedral is open, airy, and majestic. Items of interest include a painting above the sacristy ascribed to the renowned 17th-century Spanish artist Bartolomé Murillo (1617–82).

To the cathedral's left is the **Plaza de Armas,** the oldest of the plazas and the loveliest. It's recognizable by the Art Nouveau bandstand in its center. This bandstand, made in France, was a gift to the city from the dictator Porfirio Díaz in the 1890s. The female figures on the bandstand exhibited too little clothing for conservative

Guadalajarans, who then dressed the figures in cloth apparel. The dictator, recognizing when it's best to let the people have their way, said nothing.

Facing the plaza is the ✪ **Palacio del Gobierno.** This handsome palace, built in 1774, blended Spanish and Moorish elements, a popular style at the time. Inside the central courtyard, above the beautiful staircase to the right, is a spectacular mural of Hidalgo by the modern Mexican master José Clemente Orozco (1883–1949). The Father of Independence appears high overhead, bearing directly down on the viewer and looking as implacable as a force of nature. Guadalajara's native son achieved this effect through the dramatic use of proportion and perspective that are the earmarks of his work. On one of the adjacent walls is another mural, *The Carnival of Ideologies,* a dark satire on the prevailing fanaticisms of Orozco's day. There is another mural by Orozco inside the second-floor chamber of representatives. It shows Hidalgo again, but this time in a more conventional posture, writing the proclamation to end slavery in Mexico. It's open 10am to 8pm.

On the opposite side of the cathedral from the Plaza de Armas is the **Rotonda de los Hombres Ilustres.** Sixteen gleaming-white columns, sans bases or capitals, each supporting a bronze statue, stand as monuments to Guadalajara's, and the state of Jalisco's, distinguished sons.

Facing the east side of the rotonda is the **Museo Regional de Guadalajara,** Liceo 60 (☎ **3/614-9957**). Originally a convent, built in 1701 in the *churrigueresque* style (Mexican baroque, derived from a Spanish architect, Churriguera), it contains some of the region's important archaeological finds, fossils, historic objects, and art. Among the highlights are a giant reconstructed mammoth's skeleton and a meteorite weighing 1,715 pounds, discovered in Zacatecas in 1792. On the first floor there's also a fascinating exhibit of pre-Hispanic pottery; it features unusual pieces from the collection and some exquisite pottery and clay figures recently unearthed near Tequila during the construction of the toll road. On the second floor is a small but interesting ethnography exhibit of the contemporary dress of the state's indigenous peoples, including the Coras, Huicholes, Mexicaneros, Nahuas, and Tepehuanes. It's open Tuesday through Saturday from 9am to 6:45pm and Sunday from 9am to 2:45pm. Admission is $2.50 for adults; $1 for children (children enter free Sunday); Tuesday admission is free for all.

Behind the Cathedral is the Plaza de la Liberación with the ✪ **Teatro Degollado** (deh-goh-*yah*-doh) on the opposite side. This

Downtown Guadalajara

Catedral **3**
Hospicio Cabañas **11**
Iglesia de Santa María de Gracia **7**
Mercado Libertad **12**
Museo Regional de Guadalajara **5**
Palacio de Justicia **6**
Palacio del Gobierno **2**

Plaza de Armas **1**
Quetzalcoatl Fountain **10**
Rotonda de los Hombres Ilustres **4**
Teatro Degollado **8**
Universidad de Guadalajara
  Facultad de Música &
  Iglesia de San Agustín **9**

beautiful neoclassical 19th-century opera house was named for Santos Degollado, a local patriot who fought with Juárez against Maximilian and the French. Notice the seven muses above the columns in the theater's portico. This theater is justifiably famous for both the acoustics and the beauty of its interior. It hosts a variety of performances during the year, including the excellent Ballet Folklórico on Sunday at 10am. It's open Monday through Friday from 10am to 2pm and during performances (see "Guadalajara After Dark," below, for more information).

To the theater's right and across the street is the sweet little **church of Santa María de Gracia,** built in 1573 as part of a convent for Dominican nuns. On the opposite side of the Teatro Degollado is the **church of San Agustín** and the **University of Guadalajara School of Music.**

Behind the Teatro Degollado is a frieze that depicts Mexican history in low relief. Walking in that same direction, away from the cathedral, you'll next pass a charming children's fountain, followed

Special Events in Guadalajara

In September, when Mexicans celebrate independence from Spain, Guadalajara goes all out with a full month of festivities. Look for poster-sized calendars listing attractions that include performances in theaters all over the city. The celebration kicks off with the *Encuentro Internacional del Mariachi*, in which mariachi bands from around the world come to their Mecca to strut their stuff and acquire a little polish. Bands come from as far as Japan and Russia, and the event takes on a curiously postmodern hue. There are concerts in several venues, including a night of chamber music a la mariachi. The Degollado Theater and the tourism office provide information. The culmination of this affair is a parade of mariachis and charros, which would be a shame to miss if you find yourself in town during the first week in September. On **September 15,** a massive crowd assembles in front of the Governor's Palace to await the shouting of the traditional *grito* (shout for independence) at 11pm. The grito commemorates Fr. Miguel Hidalgo de Costilla's cry for independence in 1810. The celebration features live music on a street stage, spontaneous dancing, fireworks, of course, and shouts of *"[ue]Viva México!"* and *"[ue]Viva Hidalgo!"* The next day is the official Independence Day with a traditional parade; the plazas downtown resemble a country fair and Mexican market, with booths, games of chance, stuffed-animal prizes, cotton candy,

by the unusual sculpture of a tree with lions. Nearby are stone slabs engraved with Charles V's proclamation of Guadalajara's inalienable right to be recognized as a city.

The plaza opens into a huge pedestrian expanse called **Plaza Tapatía,** now framed by department stores and offices, and dominated by the abstract modern **Quetzalcoatl Fountain.** This fluid steel structure represents the mythical plumed serpent Quetzalcoatl, which figured so prominently in pre-Hispanic religion and culture, and exerts a presence even today. The smaller pieces represent the serpent and birds; the centerpiece is the serpent's fire.

At the far end of the plaza is the Hospicio Cabañas, formerly called the Cabañas Orphanage and known today as the ✪ **Instituto Cultural Cabañas,** Cabañas 8 (☎ **3/617-4322**). This vast structure is impressive for both its size (more than 23 courtyards) and its grandiose architecture, especially the cupola. Created by the famous and candied apples. Live entertainment stretches well into the night.

On **October 12,** the feast day of the Virgin of Zapopan is celebrated with a procession honoring Our Lady of Zapopan. Around dawn, the small, dark figure of Our Lady of Zapopan begins her 5-hour ride from the Cathedral of Guadalajara to the suburban Basilica of Zapopan (see "Other Attractions," below). The original icon dates from the mid-1500s; the procession began 200 years later. Today, crowds spend the night all along the route and vie for position as the Virgin approaches. She does so in a gleaming new car, virginal in the sense that it must never have had the ignition turned on. This virgin-mobile is pulled through the streets by the Virgin's caretakers. During the previous months, the figure visits churches all over the city. You will likely see neighborhoods decorated with paper streamers and banners honoring the passing of the figure to the next church.

The celebration has grown into a monthlong event, **Fiestas de Octubre,** which kicks off with an enormous parade, usually on the first Sunday (or possibly Saturday) of the month. Festivities include performing arts, rodeos (*charreadas*), bullfights, art exhibits, regional dancing, a food fair, and a Day of Nations incorporating all the consulates in Guadalajara.

Mexican architect Manuel Tolsá, it housed homeless children from 1829 until 1980. Today, it's a thriving cultural center offering art shows and classes. The interior walls and ceiling of the main building display murals painted by Orozco in 1937, at the height of his powers. His *Man of Fire,* occupying the dome, is said to represent the spirit of humanity projecting itself toward the infinite. Other rooms hold additional Orozco works, as well as excellent temporary displays. A contemporary art collection in the south wing features fascinating and unusual paintings by Javier Arévalo. The institute's own Ballet Folklórico performs here every Wednesday at 8:30pm (see "Guadalajara After Dark," below, for more info). Hours are Tuesday through Saturday 10:30am to 6pm; Sunday 10:30am to 3pm; closed Monday. Admission is $1.

Just to the south of the Hospicio Cabañas (to the left as you exit the door) is the ✪ **Mercado Libertad,** Guadalajara's gigantic covered central market, said to be the largest in Latin America. This site has been a market plaza since the 1500s; the present buildings date from the early 1950s (see "Shopping," below).

OTHER ATTRACTIONS

At the **Parque Agua Azul** (Blue Water Park), the plants, trees, shrubbery, statues, and fountains create a perfect refuge from the bustling city. Many people come here to exercise early in the morning. The park is open daily from 7am to 6pm. Admission for adults is $1; children 50¢.

Across Independencia, cater-cornered from a small flower market in a small one-story rock building, is the **Museo de Arqueología del Occidente de Mexico,** calzada Independencia con avenida del Campesino. It houses a fine collection of pre-Hispanic pottery from Jalisco, Nayarit, and Colima. The museum is open Tuesday through Sunday from 10am to 2pm and 4 to 7pm. There's a small admission charge.

The state-run **Casa de las Artesanías** (☎ 3/619-4664) is just past the park entrance at the crossroads of calzada Independencia and Gallo (for details, see "Shopping," below).

✪ **The Basílica of the Virgin of Zapopan.** Main Plaza, Zapopan (6 miles northwest of downtown), Jalisco. No phone. Free admission. Daily 7am–7pm.

The center of Zapopan has been refurbished with a wide promenade leading up to a broad plaza and the basilica. This is the true religious center of Guadalajara, with the plaza holding hundreds of thousands of people on the Virgin's feast day (see "Special Events in Guadalajara," above). The church dates from the 18th century and is a lovely (and somewhat anachronistic) combination of baroque and plateresque styles. The cult of the virgin of Zapopan practically began with the foundation of Guadalajara itself. She is much revered and the object of many pilgrimages. In front of the church you will find several stands selling religious figures and paraphernalia. To one side of the church is a lovely museum and store dedicated to the betterment of the Huichol Indians. It is well worth a visit.

✪ **Museo de las Artes de la Universidad de Guadalajara.** Juárez 975. ☎ 3/625-7553. Admission $2. Tues–Sat 10am–8pm, Sun and holidays noon–8pm. To reach the museum, take the Par Vial west on Independencia/Hidalgo. Get off after it makes the right turn onto Vallarta/Juárez. From the bus stop on Juárez, walk back (east) 2 or 3 blocks; it's on the right opposite the University of Guadalajara. It's about an 11-block walk from Alcalde/16 de Septiembre, straight west on Juárez, and 4 blocks beyond the Parque Revolución, which will be on your left.

This museum gets many important traveling exhibitions. An early show featured contemporary artists from all over the Americas. Several rooms house the university's permanent collection, consisting mainly of Mexican and Jaliscan artists. There are also some bold Orozco murals: on one wall of the auditorium and the cupola above are *Man, Creator and Rebel* and *The People and Their False Leaders*.

Museo de la Ciudad. Independencia 684 at M. Barcena. ☎ **3/658-2531.** Admission 50¢. Wed–Sat 10am–5:30pm, Sun 10am–2:30pm.

This fine museum, which opened in 1992 in a wonderful old stone convent, chronicles Guadalajara's fascinating past. The eight rooms, beginning on the right and proceeding in chronological order, cover the period from just before the city's founding to the present. Unusual artifacts, including rare Spanish armaments and equestrian paraphernalia, give a sense of what day-to-day life was like in Guadalajara's past. As you browse, dust off your Spanish and read the explanations, which give details not otherwise noted in the displays.

2 Shopping

Many visitors to Guadalajara come specifically for the shopping in Tlaquepaque and Tonalá (see below). But if you have little free time to shop, try the government-run ✪ **Casa de las Artesanías** in Agua Azul, just south of downtown. It's at the intersection of calzada Independencia and Gallo, Gallo 20 (☎ **3/619-4664**). This place is perfect for one-stop shopping, with two floors of pottery, silver jewelry, dance masks, glassware, leather goods, and regional clothing from around the state and the country. As you enter, on the right are museum displays showing crafts and regional costumes from the state of Jalisco. The craft store is open Monday through Friday from 10am to 6pm, Saturday from 10am to 5pm, and Sunday from 10am to 3pm.

Guadalajara is known for its shoe industry, so if you're in the market for a pair, try the **Galería del Calzado**—a shopping center made up exclusively of shoe stores. It's on the west side, about 6 blocks from the Minerva Circle, at the intersection of avenida México and Yaquis.

Mariachis and charros come to Guadalajara from all over Mexico to buy their highly worked belts and boots, wide-brimmed sombreros, and embroidered shirts. There are several tailor shops and stores that specialize in these outfits, but the best known is **El Charro,** which has a store in the Plaza del Sol shopping center, across the street from the Hotel Presidente Intercontinental, and one downtown on Juárez.

And if you're interested in viewing a good slice of what constitutes the material world for most Mexicans, try the mammoth **Mercado Libertad** downtown. Besides food and produce, you will find some crafts, household goods, clothing, magical preparations, and much, much more. Although it opens at 7am, the market doesn't get in full swing until around 10am. Come prepared to haggle.

SHOPPING IN TLAQUEPAQUE & TONALÁ

Almost everyone who comes to Guadalajara for the shopping has Tlaquepaque and Tonalá in mind. These two suburbs are traditional pottery and glassblowing centers that have richly expanded their repertoires into many other crafts.

TLAQUEPAQUE

Located about 20 minutes from downtown, Tlaquepaque (Tlah-Keh-*Pah*-Keh) has the best shopping for handcrafts and the decorative arts in all of Mexico. Over the years, it has become a fashionable center for shopping, attracting talented designers in a variety of fields. Even though it's a suburb of a large city, there is a cozy, small-town feel to Tlaquepaque, and since the town is compact, it's a pleasure simply to stroll down the street from shop to shop without anyone hassling you. There are some excellent places to eat (see "Where to Dine," above), or you can grab some simple fare at El Parián, a building in the middle of town housing a number of small eateries.

A taxi from downtown Guadalajara will cost you $3 to $4, or you can take one of the deluxe **Turquesa buses** that make a fairly quick run from downtown to Tlaquepaque and Tonalá (see "Getting Around," in chapter 6). Look for buses numbered 275. They leave every 10 minutes from Alcalde between Juárez and López Cotilla (50¢).

The **Tlaquepaque Tourism Office** has a very helpful, English-speaking staff. It's located at Pila Seca, Local 15 (☎ 3/635-5553); open Monday through Friday from 9am to 3pm and Saturday from 9am to 1pm. Most stores in Tlaquepaque close in the afternoon between 2 and 4pm and stay open in the evening until 7 or 8pm. Most are either closed or have reduced hours on Sunday.

If you are interested in pottery and ceramics, there are two museums well worth a visit. The **Regional Ceramics Museum,** Independencia 237 (☎ 3/635-5404), teaches something about traditional Jalisco pottery as produced in Tlaquepaque and Tonalá.

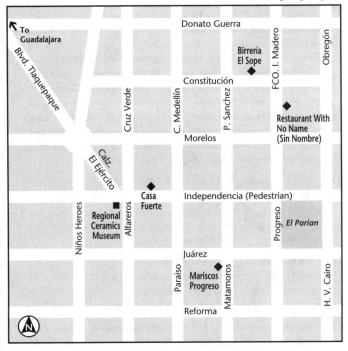

There are high-quality examples dating back several generations.
Note the crosshatch design known as *petatillo* on some of the pieces;
it's one of the region's oldest traditional motifs. Look for the wonderful old kitchen and dining room, complete with pots, utensils,
and dishes. The museum is open Tuesday through Saturday from
10am to 4pm and Sunday from 10am to 1pm; free admission. The
✪ **Museo Pantaleón Panduro** (named after a famous local artisan
of the 19th century) at P. Sánchez 191 (☎ **3/635-1089,** ext. 17),
displays prize-winning pieces from the national ceramics contest held
each year in Tlaquepaque. There are several categories including
miniatures, traditional designs, and original designs. Many of these
display a virtuosity that is truly astounding. I really liked this
museum. It's open Tuesday to Sunday from 10am to 6pm; admission is free. If you still haven't had your fill, there is also the Museo
Nacional de Cerámica in Tonalá (see below).

There are also a number of workshops where you are permitted
to watch the creative process unfold. A popular workshop is **La Rosa**

de Cristal, a glass-blowing factory at Contreras Medillín 173. It's open from 10am to 7pm Monday through Saturday. If there is a particular craft that you're interested in, talk to the city tourism office; they can help locate workshops open to the public.

The following list of Tlaquepaque shops will give you an idea of what to expect. However, this is just a small fraction of what you'll find here; the best thing might be to just follow your nose. The main shopping is along **Independencia,** a pedestrian-only street that starts at El Parián. You can go door to door visiting the shops along Independencia until it ends, and then work your way back towards El Parián along **calle Juárez,** another good shopping street, 1 block north.

✪ Agustín Parra. Independencia 158. ☎ **3/657-8530.**

So you bought an old hacienda and are trying to restore its chapel—where do you go to find traditional baroque sculpture, religious art, gold-leafed objects, and even entire retablos? Parra is famous for exactly this kind of work, and the store is lovely.

Bazar Hecht. Juárez 162. ☎ **3/657-0316.**

One of the village's longtime favorites, here you'll find wood objects, handmade furniture, and a few antiques. Open Monday through Saturday from 10am to 2:30pm and 3:30 to 7pm.

✪ Casa Canela. Independencia 258, near calle Cruz Verde. ☎ **3/635-3717.**

One of the most elegant stores in Tlaquepaque, it is a feast for the eyes. Browse through the rooms full of furniture and decorative objects. Open Monday through Friday from 10am to 2pm and 3 to 7pm, Saturday from 10am to 6pm, and Sunday from 11am to 3pm.

Ken Edwards. Madero 70. ☎ **3/635-5456.**

Ken was among the first artisans to produce high-fired, lead-free stoneware in Tonalá, and his blue-on-blue pottery is now sold all over Mexico. This showroom has a fine selection of his work, which is not usually seen in such size or quantity elsewhere. There's a section of seconds for bargain hunters. The shop is next door to the "Restaurant with No Name." Open Monday to Saturday from 10:30am to 7pm. His factory is in Tonalá.

Sergio Bustamante. Independencia 236 at Cruz Verde. ☎ **3/639-5519.**

Sergio Bustamante's imaginative and original bronze, ceramic, and papier-mâché sculptures are among the most sought after in Mexico—as well as the most copied. He also designs silver jewelry. This is an exquisite gallery showcasing his work. Open Monday through Saturday from 10am to 7pm and Sunday from 11am to 4pm.

Tete Arte y Diseño. Juárez 173. ☎ **3/635-7347.**

Architectural decorative objects are mixed in with pottery, antiques, glassware, and paintings at this shop. Open Monday through Saturday from 10am to 7pm.

Tierra Tlaquepaque. Independencia 156. ☎ **3/635-9770.**

Here you'll find unusual, rustic, and finely finished pottery, as well as wood sculptures, table textiles, and decorative objects. Open Monday through Saturday from 10am to 7pm, Sunday from 11am to 5pm.

TONALÁ: A TRADITION OF POTTERY MAKING

Tonalá is a pleasant, modest town not far from Tlaquepaque. The streets were paved only recently, and there aren't any pedestrian-only thoroughfares yet. Of the two, you might find Tonalá easier on the wallet. The village has been a center of pottery making since pre-Hispanic times; half of the more than 400 workshops here produce a wide variety of high- and low-temperature pottery. Other local artists work with forged iron, cantera stone, brass and copper, marble,

---

Packing It In

If you need your purchases packed safely for the ride home, or if you buy so much that you want it shipped back (which can be very expensive), talk to Margaret del Rio. She is an American who runs a large packing and shipping company in Tlaquepaque at Juárez 347 (☎ 3/657-5652). The cheapest way to get merchandise home is to check it as baggage and pay the extra fee; however, with large items this isn't possible.

---

miniatures, papier-mâché, textiles, blown glass, and gesso. This is a good place to look for custom work in any of these materials; a large pool of craftsmen can be located by just asking around a little.

Market days are Thursday and Sunday: You can expect large crowds and blocks and blocks of stalls displaying locally made pottery and glassware, as well as cheap manufactured goods, food, and all kinds of bric-a-brac. "Herb-men" sell a rainbow of dried medicinal herbs from wheelbarrows; magicians entertain crowds with sleight-of-hand; and craftspeople spread their colorful wares on the plaza's sidewalks. I really prefer to visit Tonalá on nonmarket days, when it's much easier to get around and see the glass and pottery stores. Lovers of hand-blown Mexican glass and folksy ceramics will wish they had a truck to haul home the gorgeous and inexpensive handmade items available here.

The **Tonalá Tourism Office** (☎ 3/683-1740; fax 3/683-0590) is in the Artesanos building set back from the road at Atonaltecas 140 Sur (the main street leading into Tonalá), at Matamoros. Hours are Monday through Friday from 9am to 3pm and Saturday from 9am to 1pm. They offer free walking tours Monday, Tuesday, Wednesday, and Friday at 9am and 2pm and Saturday at 9am and 1pm. These include visits to artisans' workshops (where you'll see ceramics, stoneware, blown glass, papier-mâché, and the like). Tours last between 3 and 4 hours and require a minimum of five people. Visitors can request an English-speaking guide. Also in Tonalá, cater-cornered from the church, you'll see a small tourism information kiosk that's staffed on market days and provides maps and useful information.

Tonalá is also the home of the **Museo Nacional de Cerámica,** Constitución 104, between Hidalgo and Morelos (☎ 3/683-0494). The museum occupies a huge two-story mansion and displays work from Jalisco and pottery from all over the country.

There's a large shop in the front on the right as you enter. The museum is open Tuesday through Friday from 10am to 5pm and Saturday and Sunday from 10am to 2pm. Admission is free, but a fee of $8.50 per camera will be charged for use of any video or still cameras.

If you feel hunger pangs coming on, try **Los Geranios** (☎ 3/ **683-0010**) at Hidalgo 71, next to El Bazar de Sermel. Try the fish with almonds and mushrooms or the pork baked in orange sauce with baked potato and vegetables. You can also grab something quick like nachos. To get here, face the church on the plaza, walk to the right, and turn down Hidalgo for about half a block; look on the left for a pretty stained-glass sign with red flowers. It's closed on Saturdays, and the rest of the week it's open only from 11am to 5pm.

3 Guadalajara After Dark

FOLKLORIC BALLET

Ballet Folklórico de la Universidad de Guadalajara. Degollado Theater, Plaza Tapatía. ☎ **3/614-4773** or 3/613-1115. Tickets $3–$12. Ticket office open daily 10am–1pm and 4–7pm.

This wonderful dance company, acclaimed as the finest folklórico company in all of Mexico, is pure Jalisco. For more than a decade it has been performing at the Degollado Theater. Performances are on Sunday at 10am.

Ballet Folklórico Nacional del Instituto Cultural Cabañas. At the far end of the Plaza Tapatía. ☎ **3/618-6003.** Tickets $6–$8.

Performances are every Wednesday at 8:30pm at the theater of the Instituto Cultural Cabañas (see "Downtown Guadalajara," above).

MARIACHIS

You can't go far in Guadalajara without coming across some mariachis, but to see really talented performances takes some effort (see "La Feria," below). If what you're really interested in is the flavor and atmosphere of the music, try ✪ **El Parián** in Tlaquepaque, where mariachis serenade diners under the archways. At **Plaza de los Mariachis,** down by the San Juan de Dios Church and the Mercado Libertad, at the junction of calzada Independencia and avenida Juárez/calle Javier Mina, colorfully dressed mariachis, sometimes a little tipsy, play every evening for money (if they can get it). Otherwise they'll just play for free. Grab something to eat and drink, or just soak up the ambiance. Ask the price before you request a song.

THE CLUB & MUSIC SCENE

✪ **El Cubilete.** Gral. Río Seco 9. ☎ **3/658-0406.** $3 cover on weekends. Mon–Sat 2pm–1am, Tues–Sat live salsa 10pm–1am.

El Cubilete ("the dice cup") is a small club tucked away in an old downtown neighborhood called Las nueve esquinas (the nine corners). This is an up-and-coming neighborhood that has a couple of other clubs worth checking out, as well as the Siglo XV restaurant (see chapter 6). The house band at El Cubilete is very tight, and the club gets some excellent traveling Cuban bands; but on weekends the place really gets cookin' when Rosalía takes the stage. This talented Cuban diva has an easy and natural stage presence, and an ability to ad-lib that makes her a joy to watch. When Rosalía is singing, the club can get very crowded. El Cubilete serves drinks and Cuban and regional foods including birria, tortas ahogadas, and carne asada.

✪ **La Feria.** Corona 291. ☎ **3/613-7150** or 3/613-1812. No cover. Daily noon–3am. Variety show at 3:30 and 10pm. Call for reservations.

To get a good sampling of local color, try this multilevel restaurant-bar with a stage in the middle. The afternoon and nighttime shows feature a variety of acts including a great mariachi band, some very impressive (and expressive) singers, a charro who performs rope tricks, and some ballet folklórico dancers. When I was there, the audience was entirely Mexican. The owner promised a free drink to anyone who shows a Frommer's book. Hold him to it. I recommend having a "paloma," the most popular drink in Guadalajara right now, made with tequila, lime juice, and grapefruit soda. The menu is standard Mexican with emphasis on grilled meats. La Feria is downtown, 5 blocks south of the Plaza de Armas.

✪ **Restaurant/Bar Copenhagen 77.** Marcos Castellanos 140-Z. ☎ **3/826-7306.** No cover. Restaurant Mon–Sat 2pm–1am, jazz 8:30pm–1am.

This dark, snug little den with upholstered walls and wood trim is the perfect setting for listening to jazz. The house band is led by the pianist Carlos de la Torre, whose elegant and economic style infuses his interpretations of bebop, modern, and Latin jazz. This is the real stuff, a fact demonstrated by the number of jazz heavyweights who come to sit in with the band or just listen. The club faces the Parque de la Revolución (along Juárez, 9 blocks west of the Plaza de Armas), on your left as you walk down López Cotilla. You can just have drinks, or you can order from the small but well-thought-out menu; the specialty is paella.

Rock-cocó. Pedro Moreno 532. ☎ **3/613-5632** or 3/614-3034. Wed, Fri, Sat 10pm–3am. $5 cover for men, $4 for women. Wed open bar, $10 cover for men, free for women.

And now for something completely different. The name of this club, in English or Spanish, is a play on the word *rococo*, a later, decadent form of baroque—and it couldn't be more appropriate. This amazing club occupies a 17th-century convent for Carmelite nuns. It has two stories of rooms and galleries that open onto a courtyard with a graceful stairway of stone and wrought iron. Set in the wall above the stairway is a small stage with a red velvet curtain. This is for the nightly show by a variety of circus performers. When I was there, it was a trapeze artist. The decor, as you might imagine, is baroque. The DJ plays rock, pop, and rock en Español. There are four bars scattered among the several rooms.

4 Side Trips from Guadalajara

RÍO CALIENTE: A NEARBY SPA

About 20 miles out of town in the same direction as Tequila, you'll find this spa, beautifully located in a hilly pine forest with a river of steaming hot water cutting right through the place. Temperatures here average 80°F year-round, and the elevation is 5,550 feet.

✪ **Río Caliente Spa.** Primavera Forest, La Primavera, Jal. No phone. (Reservations: Spa Vacations Limited, P.O. Box 897, Millbrae, CA 94030; ☎ **650/ 615-9543**; fax 650/615-0601.) www.riocaliente.com. 48 units. Patio area $202 double. Pool area $232 double. Rates include all meals. Discounts Apr 15– Dec 15; 7- and 10-night packages available. No credit cards.

Without phones or TVs in the rooms, a visit to Río Caliente Spa amounts to a refuge from the modern world and all its preoccupations. This is the perfect place to regain a sense of peace, enjoy relaxing massages and other spa treatments, and dedicate some time to yourself.

The simply furnished rooms near the activity area are smaller and cost less than the newer and more stylish rooms with patios near the river and pool. All rooms, however, have one double and one single bed, a fireplace, a full-length mirror, an in-room safe-deposit box, a desk, a chest, and bedside reading lamps. Water is purified in the pools and kitchen, and jars of fresh purified water are supplied daily in each room.

Guests have a choice of two outdoor thermal pools that are kept at different temperatures, as well as two private pools and sunning areas (separate for men and women). There is also an outdoor whirlpool.

Aside from the normal spa treatments listed below, there are a variety of programs offered throughout the year; they might include special instructors for Spanish and nutrition, or electro-acupuncture facelifts at an extra cost. Huichol Indians sell crafts on Sunday.

Arranged pickup from the airport is available upon request for around $35 one way, or you can take a taxi for around $45 one way. If you're driving, follow avenida Vallarta west, which becomes Highway 15. Go straight for almost 10$^1/_2$ miles and pass the village of La Venta del Astillero. Take the next left after La Venta and follow the rough road through the village of La Primavera for almost 5 miles. Keep bearing left through the forest until you see the hotel's sign on the left. There's no phone at the spa; reservations must be made through the United States.

Dining/Diversions: The self-serve vegetarian meals are taken in the cozy dining room. There's an activities room with nightly video movies or satellite TV, plus bingo and a library.

Amenities: Daily guided hikes, yoga and pool exercises, and use of scented steam room with natural steam from an underground river, are available free of charge. At extra cost, the spa offers massages, mud wraps, anti-stress and anti-aging therapies, live-cell therapy, horseback riding, and sightseeing and shopping excursions.

TEQUILA: THE NAME SAYS IT ALL

Tequila is an entertaining (and intoxicating) town, well worth a day trip from Guadalajara. The most fun way of visiting Tequila is to take the ✪ **Tequila Express,** which leaves from the train station every Saturday at about 10am. This trip is organized by the Guadalajara Chamber of Commerce (Cámara de Comercio), located at the intersection of Vallarta and Niño Obrero (☎ **3/122-7920**). This is where you have to buy your tickets. A ticket costs about $42 for an adult and includes an open bar and tequila tasting that begins while still on the train, a variety show, a tour of a distillery and a maguey plantation, and dinner, before returning to Guadalajara at about 7:30pm.

If you're not going to be around on Saturday, there are several taxi drivers (a few of whom speak English) who charge about $50 to take you to the town, get you into a tour of a distillery, take you to a restaurant, and then haul you back to Guadalajara. There are also plenty of tour companies who have bus trips to Tequila.

Tequila has many distilleries, including the famous brands **Sauza** and **José Cuervo.** All the distilleries—the big, modern ones and the smaller, more traditional factories—offer tours. If you're on your

Guadalajara & Environs

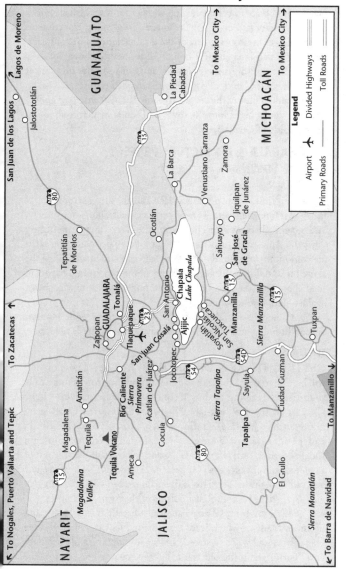

own, a good place to get hooked up with a tour is at the little booth outside the city hall on the main square. Two young women who speak English run tours to any of the local factories. The tour costs only $2.50 and lasts about 2 hours. All tours show how tequila is made, what traditions are followed, and what are the differences among them; they end, of course, with a tequila tasting.

The same highway that heads towards Río Caliente (see above) will take you straight into the town of Tequila, which is about an hour outside of Guadalajara.

LAKE CHAPALA & ITS PICTURE-PERFECT LAKESIDE TOWNS

26 miles S of Guadalajara

For a long time, Mexico's largest lake and the area surrounding it has drawn foreigners with its near-perfect climate, gorgeous scenery, and several distinct and charming lakeshore towns, including Chapala, Ajijic, and Jocotepec. In fact a large, permanent expatriate community of around 4,000 people live in settlements along the shoreline and in the villages stretching all the way from Chapala to Jocotepec. The lake is a stunning sight, ringed by fishing villages set against high, forested mountains.

Note: The year-round climate is so pleasant that few hotels offer air-conditioning and only a handful have fans; neither is necessary.

ESSENTIALS

GETTING THERE & DEPARTING   By Car   Those driving will be able to enjoy the lake and the surrounding towns more fully than those traveling by bus. From Guadalajara, drive to Lake Chapala via the new four-lane Highway 15/80. Leave Guadalajara via avenida González Gallo, which intersects with calzada Independencia just before Agua Azul Park. Going south on Independencia, turn left onto Gallo and follow it all the way out of town past the airport, where it becomes Highway 15/80 (signs may also call it Highway 44). This is the main road to Chapala. The first view of the lake isn't until just outside of the town of Chapala.

The highway from Guadalajara leads directly into Chapala and becomes Madero, which leads straight to Chapala's pier, *malecón* (waterfront walkway and street), and small shopping and restaurant area. Turn right at the one traffic light in town (a block before the pier) to go towards Ajijic, San Antonio, San Juan Cosalá, and Jocotepec. Chapala's main plaza is 3 blocks north of the pier, and the central food market flanks the park's back side.

Lake Chapala

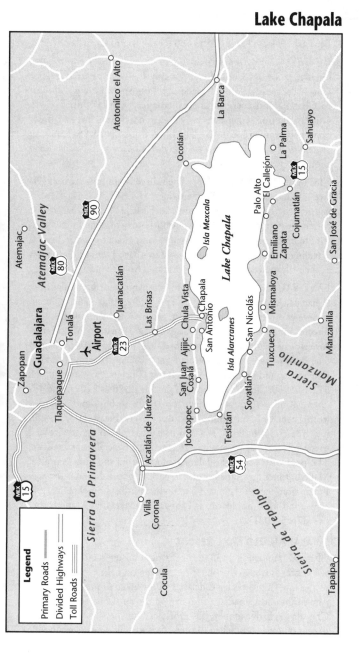

By Taxi   Taxis charge $25 to $30 for the trip to Chapala or Ajijic.

By Bus   Buses to Chapala (a 45-minute ride) leave from Guadalajara's old Central Camionera; Transportes Guadalajara-Chapala serves the route. Buses and minibuses run every half hour to Chapala and every hour to Jocotepec. The last bus back to Guadalajara from Chapala is at 9pm. From Chapala, there are buses every half hour to Jocotepec. The buses from Chapala to San Juan Cosalá stop in Ajijic. There are also direct buses to Ajijic that leave about every other hour.

VISITOR INFORMATION   The Jalisco State Information Office in Chapala is at Aquiles Serdán 26 (☎ **376/5-3141**). Serdán is a narrow side street going toward the lake, 1 block before the correo (post office). The office is open Monday through Friday from 9am to 6pm and Saturday and Sunday from 10am to 6pm. The staff is willing to help and, although they don't have a lot of information at their disposal, you can try to get a map from them.

FAST FACTS   The **area code** for the whole northern lakeshore (Chapala, Ajijic, San Juan Cosalá, and Jocotepec) is **376.**

Several outlets offer communications services, including fax, telephone, mail, and messages. **Centro de Mensajes Mexicano-Americano** is the local affiliate for UPS. They also have 24-hour telephone message and fax-receiving service, court-certified translation ability, and secretarial service. It's at Hidalgo 236 (Apdo. Postal 872), 45900 Chapala, Jalisco (☎ and fax **376/5-2102**), and it's open Monday through Friday from 10am to 6pm and Saturday from 10am to 2pm. Almost next door, **Aero Flash,** Hidalgo 236 (☎ **376/5-3696;** fax 376/5-3063), has a 24-hour fax service and specializes in package mailing. It's the local Federal Express office. The **post office** is on Hidalgo, 2 blocks from the intersection of Madero. Enter down the hill and in back. It's open Monday through Friday from 9am to 1pm and 3 to 6pm; Saturday from 9am to 1pm.

A good local bookstore is **Libros y Revistas,** at Madero 230 (☎ **376/5-2021**).

CHAPALA: AN OLD LAKE RESORT

Chapala, founded in 1538, is the district's business and administrative center as well as the oldest resort town on Lake Chapala. Much of the town's prosperity is derived from the community of retired Americans and Canadians who live on the outskirts and come into Chapala to change money, buy groceries, and check the stock ticker. Except on weekends, when throngs of visitors fill the area around the pier and lake's edge, the town of 36,000 can be a pretty sleepy place. There are a couple of hotels in Chapala, but Ajijic is the best place to stay in the area. Good restaurants on the lake include Cozumel and Mariscos Guicho.

AJIJIC: A QUIET FISHING & ARTIST VILLAGE

Ajijic (ah-hee-*heek*), a quaint lakeside village, is quietly inhabited by mostly fishermen, artists, and retirees. As you reach Ajijic, the highway becomes a wide, tree-lined boulevard through La Floresta, a wealthy residential district. The LA_FLORESTA sign signals you've entered Ajijic, but the central village is still about a mile farther on the left. To reach Ajijic's main street, Colón (which changes to Morelos), turn left when you see the SIX (corner grocery) sign on the left. Colón/Morelos leads straight past the main plaza and ends at the lake and the popular Restaurant La Posada Ajijic. The cobblestone streets and arts-and-crafts stores give the town its charm. (See "Essentials," above, for bus information to Ajijic.)

The **Clínica Ajijic** (☎ 376/6-0662; for emergencies 376/6-0875 or 376/6-0500), on the main highway at the corner of Javier and Mina, has a two-bed emergency section with oxygen and electrocardiogram, ambulance, and five doctors with different specialties. Their 16-bed hospital opened in 1993. The pharmacy there is available after hours for emergencies.

Línea Profesional (☎ 376/6-0187; fax 376/6-0066) is a locally owned car-rental agency in Ajijic. Make reservations as soon as you can, as cars are often all booked.

Exploring Ajijic

In La Floresta, immediately after the modern sculpture on the left, you'll see a cluster of buildings, one of which is marked ARTESANÍAS. The **state-owned crafts shop** (☎ 376/6-0548) has a good selection of pottery from all over Mexico and local crafts such as pottery, glassware, rugs, and wall tapestries. The shop is open Monday through Saturday from 10am to 6pm and Sunday from 10am to 2pm.

Ajijic has long been a center for weavers, but now there are few left. There are a number of stores selling handcrafts; most are on Colón and the streets leading immediately off of it for a block or so. You'll find designer clothing and decorative accessories such as hand-loomed fabrics made into pillows and bedspreads, furniture, and pottery.

As for performing arts in the region, productions of the Lakeside Little Theater are usually announced in the local paper or on the bulletin board at the Nueva Posada Ajijic (see "Where to Stay," below).

Ajijic

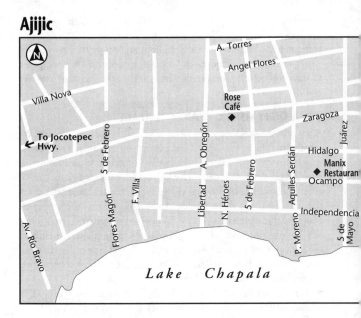

Meeting local foreign residents is easy; just go to the popular hangouts: the Restaurant Posada Ajijic, La Nueva Posada Ajijic, the Rose Café, and Los Veleros Restaurant and Sports Bar.

Where to Stay

La Laguna Bed and Brunch. Zaragoza 29, 45900 Ajijic, Jal. ☎ **376/6-1174** or 376/6-1186. Fax 376/6-1188. E-mail: laguna@laguna.com.mx. 4 units. $30 double (including brunch). No credit cards.

The rooms in this small inn are handsomely furnished: king-size beds with bright loomed bedspreads, thick tile floors, and fireplaces. Breakfast/brunch is served Monday through Saturday from 8:30am to noon, Sunday from 9am to noon; it is quite substantial and excellently prepared. The glassed-in dining area faces the back patio. Nonguests can also have brunch ($4 to $5). To find La Laguna from the main highway, turn left on Colón and left again on the first street. It's 1¹/₂ blocks down on the left behind the Laguna Ajijic Real Estate Office (which faces the main highway).

✪ **La Nueva Posada.** Donato Guerra no. 9 (Apdo. Postal 30), 45900 Ajijic, Jal. ☎ 376/6-1444. Fax 376/6-1344. E-mail: nuevaposada@laguna.com.mx. 16 units. TV, TEL. $50–$60 double. Rates include full breakfast. AE, MC, V. Free parking.

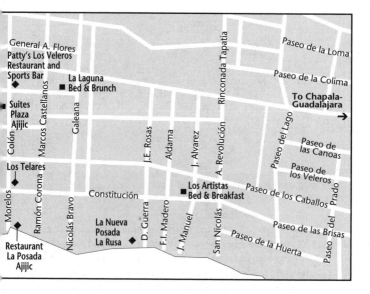

This new posada (inn) was built by Michael and Elena Eager, the former owners of the popular Posada Ajijic (now a restaurant and bar under different ownership). Modeled after a gracious, traditional hacienda, La Nueva Posada looks a lot more expensive than it is. French doors, marble bathrooms, a wine cellar, and a small swimming pool are just some of the amenities. Original paintings hang in all the color-coordinated rooms and public areas. Some rooms overlook the lake, and others have intimate patios; but those in the former will be less disturbed by the after-hours kitchen crew. Three rooms are equipped for people with disabilities. A paperback-exchange library is at the reception area. The hotel's restaurant, La Rusa, and casual bar (see "Where to Dine," below) are among the most popular meeting places in the village. The elegant dining room looks gloriously out onto the view. There's live music most evenings and some afternoons. La Nueva Posada is often booked up way in advance for holidays. The hotel is east of the Plaza at the lakeshore corner of Independencia/Constitución and Donato Guerra. You'll see the hotel's blue facade on the right by the lake.

✪ **Los Artistas B&B.** Constitución 105, 45900 Ajijic, Jal. ☎ **376/6-1027.** Fax 376/6-1762. E-mail: artistas@laguna.com.mx. 6 units. $40–$55 double (including breakfast). No credit cards.

One of Ajijic's loveliest homes also offers one of the best, most relaxing lodging values in Mexico. The inn has a beautiful garden setting with a swimming pool and a view of the mountains in the background. Rooms of varying size and arrangement are colorfully and individually decorated. Guests have use of the pool and run of the downstairs, which includes a comfortable living room with stereo, and the dining room. Breakfast can be served out by the pool and patio. The inn is $5^1/_2$ blocks east of the main square between Aldama and J. Álvarez. You'll see the name on a small tile plaque on the brick wall beside the iron gate.

Where to Dine

Ajijic Grill. Morelos 5. ☎ **376/6-2458.** Main courses $9–$20. MC, V. Sun–Thur 1–8pm, Fri–Sat 1–9pm. GRILL/JAPANESE.

This pleasant open-air patio, with tile roofs and adobe walls, is furnished with *equipal* chairs and tables. Such modest surroundings in such an out-of-the-way town as Ajijic give no hint that you will find some of the best Japanese food in Mexico here. The chef lives in Guadalajara and does the daily shopping there for the restaurant. The food is very fresh, and the specialties are mesquite-grilled salmon and several varieties of teppanyaki.

✪ **La Rusa.** Donato Guerra no. 9. ☎ **376/6-1444** or 376/6-1344. Reservations recommended Dec–Apr. Breakfast $3.50–$5, lunch $4.75–$8, dinner main courses $5–$12, Sun brunch $5–$6.50. MC, V. Mon–Sat 8am–9pm, Sun 9am–8pm (Sun brunch served 9am–1pm). INTERNATIONAL.

La Rusa, the dining and drinking area of La Nueva Posada, offers wonderful settings, whether in the *equipales*-furnished bar, the elegant dining room with garden and lake view, or the garden itself. This is a popular dining spot with locals and tapatíos alike. The lunch menu is simple: crepes, sandwiches, and salads. The dinner menu, printed on a large poster, has a dozen meat, seafood, and chicken main courses, plus soup, salad, and dessert. The Sunday brunch, which includes wine, offers an entirely different selection. There's live music on Friday and Saturday. To reach the restaurant from the Ajijic plaza, walk toward the lake on Colón, turn left on Independencia/16 de Septiembre, and look for Donato Guerra. Turn right; La Rusa is on the right by the lake.

✪ **Manix Restaurant.** Ocampo 57. ☎ **376/6-0061.** Comida corrida $9–$10. MC, V. Mon–Sat 1–9pm. INTERNATIONAL.

This is one of my favorite restaurants in Mexico, and it has nothing to do with the 1970s TV show. I can always count on a delicious meal that's politely served in a pleasant, serene setting. Rainbow-colored napkins brighten the dark carved-wood furniture. The restaurant includes a nonsmoking section. There are usually two different international meals offered daily. Seafood, beef, and sometimes chicken cordon bleu, osso buco, or chicken Parmesan are served. Portions are generous and each meal comes with soup or salad and dessert. To get here from the plaza, turn your back to the church, walk straight ahead on Colón for 2 blocks, and turn right on Ocampo; the restaurant is down the street on the right, but the sign is obscured by the lone tree on the street.

Restaurant La Posada Ajijic. Morelos and Independencia. ☎ **376/6-0744.** Sandwiches $2.75–$4; main courses $3.90–$8. AE, MC, V. Sun–Thurs noon–9pm; Fri–Sat noon–1:30am. MEXICAN/INTERNATIONAL.

Formerly managed by the owners of La Nueva Posada, this restaurant facing the lake has reopened with graceful Mexican decor and good service. The menu covers traditional fare, including soups, salads, sandwiches, more filling Mexican specialties, and imaginatively prepared main courses. The bar, opposite the restaurant, is a favorite Ajijic hangout. The restaurant is at the end of Colón/Morelos; you enter through the back by the lake, where there's parking.

Appendix:
Useful Terms & Phrases

1 Telephones & Mail

USING THE TELEPHONES

In 1999, an important change in local telephone service took place. Where previously you would dial a five- or six-digit number within a city for local calls, these now all conform to international standards of seven-digit numbers. In order to **call any local number in this book,** dial the last seven digits listed (most numbers listed in this book are a total of eight digits—the number plus the area code within Mexico). For local numbers within Mexico City, Guadalajara, and Monterrey, eight digits are required: dial the city code (in Mexico City, **5;** in Guadalajara, **3;** in Monterrey, **8**), and the remaining seven digits of the number.

To call long distance within Mexico, you'll need to dial the national long-distance code **01** prior to dialing the two- or three-digit area code, and then the number. In total, Mexico's telephone numbers are eight digits in length. Mexico's area codes (*claves*) are usually listed in the front of telephone directories. Area codes are listed before all phone numbers in this book. For long-distance dialing you will often see the term "LADA," which is the automatic long-distance service offered by Telmex, Mexico's former telephone monopoly and the largest phone-service company in Mexico.

International long-distance calls to the United States or Canada are accessed by dialing **001,** then the area code and seven-digit number. For other international dialing codes, dial the operator at **090** (though you're not assured of getting an English-speaking operator).

To call Mexico from another country: Dial international access code (U.S. or Canada 011, U.K. or New Zealand 00, Australia 0011), followed by the country code 52, then the area code, then the local number.

To make a direct international call to the U.S. or Canada from Mexico: Dial **001** followed by the area code and number.

To make a direct international call to elsewhere from Mexico: Dial **00,** the country codes (U.K. 44, Australia 61, New Zealand 64) the area code, and the local number.

To charge international calls: You can reach an **AT&T** operator by dialing ☎ **01-800-288-2872,** MCI by dialing ☎ **01-800-021-8000, Sprint** by dialing ☎ **001-800-877-8000,** and **British Telecom (BT)** by dialing ☎ **01-800-123-0244** (pay phones may sometimes require a coin deposit).

For additional details on making calls in Mexico and to Mexico, see chapter 1, "Planning a Trip to Mid-Pacific Mexico."

POSTAL GLOSSARY

Airmail **Correo Aéreo**
Customs **Aduana**
General Delivery **Lista de Correos**
Insurance (insured mail) **Seguro (correo asegurado)**
Mailbox **Buzón**
Money Order **Giro Postal**
Parcel **Paquete**
Post Office **Oficina de Correos**
Post Office Box **Apartado (Apdo.) Postal**
Postal Service **Correos**
Registered Mail **Registrado**
Rubber Stamp **Sello**
Special Delivery, Express **Entrega Inmediata**
Stamp **Estampilla or Timbre**

2 Basic Vocabulary

Most Mexicans are very patient with foreigners who try to speak their language; it helps a lot to know a few basic phrases.

I've included a list of certain simple phrases for expressing basic needs, followed by some common menu items.

ENGLISH-SPANISH PHRASES

English	Spanish	Pronunciation
Good day	**Buenos días**	*bway*-nohss *dee*-ahss
How are you?	**¿Cómo está?**	*koh*-moh ess-*tah*?
Very well	**Muy bien**	mwee byen
Thank you	**Gracias**	*grah*-see-ahss
You're welcome	**De nada**	day *nah*-dah
Goodbye	**Adiós**	ah-*dyohss*
Please	**Por favor**	pohr fah-*vohr*
Yes	**Sí**	see
No	**No**	noh
Excuse me	**Perdóneme**	pehr-*doh*-ney-may

English	Spanish	Pronunciation
Give me	**Déme**	*day*-may
Where is . . . ?	**¿Dónde está . . . ?**	*dohn*-day ess-*tah*?
the station	**la estación**	lah ess-tah-*seown*
a hotel	**un hotel**	oon oh-*tel*
a gas station	**una gasolinera**	*oon*-uh gah-so-lee-*nay*-rah
a restaurant	**un restaurante**	oon res-tow-*rahn*-tay
the toilet	**el baño**	el *bahn*-yoh
a good doctor	**un buen médico**	oon bwayn *may*-thee-co
the road to . . .	**el camino a/hacia**	el cah-*mee*-noh ah/*ah*-see-ah
To the right	**A la derecha**	ah lah day-*reh*-chuh
To the left	**A la izquierda**	ah lah ees-ky-*ehr*-thah
Straight ahead	**Derecho**	day-*reh*-cho
I would like	**Quisiera**	key-see-*ehr*-ah
I want	**Quiero**	*kyehr*-oh
to eat.	**comer**	ko-*mayr*
a room.	**una habitación**	*oon*-nuh ha-bee-tah-*seown*
Do you have?	**¿Tiene usted?**	tyah-nay oos-*ted*?
a book.	**un libro**	oon *lee*-bro
a dictionary.	**un diccionario**	oon deek-seown-*ar*-eo
How much is it?	**¿Cuánto cuesta?**	*kwahn*-to *kwess*-tah?
When?	**¿Cuándo?**	*kwahn*-doh?
What?	**¿Qué?**	kay?
There is (Is there . . . ?)	**(¿)Hay (. . . ?)**	eye?
What is there?	**¿Qué hay?**	kay eye?
Yesterday	**Ayer**	ah-*yer*
Today	**Hoy**	oy
Tomorrow	**Mañana**	mahn-*yahn*-ah
Good	**Bueno**	*bway*-no
Bad	**Malo**	*mah*-lo
Better (best)	**(Lo) Mejor**	(loh) meh-*hor*
More	**Más**	mahs
Less	**Menos**	*may*-noss
No smoking	**Se prohíbe fumar**	say pro-*hee*-bay foo-*mahr*

English	Spanish	Pronunciation
Postcard	**Tarjeta postal**	tar-*hay*-ta pohs-*tahl*
Insect repellent	**Rapelente**	rah-pey-*yahn*-te
	contra insectos	*cohn*-trah een-*sehk*-tos

MORE USEFUL PHRASES

English	Spanish	Pronunciation
Do you speak English?	**¿Habla usted inglés?**	*ah*-blah oo-*sted* een-*glays*?
Is there anyone here who speaks English?	**¿Hay alguien aquí qué hable inglés?**	eye *ahl*-ghee-en kay *ah*-blay een-*glays*?
I speak a little Spanish	**Hablo un poco de español.**	*ah*-blow oon *poh*-koh day ess-pah-*nyol*
I don't understand Spanish very well.	**No (lo) entiendo muy bien el español.**	noh (loh) ehn-tee-*ehn*-do moo-ee bee-ayn el ess-pah-*nyol*
The meal is good.	**Me gusta la comida.**	may *goo*-sta lah koh-*mee*-dah
What time is it?	**¿Qué hora es?**	kay *oar*-ah ess?
May I see your menu?	**¿Puedo ver el menú (la carta)?**	*puay*-tho veyr el may-*noo* (lah *car*-tah)?
The check please.	**La cuenta por favor.**	lah *quayn*-tah pohr fa-*vorh*
What do I owe you?	**¿Cuánto le debo?**	*Kwahn*-toh loh *day*-boh?
What did you say?	**¿Mande? (colloquial expression for American "Eh?")**	*Mahn*-day?
More formal:	**¿Cómo?**	*Koh*-moh?
I want (to see) a room	**Quiero (ver) un cuarto** or **una habitación**	Key-*yehr*-oh vehr oon *kwar*-toh *oon*-nuh ha-bee-tah-*seown*
for two persons.	**para dos personas**	*pahr*-ah doss pehr-*sohn*-as
with (without) bathroom.	**con (sin) baño.**	kohn (seen) *bah*-nyoh

English	Spanish	Pronunciation
We are staying here	Nos quedamos aquí	nohs kay-*dahm*-ohss ah-*key*
only . . .	solamente . . .	sohl-ah-*mayn*-tay
one night.	una noche.	oon-ah *noh*-chay
one week.	una semana.	oon-ah say-*mahn*-ah
We are leaving	Partimos (Salimos)	Pahr-*tee*-mohss (sah-*lee*-mohss)
tomorrow.	mañana.	mahn-*nyan*-ah
Do you accept traveler's checks?	¿Acepta usted cheques de viajero?	Ah-*sayp*-tah oo-sted *chay*-kays day bee-ah-*hehr*-oh?
Is there a Laundromat near here?	¿Hay una lavandería cerca de aquí?	Eye *oon*-ah lah-*vahn*-day-*ree*-ah *sehr*-ka day ah-*key*?
Please send these clothes to the laundry.	Hágame el favor de mandar esta ropa a la lavandería.	*Ah*-ga-may el fah-*vhor* day mahn-*dahr* ays-tah *rho*-pah a lah lah-*vahn*-day-*ree*-ah

NUMBERS

1	uno (*ooh*-noh)		17	diecisiete (de-*ess*-ee-*syeh*-tay)
2	dos (dohs)		18	dieciocho (dee-*ess*-ee-*oh*-choh)
3	tres (trayss)		19	diecinueve (dee-*ess*-ee-*nway*-bay)
4	cuatro (*kwah*-troh)		20	veinte (*bayn*-tay)
5	cinco (*seen*-koh)		30	treinta (*trayn*-tah)
6	seis (sayss)		40	cuarenta (kwah-*ren*-tah)
7	siete (*syeh*-tay)		50	cincuenta (seen-*kwen*-tah)
8	ocho (*oh*-choh)		60	sesenta (say-*sen*-tah)
9	nueve (*nway*-bay)		70	setenta (say-*ten*-tah)
10	diez (dee-ess)		80	ochenta (oh-*chen*-tah)
11	once (*ohn*-say)		90	noventa (noh-*ben*-tah)
12	doce (*doh*-say)		100	cien (see-*en*)
13	trece (*tray*-say)		200	doscientos (*dos*-se-en-tos)
14	catorce (kah-*tor*-say)		500	quinientos (keen-ee-*ehn*-tos)
15	quince (*keen*-say)		1,000	mil (meal)
16	dieciseis (de-*ess*-ee-sayss)			

TRANSPORTATION TERMS

English	Spanish	Pronunciation
Airport	**Aeropuerto**	Ah-ay-row-*por*-tow
Flight	**Vuelo**	Boo-*ay*-low
Rental Car	**Arrendadora de Autos**	Ah-rain-da-dow-rah day autos
Bus	**Autobús**	ow-toh-*boos*
Bus or truck	**Camión**	ka-mee-*ohn*
Lane	**Carril**	kah-*rreal*
Nonstop	**Directo**	dee-*reck*-toh
Baggage (claim area)	**Equipajes**	eh-key-*pah*-hays
Intercity	**Foraneo**	fohr-ah-*nay*-oh
Luggage storage area	**Guarda equipaje**	gwar-daheh-key-*pah*-hay
Arrival gates	**Llegadas**	yay-*gah*-dahs
Originates at this station	**Local**	loh-*kahl*
Originates elsewhere;	**De Paso**	day *pah*-soh
stops if seats available	**Para si hay lugares**	*pah-rah-see-aye-loo-gahr-ays*
First class	**Primera**	pree-*mehr*-oh
Second class	**Segunda**	say-*goon*-dah
Nonstop	**Sin Escala**	seen ess-*kah*-lah
Baggage claim area	**Recibo de Equipajes**	ray-see-boh day eh-key-*pah*-hayes
Waiting room	**Sala de Espera**	*Saw*-lah day ess-*pehr*-ah
Toilets	**Baños**	*bahn*-yos
	Sanitarios	sahn-ee-tahr-*ee*-oss
Ticket window	**Taquilla**	tah-*key*-lah

3 Menu Glossary

Achiote   Small red seed of the annatto tree.

Agua fresca   Fruit-flavored water, usually watermelon, cantaloupe, chia seed with lemon, hibiscus flower, rice, or ground melon-seed mixture.

Antojito   A Mexican snack, usually masa-based with a variety of toppings such as sausage, cheese, beans, and onions; also refers to tostadas, sopes, and garnachas.

Atole   A thick, lightly sweet, warm drink made with finely ground rice or corn and usually flavored with vanilla, pecan, or chocolate.

Birria   Goat, or beef meat cooked in a tomato broth, spiced with garlic, chiles, cumin, oregano, cloves, cinnamon, and thyme and garnished with onions, cabbage, cilantro, and fresh lime juice to taste; a specialty of Jalisco state.

Botana   A light snack—an antojito.

Buñuelos   Round, thin, deep-fried crispy fritters dipped in sugar.

Cabrito   Grilled kid; a northern Mexican delicacy.

Carnitas   Pork that's been deep-cooked (not fried) in lard, then steamed and served with corn tortillas for tacos.

Ceviche   Fresh raw seafood marinated in fresh lime juice and garnished with chopped tomatoes, onions, chiles, and sometimes cilantro and served with crispy, fried whole corn tortillas, or crackers.

Chayote   Vegetable pear or merleton, a type of spiny squash boiled and served as an accompaniment to meat dishes.

Chile en nogada   Poblano peppers stuffed with a mixture of ground pork and chicken, spices, fruits, raisins, and almonds, fried in a light batter and covered in a walnut and cream sauce.

Chiles rellenos   Poblano peppers usually stuffed with cheese, rolled in a batter, and fried; other stuffings include ground beef spiced with raisins.

Churro   Tube-shaped, breadlike fritter, dipped in sugar and sometimes filled with cajeta or chocolate.

Corunda   A triangular tamal wrapped in a corn leaf; a Michoacán specialty.

Enchilada   Tortilla dipped in a sauce and usually filled with chicken or white cheese and sometimes topped with tomato sauce and sour cream (enchiladas Suizas—Swiss enchiladas), or covered in a green sauce (enchiladas verdes), or topped with onions, sour cream, and guacamole (enchiladas Potosinas).

Epazote   Leaf of the wormseed plant, used in black beans and with cheese in quesadillas.

Escabeche   A lightly pickled sauce used in Yucatecan chicken stew.

Frijoles charros   Beans flavored with beer; a northern Mexican specialty.

Frijoles refritos   Pinto beans mashed and cooked with lard.

Garnachas   A thickish small circle of fried masa with pinched sides, topped with pork or chicken, onions, and avocado or sometimes chopped potatoes, and tomatoes, typical as a botana in Veracruz and Yucatán.

Gorditas   Thickish fried-corn tortillas, slit and stuffed with choice of cheese, beans, beef, chicken, with or without lettuce, tomato, and onion garnish.

Gusanos de maguey   Maguey worms, considered a delicacy, and delicious when deep-fried to a crisp and served with corn tortillas for tacos.

Horchata   Refreshing drink made of ground rice or melon seeds, ground almonds, and lightly sweetened.

Huevos Mexicanos   Scrambled eggs with chopped onions, hot peppers, and tomatoes.

Huevos Motuleños   Fried eggs atop a tortilla, garnished with beans, peas, ham, sausage, plantain, and grated cheese; a Yucatecan specialty.

Huevos rancheros   Fried eggs on top of a fried corn tortilla covered in a spicy or mild tomato sauce.

Huitlacoche   Sometimes spelled "cuitlacoche," mushroom-flavored black fungus that appears on corn in the rainy season; considered a delicacy.

Machaca   Shredded dried beef scrambled with eggs or as salad topping; a specialty of northern Mexico.

Manchamantel   Translated means "tablecloth stainer," a stew of chicken or pork with chiles, tomatoes, pineapple, bananas, and jicama. Sometimes listed as "mancha manteles."

Masa   Ground corn soaked in lime used as basis for tamales, corn tortillas, and soups.

Mixiote   Rabbit, lamb, or chicken cooked in a mild chile sauce (usually chile ancho or pasilla), then wrapped like a tamale and steamed. It is generally served with tortillas for tacos, with traditional garnishes of pickled onions, hot sauce, and lime wedges.

Pan de muerto   Sweet bread made around the Days of the Dead (November 1 to 2), in the form of mummies, dolls, or round with bone designs.

Pan dulce   Lightly sweetened bread in many configurations, usually served at breakfast or bought at any bakery.

Papadzules   Tortillas are stuffed with hard-boiled eggs and seeds (pumpkin or sunflower) in a tomato sauce.

Pavo relleno negro   Stuffed turkey Yucatán-style, filled with chopped pork and beef, cooked in a rich, dark sauce.

Pibil   Pit-baked pork or chicken in a sauce of tomato, onion, mild red pepper, cilantro, and vinegar.

Pipián   Sauce made with ground pumpkin seeds, nuts, and mild peppers.

Poc chuc   Slices of pork with onion marinated in a tangy sour orange sauce and charcoal broiled; a Yucatecan specialty.

Pollo Calpulalpan   Chicken cooked in pulque; a specialty of Tlaxcala.

Pozole   A soup made with hominy and pork or chicken, in either a tomato-based broth Jalisco-style, or a white broth Nayarit-style, or green chile sauce Guerrero-style, and topped with choice of chopped white onion, lettuce or cabbage, radishes, red pepper, and oregano.

Pulque   Drink made of fermented sap of the maguey plant; best in state of Hidalgo and around Mexico City.

Quesadilla   Corn or flour tortillas stuffed with melted white cheese and lightly fried.

Queso relleno   "Stuffed cheese" is a mild yellow cheese stuffed with minced meat and spices; a Yucatecan specialty.

Rompope   Delicious Mexican eggnog, invented in Puebla, made with eggs, vanilla, sugar, and rum.

Salsa verde   A cooked sauce using the green tomatillo and puréed with spicy or mild hot peppers, onions, garlic, and cilantro; on tables countrywide. As a rule green sauce is hotter than red sauce.

Sopa de calabaza   Soup made of chopped squash or pumpkin blossoms.

Sopa de lima   A tangy soup made with chicken broth and accented with fresh lime; popular in Yucatán.

Sopa seca   Translated means "dry soup." Any pasta or rice served as a first or second course.

Sopa Tarasca   A rib-sticking pinto bean–based soup, flavored with onions, garlic, tomatoes, chiles, and chicken broth and garnished with sour cream, white cheese, avocado chunks, and fried tortilla strips; a specialty of Michoacán state.

Sopa Tlalpeña   A hearty soup made with chunks of chicken, chopped carrots, zucchini, corn, onions, garlic, and cilantro.

Sopa Tlaxcalteca   A hearty tomato-based soup filled with cooked nopal cactus, cheese, cream, and avocado with crispy tortilla strips floating on top.

Sopa de Tortilla   A traditional chicken broth–based soup, seasoned with chiles, tomatoes, onion, and garlic, bobbing with crisp fried strips of corn tortillas.

Sope   Pronounced "*soh*-pay," a botana similar to a garnacha, except spread with refried beans and topped with crumbled cheese and onions.

Tacos al pastor   Thin slices of flavored pork roasted on a revolving cylinder dripping with onion slices and juice of fresh pineapple slices. Served in small corn tortillas, topped with chopped onion and cilantro.

Tamal   Incorrectly called tamale (tamal singular, tamales plural); meat or sweet filling rolled with fresh masa, then wrapped in a corn husk or banana leaf and steamed; many varieties and sizes throughout the country.

Tepache   Drink made of fermented pineapple peelings and brown sugar.

Tikin xic   Also seen on menus as "tikik chick," charbroiled fish brushed with achiote sauce.

Tinga   A stew made with pork tenderloin or chicken, sausage, onions, garlic, tomatoes, chiles, and potatoes; popular on menus in Puebla and Hidalgo states.

Torta   A sandwich, usually on bolillo bread, usually with sliced avocado, onions, tomatoes, with a choice of meat and often cheese.

Torta ahogada   A specialty of Lake Chapala is made with a scooped out roll, filled with beans and carnitas and seasoned with a tomato or chile sauce.

Tostadas   Crispy fried corn tortillas topped with meat, onions, lettuce, tomatoes, cheese, avocados, and sometimes sour cream.

Venado   Venison (deer) served perhaps as pipian de venado, steamed in banana leaves and served with a sauce of ground squash seeds.

Xtabentun (shtah-ben-*toon*)   A Yucatán liquor made of fermented honey and flavored with anise. It comes *seco* (dry) or *crema* (sweet).

Zacahuil   Pork leg tamal, packed in thick masa, wrapped in banana leaves, and pit-baked, sometimes pot-made with tomato and masa; specialty of mid- to upper Veracruz.

Index

See also separate Accommodations and Restaurant indexes below.
Page numbers in italics refer to maps.

ACCOMMODATIONS

Puerto Vallarta

Costa Alegre

FROMMER'S® COMPLETE TRAVEL GUIDES

FROMMER'S® DOLLAR-A-DAY GUIDES

Australia from $50 a Day
California from $60 a Day
Caribbean from $70 a Day
England from $70 a Day
Europe from $60 a Day
Florida from $60 a Day

Hawaii from $70 a Day
Ireland from $50 a Day
Israel from $45 a Day
Italy from $70 a Day
London from $85 a Day
New York from $80 a Day

New Zealand from $50 a Day
Paris from $85 a Day
San Francisco from $60 a Day
Washington, D.C.,
    from $60 a Day

FROMMER'S® PORTABLE GUIDES

Acapulco, Ixtapa &
    Zihuatanejo
Alaska Cruises & Ports of Call
Bahamas
Baja & Los Cabos
Berlin
California Wine Country
Charleston & Savannah
Chicago

Dublin
Hawaii: The Big Island
Las Vegas
London
Maine Coast
Maui
New Orleans
New York City
Paris

Puerto Vallarta, Manzanillo
    & Guadalajara
San Diego
San Francisco
Sydney
Tampa & St. Petersburg
Venice
Washington, D.C.

FROMMER'S® NATIONAL PARK GUIDES

Family Vacations in the
    National Parks
Grand Canyon

National Parks of the
    American West
Rocky Mountain

Yellowstone & Grand Teton
Yosemite & Sequoia/
    Kings Canyon
Zion & Bryce Canyon

FROMMER'S® GREAT OUTDOOR GUIDES

New England
Northern California

Southern California & Baja
Washington & Oregon

FROMMER'S® MEMORABLE WALKS

Chicago
London

New York
Paris

San Francisco
Washington D.C.

FROMMER'S® IRREVERENT GUIDES

Amsterdam
Boston
Chicago
Las Vegas

London
Los Angeles
Manhattan

New Orleans
Paris
San Francisco

Seattle & Portland
Vancouver
Walt Disney World
Washington, D.C.

FROMMER'S® BEST-LOVED DRIVING TOURS

America
Britain
California

Florida
France
Germany

Ireland
Italy
New England

Scotland
Spain
Western Europe

THE COMPLETE IDIOT'S TRAVEL GUIDES

Boston
Chicago
Cruise Vacations
Planning Your Trip to Europe
Florida
Hawaii

Ireland
Las Vegas
London
Mexico's Beach Resorts
New Orleans
New York City

Paris
San Francisco
Spain
Walt Disney World
Washington, D.C.

THE UNOFFICIAL GUIDES®